About Faces

ABOUT FACES

Physiognomy in Nineteenth-Century Britain

SHARRONA PEARL

Harvard University Press
Cambridge, Massachusetts, and London, England 2010

Library of Congress Cataloging-in-Publication Data

Pearl, Sharrona.
    About faces : physiognomy in nineteenth-century Britain / Sharrona Pearl.
        p.   cm.
    Includes bibliographical references and index.
    ISBN 978-0-674-03604-8 (alk. paper)
    1. Physiognomy—Great Britain—History—19th century.   2. Facial
expression—Great Britain—History—19th century.   3. Face perception—Great
Britain—History—19th century.   I. Title.
    BF851.P35 2010
    138.0941'09034—dc22   2009017608

Contents

Figures

Acknowledgments

Writing this book has shown me, among other things, that many people did and do believe that one can judge a book by its cover. If that is indeed the case, I hope that you have found my cover pleasing, and that the contents live up to the promise of the outside. Although (as will become evident throughout the text) I take no stand on the predictive power of the external, I do hope that one can be judged by one's surroundings, in particular, by one's friends and teachers. If this is so, I consider myself lucky beyond belief and placed in excellent stead for scrutinizing eyes.

This project has been rewarding beyond my wildest expectations, in no small part because of the people toward whom it led me. I am grateful for the opportunity to list my debts here, in hopes that this recognition goes some small way toward expressing my great gratitude. My graduate advisors offered not just advice and guidance but true mentorship. Anne Harrington first urged me to look into physiognomy, and her constant enthusiasm gave this work its shape. Mario Biagioli kept the project and the experience of researching it interesting and has remained a steadfast source of guidance and inspiration. Harriet Ritvo, scholar, teacher, and true friend, taught me to be a historian and helped me always find my own voice. Simon Schaffer continues to be a role model for me and countless others, and I am grateful for every conversation we have had, all of which have found their way into these pages.

The community of historians of British science is a generous and welcoming one, and I count myself fortunate to be among its members. Anne Secord, Alison Winter, Jennifer Tucker, Peter Galison, Iwan Morus, Bernie Lightman, and James Secord have offered the dual blessings of personal encouragement and intellectual guidance, without which both this book and my feelings toward it would be much poorer.

Like any work, this book was written (and rewritten) in stages; many friends and advisors offered eagerly accepted help along the way. It would be impossible to list every conversation that found its way into these pages and vastly improved its contents. I am grateful to have been surrounded by many brilliant colleagues who are also friends from the first day of graduate school, and I hope that they recognize my debts to them in these pages. Orit Halpern, Matthew Stanley, Nasser Zakariya, Tom Stapleford, Debbie Coen, Debbie Weinstein, Colin Milburn, Ben Hurlbut, Lambert Williams, Denise Phillips, Theresa Levitt, Nadine Knight, Jeremy Goldhaber-Fiebert, Ziva Mann, and Joshua Meyer: I thank you and I admire you.

One of the joys of scholarship is the generosity and support of those enormously clever colleagues and students one meets along the way. My students have energized me, excited me, and, always, taught me, and I am a better scholar for being their teacher. This work has been improved immeasurably by feedback from conference participants at the History of Science Society annual meetings, the North American Conference on British Studies in 2005 and 2007, the European History Working Group at Harvard University, the Dissertation Writers' Group (DaWGs) in the History of Science Department at Harvard, and the 2006 Talking Shop History and Literature Conference. I particularly appreciate the careful and close readings from members of the audiences at the Philadelphia Area Center for History of Science Regional Colloquium and the participants in the Delaware Valley British Studies Group. Their many thoughtful comments helped me reframe the project at crucial stages. Jordanna Bailken and David Feldman commented on chapter drafts, and their knowledge and insight enriched this work considerably. Katey Anderson, Tom Conolly, Serena Dessen, and Michael Gordin heroically read the entire manuscript in its early stages, and their detailed, careful, and kind critiques guided me through every stage of the process. I am grateful also for the comments of the two anonymous referees for Harvard University Press, as well as for the attention and support of my editors, Ann Downer-Hazell and Elizabeth Knoll.

I remain indebted to the faculty and staff of the Harvard Department of the History of Science for their support from the earliest stages of this work, which made the entire process easier and much more fun. The kindness and professionalism of wonderful staff and librarians in the Cambridge University Library, the Houghton Library, the Harvard Theatre Collection, the Library of Congress, and the Yale Centre for British Art saved me countless hours and opened up new worlds. I am grateful to the following libraries and sources for allowing me to reproduce the images in this book: Alan Moss of History by the Yard; the Widener Library; Trinity College Library, Cambridge; the Harvard Theatre Collection, Houghton Library; the National Portrait Gallery, London; Yale University, Harvey Cushing/John Hay Whitney Medical Library; Professor James Secord; Tate, London; the Trustees of the British Museum; the Jewish Museum, London; the Royal Society of Medicine; the Mary Evans Picture Library; John Van Wyhe; and the National Library of Medicine. Parts of Chapter 5 of this book originally appeared as the article "Through a Mediated Mirror: The Photographic Physiognomy of Dr. Hugh Welch Diamond" in *History of Photography* 33, no. 3 (August 2009).

I was very lucky to be able to be in those libraries, thanks to the generosity of the Social Science and Humanities Research Council of Canada, the Krupp Foundation at the Harvard Centre for European Studies, the Harvard Department of the History of Science, the Yale Centre for British Art, and the Caroline and Erwin Swann Foundation for Caricature and Cartoon. The project was supported in its earliest stages by the Department of the History of Science at Harvard and made it to completion—much improved—because of the generosity of the Annenberg School for Communication at the University of Pennsylvania.

Philadelphia and the University of Pennsylvania have welcomed me with open arms, making the final stages of this book project (mostly) a joy and a delight. My new colleagues in the Annenberg School for Communication and in the university as a whole have, in just a few short months, enriched this work and my own scholarship immeasurably with their creativity, enthusiasm, and insights. The staff at Annenberg has made the transition seamless, freeing up time for me to finish this work and dive into the next one. I wish to thank my amazingly competent research assistants Carolyn Sofman and Adrienne Shaw, who showed considerable patience and diligence in bringing this book to its final form.

The peculiarly pleasurable tortures of academia are enhanced and also mitigated when shared. For their undying support and love for me and my work, and for helping me find the boundaries between the two, I extend my own equal promise of support and love to Shiamin Kwa Roses, Anna Deeny, Adina Isenberg, Nina Rabinovitch Blecker, and Carrie Endries. This book has a kind of twin, born at exactly the same time after exactly the same deadlines, and for her support during her own book's gestation, I am grateful for the warmth, wisdom, and friendship of Carla Nappi.

Last—but also first, second, and always—I would like to express my gratitude and love for my family, without whom this, and everything else, would have been impossible. My grandparents, Harold and Eva Dessen, and my parents, Susan and Ernest Pearl, instilled in me their lifelong dedication to learning and teaching, and I am honored to be able to continue their great work. My brother Mayeer has supported me unstintingly and unceasingly from day one. And my husband, Ben Knepler, who has lived with this book and its judgments as much as I, has been my greatest cheerleader, questioner, sounding board, and silent sympathizer, always showing that he does, in every possible way, understand.

It is written in Pirkei Avot, the Ethics of the Ancestors, 4:15: "Let the honor of your student be as precious to you as your own; and the honor of your colleague as the respect due your teacher; and the respect towards your teacher as your reverence for the universe." I offer this work as a humble sign of my respect and reverence for students, colleagues, and teachers. Thank you for paying me the honor of reading it.

About Faces

Introduction

Face Facts

CALL IT GUT INSTINCT. Call it a sense. Call it experience. Call it what you will, but acknowledge that it is there—we judge others when we look at them. For a long time, it was called physiognomy, and it needed no reason to hide behind any other name. In fact, in its very naming—and the universalizing of that name—was great power. This power was used to expand the purview of this looking and judging in many sites and in many ways, especially in England in the long nineteenth century.[1]

As I follow physiognomy—the study of facial traits and their relationship to character—through time, I take us through various sites and spaces of the nineteenth century. We will walk through the streets of London and browse the galleries of Madame Tussaud's wax museum. We will go to the theatre and to art exhibits, where we will try to look at Victorian entertainment through physiognomic eyes. We will strive to capture the surprise and shock of those looking at asylum inmates by using images to peek behind closed doors. We will attempt to see faces as Londoners saw them, mediated through photographs, caricatures, and their own assumptions. We will also look outward, toward the world at large, and observe how the act of seeing made the boundaries of country and nation change. While we take this journey, we will think about ways of describing, and how those ways changed as the subjects—and the idea of the "subject"—changed. When we first meet physiognomy in this book, it was used as a technology to make decisions about individual others. As the practice gained frequency, it grew in scope, including in its diagnostic range not just features of the face and body but also clothing, hairstyles, and other forms of self-decoration. Through time and in conjunction with shifts in ideas of nationhood, immigration, the expansion of empire, the emergence of realism, evolutionary thinking, and anthropological growth, physiognomy changed along with those who used it. Physiognomy became a way to talk about groups rather than individuals, and to paint communities in broad strokes rather than in specific detail.

Physiognomy achieved almost universal penetration into the Victorian consciousness. In part because of the way in which the practice was framed, as accessible even to the inexpert, physiognomy was applied on a regular basis across all classes of English society. Vaunted for its speed, physiognomy offered a way to suture the crisis of urban interaction by providing a means of making judgments even in the most passing encounters. Through the very act of engaging in physiognomy, all who applied it developed and extended its parameters; in this way, physiognomy exemplifies James Secord's claim that there need be no distinction between the making and the communicating of knowledge.[2] In elite education settings and daily street applications, physiognomy was disseminated through learned monographs, guidebooks, graphic print, and training manuals and in a variety of entertainment experiences. Cultural entertainments and exchanges played an important role in the production and communication of physiognomic ideas on the part of audiences and entertainers alike.

This book takes as its subject a slippery and flexible concept that changed with every interrogation, every elucidation, every user, and every use. In this flexibility lay one of the secrets of physiognomy's longevity. The concept of physiognomy dates back to antiquity and lingers in various forms today, but its use and acceptance have had peaks and valleys, the most dramatic of which were in the same decade. As one of my starting points, I ask why physiognomy had so much appeal in the cities of the nineteenth century, and in one city in particular—London. In order even to begin exploring this question, I had to understand what physiognomy was at that time, and in trying to answer that, I quickly learned that there was no one physiognomy. There was, however, a concerted effort to talk about physiognomy in a particular and perhaps, to the historical eye, peculiar way. Educated advocates and lay users alike worked hard to cast physiognomy in a scientific framework despite centuries of its use as an artistic technique, fortune-telling mechanism, and etiquette guide. In this scientizing effort lies one of the keys to my examination, because I use the framing of physiognomy to understand the stakes for its use and the contexts in which it was applied. Even the scientizers, however, acknowledged the artistic elements in physiognomic practice and application. Physiognomy straddled both approaches and touched on many pursuits, making it a very nineteenth-century kind of thing, and a rich source of historical inquiry.

Many of the chapters of this book overlap in both time and space. The sites of physiognomy were strongly interconnected, and its moments of development were not strictly linear. A rough forward chronology starts in the early nineteenth century and ends at the century's close, but many physiognomic applications occurred in different ways and different places at the same time, so some chapters cover similar temporal ground. The connections between the cultural sites—including the streets, the theatre, art exhibitions, newspaper images, asylums, and learned texts—are equally strong. Like physiognomy itself, the study of the topic requires flexibility of both researchers and readers. To this end, I have tried to make each chapter a stand-alone unit, although the themes and major arguments cohere far more effectively in the text as a whole.

One of the exciting aspects of studying something as flexible and embedded as physiognomy is that it opens up many new perspectives on well-trodden ground. In looking at classic paintings and photographs, in reading plays and costume lists, and especially in examining novels I had read many times before, I gained new insight with the benefit of a physiognomic perspective. I began to understand that the multitudes of physical and visual information formed a set of cues, and I discovered that there was much that I had not been coded to understand. Once I knew how to look for physiognomy, it was everywhere. The rich descriptions, the detailed faces and clothes, and the careful illustrations all contained important character information that was meaningful to the Victorians. Through today's eyes, these read as a bewildering wealth of details.

By looking at the past through physiognomically aware eyes, I was able to learn a great deal about nineteenth-century daily life: the minutiae of decision making and interaction, cultural experiences, and mundane tasks. Perhaps more important, I also was able to explore major themes prominent in the nineteenth century. The prevalence of physiognomy reveals far more about the physiognomists than about those they studied. In interrogating the construction, application, and conceptualization of this category of analysis, I excavated Victorian ideas about visual judgment, concepts of representation, modes of interaction, presentations of criminality, notions of individual and group distinction, and artistic renderings. More broadly, physiognomy allowed me to ask questions about perception and reaction and helped me formulate new constructions to describe the ways in which Victorians saw the world and made decisions about it.

Although the sites of my exploration shift, many of the themes are constant. Even as physiognomy expanded and changed, it remained an important technology of classification and description. Set against a rapidly industrializing landscape in the largest and fastest-growing city in the world, physiognomy provided Londoners a way to make quick-and-dirty judgments without the burdens (and advantages) of lengthy encounters and conversations. A swift glance was enough to start forming conclusions about others. This much perhaps is obvious. More interesting are questions that explore the framing of physiognomy and the way in which it was described, discussed, and expressed by those who used it and critiqued it. Who were the physiognomists? What were the stakes for placing physiognomy in a scientific rubric? How did people think about their own physiognomic decisions and reactions? In what ways was physiognomy manipulated to communicate very specific kinds of information? How aware were Victorians of these various processes? What was physiognomy's relationship to other practices of visual classification? Finally, where did physiognomy go? I can answer only some of these questions, and, like physiognomy itself (this will be a repeated trope), the answers change in space and time.

Let us begin to think about the major themes. Some are chronological; throughout the course of this book, I chart a shift from the discussion of individuals to the discussion of groups, or the physiognomy of one melding into the physiognomy of many of a kind. Although both applications of physiognomy existed side by side, earlier applications generally focused on describing individuals. As the nineteenth century progressed, physiognomy more frequently became the tool of social commentators, artists, and laypeople to discuss what characterized particular groups. This change mirrors a broader Victorian trend that saw people thinking of themselves as part of a larger whole and, in so doing, creating exclusions of those who did not belong. The inside groups included the nation, the elite, the English, and the sane. On the outside were criminals, the poor, the crazy, and, of course, the non-English. I focus in particular on two groups for which physiognomy was used to assign difference in the absence of obvious physical distinction, namely, the Jews and the Irish. In Chapter 6 I turn physiognomy outward, looking at its use in anthropological classification and imperial exploration and arguing that physiognomy was used to import empire and create visual meaning.

Meaning could be made, however, only if the symbols of physiognomy offered intelligible information. Physiognomic understanding was a process of training. Throughout this book, I look at the ways in which physiognomy was used both to get and self-consciously to give meaning in representational contexts. The nature of that meaning was at times up for grabs, but rather than destabilizing the application of physiognomy, ambiguity gave it strength. One of the important factors in the power of physiognomy was its accessibility. No special training was required or even necessary. Although physiognomic skill could be honed, some were born with natural skill, and everyone was born with (variably reliable) instinct. All one really needed was the ability to see and then judge.

But for these judgments to have meaning beyond the strictly personal, for the outcomes to have justification, and for deliberate physiognomic messaging (by actors, writers, painters, wax sculptors, and the like), there had to be some promise of consistent understanding. Universal understanding based on individual instinct is a tricky combination, but physiognomy promised it through the compelling notion of what I call *shared subjectivity*. This approach allows me to introduce the underexamined modality of subjectivity and to offer a corrective to the narrow focus on mechanical objectivity that permeates studies of Victorian science.[3] Likewise, my emphasis on subjectivity acknowledges vision as an active and deeply personal activity. As Chris Otter has argued, the relentless historical attention paid to the Foucauldian "faceless gaze," the authorless surveillance of the panopticon, ignores the role of the individual in the observational exchange.[4] Not all forms of interaction were rooted in surveillance, and not all urban experiences involved observation of others.

Although I agree with Otter about the importance of widening our perspective on observation and visuality, I differ from him on his understanding that "the knowledge gained from judicious observation was useful largely for the subject alone."[5] Physiognomy served to disrupt precisely the idea that the conclusions drawn from seeing were meaningful only for the individual; instead, it provided a way to make observational information communal. Physiognomy offered a meaningful frame of reference for conversations and decisions about the evidence of the eyes. Although the insights gained from observation were subjective, they could be and were shared. Physiognomy helped create community and contributed to the creation of consensus, or what Alison Winter called "the phenomenon of agreement," which she situates as a particularly Victorian invention.[6]

Having acknowledged the shared nature of observation, I want to clarify my approach on a related issue. Otter, among others, has begun to push against the hegemony that Foucauldian surveillance enjoys in historical accounts of the urban experience. I follow Otter's lead on this front and also on the approach he takes toward the training of perception in the nineteenth century. Although scholars working on visuality and technology in the nineteenth century owe a tremendous debt to Jonathan Crary and the approaches he inspired, I agree with Otter that it is time to look in a different direction and to acknowledge that not everyone expected or even wanted vision to be objective.[7] Great significance lay in the eyes of the beholder.

The emphasis on individual instinct in observation was one of the great attractions of Victorian physiognomy. Combined with the rhetoric of natural philosophy, classificatory power, and scientific importance that permeated physiognomic discussions, subjectivity gave people permission to judge in a way that seemed supported by external factors. Physiognomy was accessible and nonexpert, but it seemed to draw on the kinds of authority that more rarefied pursuits enjoyed. Physiognomy was subjective science for everyone, with very practical applications in daily life. Those people whom I call "pocket physiognomists" enjoyed the advantages of drawing seemingly shared conclusions from the evidence of their eyes, conclusions that I analyze with the help of audience response theory. They could communicate their ideas to others and not sacrifice trusting in themselves. In a time of increasing automation and industrialization, the emphasis on an outcome derived solely from the self carried great currency for making physiognomy an attractive pursuit.

By the same token, the very flexibility of physiognomy served to lengthen its life span as a technology of judgment. Physiognomic analyses served to strengthen decisions already made and to reinforce and provide evidence for conclusions drawn from a variety of sources, of which instinct was only one. There was also an unsurprising trend of retroactive diagnoses, in which physiognomy was used after the fact to explain people's future that was now their past. The many valences of physiognomy allowed observations to describe a given trait in numerous ways, and features could often be read positively and negatively. Thin lips, for example, could be a sign of criminal cunning or sophisticated calculation skills. It all depended on who was looking, who was being looked at, when, and why.

Although some purists insisted that physiognomy referred only to the shape and structure of facial features and extremities, most extended the range of their analyses to include expressions (more properly called "pathognomy"), body types, and, eventually, hairstyle, clothing, and self-presentation broadly construed. The word *physiognomy* even came to stand for the face itself. One of the paths that I chart throughout this book is the metonymization of the physiognomic self as clothing and externally manipulable attributes came to convey physiognomic information. For example, in a series of photographs of asylum inmates that I explore in Chapter 5, the photographer and asylum superintendent Hugh Welch Diamond and his commentator John Conolly drew significant physiognomic conclusions from various aspects of self-presentation. On the flip side, actors were very thoughtful about their costumes and props because they conveyed important character information to their physiognomically astute audiences.

As Victorians became physiognomically literate, the purview of physiognomy shifted from a mechanism to get information to a means of self-consciously giving information. During the first half of the nineteenth century, physiognomy had become a widely understood visual language, a means of procuring immediate character detail. With the application and subversion of physiognomy on canvas and on stage, the calibrating image changed. Instead of using texts and pictures to look up people's faces, the representations of people in portraiture and on stage became the sources of information, and audiences were expected already to understand what they were reading. The bulk of this book chronicles how actors, novelists, painters, photographers, caricaturists, and others who engaged in mimesis and representation mobilized physiognomic messaging as part of their visual shorthands. This book is rich in visual images that I read through a physiognomic lens, offering new insight into the pictures themselves, as well as into the way in which they were constructed and understood. As Alan Sekula and Julie Codell have explained, the Victorian body in all its representation was a semiotic system to which physiognomy offered a key.[8] Of course, audiences and observers had to have physiognomic awareness in order to communicate their understanding of these clues. As I show, cultural figures were key contributors to the training of physiognomic vision.

Some novelists explicitly engaged in physiognomy and gave their illustrators a great deal of specific guidance about what they wanted the pictures to look like. Historian and children's writer Reverend Charles Kingsley was particularly sensitive to the physiognomic implications of literary illustrations; when he was acting as an advising editor to illustrator Charles Bennett on an edition of John Bunyan's 1678 classic *Pilgrim's Progress,* he insisted that Bennett adhere to physiognomic conventions in the illustrations. An 1859 letter from Kingsley to Bennett included a number of suggestions about ways for Bennett to improve his drawings by increasing the physiognomic agreement between the literary and visual drawings of their characters. Kingsley was very specific, noting that "Mr. Gripeman is too handsome. I think you want a more sharp, comprest [*sic*], and cruel lip. But the general shape of the face is good. It is very like Alva, who was a cruel man, and a rigid pedant." The more general typologies were also inaccurate. "The 'Lust of the Flesh,' is hardly animal enough. I have generally seen with strong animal passion, a tendency to high cheek bone; but only in a dark woman. Yours may stand for a blonde type; but even thin [*sic*] I should prefer a lower forehead." Bennett's messages were confusing because "I should take the 'Pride of Life' for an older woman, and a much stouter one." To correct this, Kingsley advised, "Give her very full features and bust." Finally, "Your 'Pride of Life' has more animal passion than the 'Lust of the Flesh;' indeed, beyond that of vacuity, she has not much. She would be gad-about and vain enough, but not pompous and magnificent. Besides, she is a low type, and you should have the highest you can get."[9]

Kingsley's comments to Bennett highlight the extent to which physiognomic notions had become normalized; rather than offering a systematic explanation of the principles underlying his suggestions, he took for granted that the validity of physiognomy was accepted. To Kingsley, like many Victorians, physiognomy was a fact of life in all relational and representational contexts; from faces in the street to drawings on the page, physiognomy was the quickest and most immediate way of understanding who people were.

Although I explore a wide range of media and their use in the growth of physiognomy, I particularly focus on performance, both on stage and as a theoretical approach. An important part of my analysis of the history of physiognomy is the contention that physiognomy itself entails performance and self-presentation. With an awareness that one's face and one's self are being visually judged comes a self-consciousness about that very self. Part of my work explores the production of the self as people considered how best to display themselves in the context of the highly surveyed urban streets. Some, I show, opted out by blending in, using the crowds to hide through facial and sartorial anonymity. Most interpersonal interactions involve a degree of performativity as people try to project particular images and impressions, and physiognomic awareness heightened this effect. As consensus was built about the meaning of visual signs—including clothing, accessories, posture, and, of course, facial features and expressions—Victorians became very thoughtful actors and audiences for the character messages they projected and observed.[10] Each chapter of this book details some aspect of performance, either explicitly, as in my explorations of the stage and various forms of portraiture, or in the many subtle and nondeliberate ways that are a necessary component of interaction.

The development and awareness of physiognomy during the nine-teenth century had an interesting by-product, namely, the rising emphasis on interior space. Any understanding of physiognomy entails a commit-ment to the idea that exterior signs signify a less visible interior correlate. Performativity is in some ways an attempt to subvert the correlation be-tween the internal and the external, but even that subversion provides important information. One of my goals in this book is to chronicle the growing landscape of interior space, which provided the conditions of possibility for fin de siècle developments, including fingerprinting and psychoanalysis. These developments, however, form only a very minor part of this book because they are in many ways unearthed only in private spaces. Much of this text is concerned with the public and with the ways in which physiognomy offered a way to navigate large arenas of interac-tion and make them manageable.

Tom Crook has noted that the Victorian era was in many ways a time of privacy and liberalism. That privacy, however, often enabled a kind of deviance that crossed the line of what Crook called "civilized indul-gence."[11] Part of the power of physiognomy lay in its ability to penetrate privacy in order to predict those moments when indulgence could be-come deviance. Physiognomy was a useful way to peek behind the meta-phorical and actual closed doors behind which urban dwellers lived their lives. Therefore, the study of physiognomy helps reveal the tension be-tween democracy and hierarchy that the Victorian city represented in both its layout and its modes of interaction. The urban experience was one of space and enclosure, freedom and limitation. The busy streets al-lowed unfettered visual access while at the same time constraining inter-action and often forcing physical encounter. Physiognomy was a form of perceptual access in both the highly tactile slums and the sensually rich boulevards. Importantly, cities were about movement, because inhabit-ants used their bodies and their eyes to travel from enclosed spaces to open access and from limited sight to complete visual command of the perceptual field.

As Simon Gunn has argued, the privileged classes developed strategies to deal with the fluid social conditions of the urban experience. These groups employed classification heuristics based on visual and etiquette codes that reinforced status social hierarchies.[12] These heuristics, I sub-mit, were often dependent on physiognomic signs, which themselves were highly in flux. The very accessibility of physiognomy and the flexibility of its messages served to undermine the rigid hierarchies it was deployed to support. Nevertheless, there is a pattern of physiognomic objectifica-tion in which those with great social power—the wealthy, the sane, the employed, and the male and masculine—reduced others to component parts, thereby using physiognomy as a form of belittlement and dehumanization. While Gunn is interested in the ways in which the city was demarked along points of social difference, I am concerned with the moments in which these divisions were breached. Of course, the strategies of classification with which Gunn is concerned point to the extent to which these categories were breached. As much as the city recapitulated division, it also encouraged interaction, particularly through public spaces such as pleasure gardens, museums, stores, houses of worship, transportation, and especially the streets. Jonathan Conlin has usefully proposed thinking about these spaces as arenas of "autovoyeurism," places that people inhabited in order deliberately to see and be seen.[13] This practice stands in direct contrast to panopticism, the top-down surveillance that is often used to describe the city.

Almost all the analyses in this book focus on the city. There are a number of reasons for this, many of which are connected to my choice of chronological and geographic focus. I would like to make very clear that although this book is set in nineteenth-century England, I am not claiming that there was no significant physiognomic activity elsewhere. Nor do I believe that my findings are exclusive to English urban environments. Rather, I propose that there are a number of reasons that physiognomy flourished in particular in these contexts. As my broad interest is nineteenth-century England, I use physiognomy as a way to explore it, and in so doing, I have accessed both broad themes and the nitty-gritty of daily life. Having said that, I do think that there are useful claims to be made about when and why physiognomy garnered mass attention and support.

Physiognomy was a widespread technology, applied in cities and counties, streets and stores, farms and fancy halls. That much is certainly true. The difference between city and country physiognomy was not one of degree rather than kind. Rather, it was an issue of imperative. The scale of London changed the nature of human interaction in dramatic and pressing ways. Physiognomy helped urbanites deal with the simultaneous overload and lack of human information by allowing people to make judgments on the basis of sight. The most important information physiognomy could provide was precisely what was lacking in the urban environment, namely, a system of establishing reasons to trust and, equally important, identifying whom not to trust. Without the lengthy timescale of rural life, and with the hustle and bustle of the streets, physiognomy emerged as a way to make sense of the city. From there, it grew.

An important—perhaps the most important—context for this study is the urban street. As I have already noted, a huge part of the imperative that spurred the spread of physiognomy was the confusion and novelty of the city and its sites of interaction. Most of this story takes place in London, but a similar study could be done of Manchester, Paris, Berlin, or Vienna. This, however, is not a comparative project, although such an approach could be quite fruitful. I have no doubt that a comparative Continental approach would yield many similarities, as well as important differences. In my own research, I have found that physiognomy followed a different trajectory on the Continent for a variety of reasons, including varying access to printed material and different class contexts, which work toward explaining why Continental physiognomy had a greater presence in literature and painting than in practical and accessible applications.[14] One need only look at the relative publication figures of English and English-language physiognomic texts compared with other languages to see the unique extent of physiognomy's reception and spread in England.[15]

Physiognomy, of course, was not new to the nineteenth century and not unique to London. Dating back to antiquity, physiognomy had enjoyed a long and varied tenure in the fine arts, philosophy, etiquette, fortune-telling and astrology, demonology and the mark of the cursed, and medical and religious contexts. Many scholars have treated the history of physiognomy up to and following the work of the Zürich pastor Johann Caspar Lavater, so I will leave that history in their capable hands, except to comment briefly on physiognomy's more modern manifestations, on which I build my analysis.[16] I also do not delve into the various and heated debates about physiognomic efficacy, which I have discussed in detail elsewhere.[17] What is important for the purposes of this project is that European elites became aware of physiognomy on a grand scale because of the efforts of Lavater.[18] Lavater urged his readers to embark on a system of data collection and compilation about physiognomy as a form of divine worship. For Lavater, physiognomy was a way to access the invisible internal through the external and to provide additional information about the works of the Creator. Lavater created the context for nineteenth-century urban physiognomy, and I draw from his writings to demonstrate the framework under which some of my actors were operating. However, although Lavater established the language, it was those who followed who built it.

Lavater quickly became a social broker, mediating European prestige through inclusion in his works of physiognomic analysis. The books themselves, expensive and beautifully illustrated, became status symbols to be displayed in elegant drawing rooms in Britain and on the Continent. Showpieces rather than guidebooks, Lavater's initial publications were made to be seen rather than to show how to see. But then, in the early nineteenth century in England, something happened. Lavater's ideas caught on, and his books changed accordingly. Cheap and accessible pocket books rivaled and soon replaced the display volumes.[19] In the nineteenth century, physiognomy went paperback. People began to speak in physiognomic terms, using a Lavaterian framework to describe their judgments and explain their reactions. Their judgments and reactions were not new, but their language was. It was also shared, creating a new form of communication and community, the community of physiognomists, of which anyone could become a member.

Many approaches arose to supplement and improve on Lavater's system of data compilation. Scholars and lay writers alike strove to define the elusive key to the physiognomic system and thereby to provide a failsafe way not only to diagnose but also to predict behavior. None entirely succeeded, but efforts continued. As they did, physiognomic awareness grew until it merged almost seamlessly with all forms of observation and judgment. Formal physiognomy, including the approaches of Lavater and those who followed him, was soon beside the point. Empowered by the accessibility of a system that emphasized personal instinct, people simply did physiognomy on their own.

Some of the writers who followed Lavater took seriously his call to find the key to internal physiognomic workings. The works of these scholars, all scientists and almost all doctors, represent a minority of physiognomic writings and an even smaller minority of physiognomic practice. Mechanism remained a largely unexplored arena of physiognomic doctrine, largely because it did not matter. What did matter to all the physiognomists of all types and practices was that, for their purposes of making immediate visual judgments, it seemed to work.

Not everyone agreed that it worked. The amount of ink spent justifying the legitimacy of physiognomy, from Lavater onward, speaks to the amount of opposition it received. Lavater's strategy was to identify all objections and dismantle them, a rhetorical approach that provided one of the keys to the acceptance of his doctrines.[20] Because there was never a physiognomic orthodoxy, there was no concerted opposition. Rather, objections to physiognomy were found in scattered critical reviews of the scholarly writings and in comic magazines. In part because of this hostility, and mostly because of the nature of physiognomy itself (a set of ideas that could not produce testable outcomes), physiognomy as a scholarly discourse hardly developed.

The lay objections to physiognomy were equally disparate because there were a number of different physiognomic practices and practitioners to target. Like its literary supporters, many novelists used physiognomic skepticism as a chance to play with their characters and their audiences. Rather than adhering to the physiognomic formula that the best people were the best looking, writers such as Frances Burney applied physiognomic doctrines to confound readers. In her 1796 novel *Camilla*, Burney flouted convention by making the most beautiful sister the most soulless, and the ugly sister the one with the kindest heart. Others used the literary form to criticize physiognomy directly; in a comic turn, Azilé d'Arcy's 1817 novel *Prejudice; or, Physiognomy* chronicled the experiences of the devoted Lavaterian Helen, who made a series of poor judgments based on physiognomy. Ultimately she renounced the practice, asking, "How can I presume to trust to that which has so woefully deceived me?"[21]

Aside from the scientific and literary objections to physiognomy, critical comments were few and far between. In part, there was no one against whom to direct criticism; aside from the published guides, physiognomy flourished mainly through tacit knowledge and application, seemingly having no single author. Humorous journals such as *Punch,* and serious literary and cultural publications, vacillated on the question; although they sometimes published articles strongly in favor of physiognomy and physiognomic writers, there were a number of sharp critiques of Lavater and the practice he catapulted into daily use. As a constantly changing and expanding set of ideas with such a large number of practitioners who never formed a community, physiognomy had no real body to criticize; such attacks as were found in lay periodicals only fueled the awareness of, and engagement with, physiognomy in all its forms.

It would be impossible and uninteresting to document every mention of physiognomy in nineteenth-century England. Although I have tried to present enough manifestations to demonstrate the frequency and importance of physiognomic applications, I have selected my examples to highlight the various themes that physiognomy brings to light. Common to all these examples, and central to the practice of physiognomy itself, is the privileging of vision as a mode of information gathering and evidence collection. Vision, and therefore physiognomic vision, offered the most reliable data from which to draw conclusions about the natural world, about art, and, of course, about others. It was also the sensory mode over whose deployment the individual had the most choice. Sight can be controlled and even shut off.

The superiority of vision over sound was reflected in an 1856 article in the highbrow moderate journal the *Quarterly Review*. The writer argued that the reliability of vision was universally recognized: "I cannot recollect the author of a famous saying to a stranger who stood silent in his company—'Speak that I may see thee.' But with submission I think we may be better known by our looks than by our words, and that a man's speech is much more easily disguised than his countenance."[22]

The power of observation was derived from the importance of sensory and especially visual experiences in the new modernity. An *Illustrated London News (ILN)* article reprinted from the *Economist* and titled "Speaking to the Eye" explicitly tied pictures to the power of modernity: "Will not the modern art of speaking to the eye, confined to representation of the material world . . . increase the influence of that world, and give the knowledge derived from it a vast preponderance over the mind?"[23] Speaking directly, if unknowingly, to physiognomic practice, the *ILN* argued that the evidence of the eye was superior to other forms of learning and communication.

In unembarrassed self-promotion, the *ILN* supported the notion that pictures were a universal form of communication. The written word, although a highly used source of communication and information exchange in Victorian England, followed the picture as a commodity of the new modernity. The consensus about pocket physiognomy would have been impossible without an increasing awareness of the power of vision. The *ILN* article explicitly noted the importance of images over conversation precisely for the purpose of communicating ideas and information, claiming that "written or spoken language merely suggests thought . . . But pictorial representation may at once convey totally different and totally new ideas to the mind. The artist speaks a universal language." Also, the artist—and his or her pictures—spoke quickly. Pictures thus had "the great advantage over words, that they convey immediately much new knowledge to the mind . . . [Pictures] are universally comprehended. They may make everyone participate in the gathered knowledge of all."[24]

Conversation, that is, long-term interaction, was not only unlikely and at times impossible as a means of communication but also, this article contended, inferior. Speech was less reliable and less well understood than the evidence of sight. It was also necessary; language was required to communicate and create consensus about physiognomy. Vision was but one mode of urban interaction, and it was one that could not be isolated. The sensory signs of sight are always mediated by other modes of perception and experience.

As modernity outpaced the words with which to express itself, new languages and new modes of representation emerged.[25] Lavater early understood the relationship between language and vision and argued for the production of new words to describe his physiognomic ideas. "The more observation shall be extended, [and] language enriched," Lavater wrote, "the more physiognomy shall become scientific, accurately defined, and capable of being taught."[26] But the words and pictures of others could go only so far. Secondhand vision, the sight of others, was inadequate; people trusted what they experienced personally.[27]

The "virtual witnessing" of the seventeenth and eighteenth centuries, through which the testimonial of a respected and established individual acted as sufficient evidence for all concerned, was no longer a viable source of widespread communication.[28] Powerful forces, including the printing press, the railway, and even the Great Exhibition of 1851, ceased to have authors and thus undermined the foundations of trust based on knowledge of others.[29] This trust emerged from personal knowledge of moral character cultivated through interaction. With distant and seemingly authorless phenomena, personal interaction became impossible, and this impossibility precipitated an urban crisis of social confidence.[30] For example, purchasing decisions were not made because consumers knew and trusted those who designed the advertisements.[31] New ways of developing knowledge of moral character, including and especially physiognomy, came to bridge this crisis. Without knowing whom and what to trust, urban dwellers turned to the only ones with whom they had long-standing and deep interactions—themselves.

A new form of trust emerged that depended not on the personal status of the claimant but on the status and acceptance of a system. Theodore Porter has examined the ways in which the impersonality of quantification replaced earlier notions of truth and objectivity in the nineteenth century.[32] Physiognomy drew on both forms of authority, basing its claims on systematized application and the claims of respected authorities. The rules of observation provided legitimacy for the instinctive judgments necessary for the application of physiognomy. Surgeon and physiologist Sir James Paget pointed out the authority gained from the consensus about the practice of physiognomy: "Whatever probability, therefore, a doctrine may claim on the ground that it is generally assented to, this may be claimed for the physiognomy of the human form."[33] This mass consensus was not based only on the mindless adherence of a mob but had its roots in eighteenth-century commitments to respected testimony: "But the assent is not only popular and inconsiderate. The best authorities among men, the keenest observers of all classes, have believed the doctrine, and have applied it. Those have done so who have been most eminent for 'knowledge of the world.' "[34] Once established, however, the evidence of the authorities was set aside by practitioners of pocket physiognomy, who shaped it according to their immediate and unschooled needs.

The greatest need of the nineteenth century was the classification of forms of knowledge, especially human types. Physiognomy offered a way to categorize humanity and to assign and visualize difference, both of individuals and of groups. This form of taxonomy had many values, particularly the infusion of visuality into classification, which necessarily underscored the opinion of the individual. Although this aspect of physiognomy was in many ways a failed project, it contributed to later conceptualizations of interiority and bodily expression of character and experience.

It is not the later manifestations of physiognomic thought that make it an important area of study, however. Although it is interesting to consider what buildings were erected on physiognomic foundations, the practice merits sustained examination in its own right. With this statement I betray some of my own methodological and historiographical commitments, which, for the sake of keeping the reader's interest, I outline only briefly.

Some scholars would label my subject "popular science." This is the only time that term will appear in this book. Despite the fact that physiognomy falls well into this category as it has been very broadly defined, I steer clear of this expression because it is not useful; as James Secord has pointed out, it encompasses too much.[35] By the same token, the expression implies that science in the public realm is less legitimate and less rigorous than that with which scientists exclusively are engaged, or that it is a dilution of the real thing.[36] This is explicitly *not* a story of the lower or middle classes laying claim to ideas that were either taken by or developed in elite circles. Rather, I look at the ways in which members of all social classes participated in this endeavor on equal terms, in its application and so, by definition, its development. The physiognomic instinct, like the act of looking on which it was based, was unclassed.[37] Scholars interested in the relationship between cultural entertainment and science, and in the practical application of scientific ideas, continue to struggle to find a term that adequately defines these endeavors.[38]

Culture—by which I mean entertainment events and experiences rather than attitudes and behaviors characteristic of a given group—matters.[39] It was not just in rarefied intellectual environments, or in laboratories, or in pubs, that science was communicated and produced, but also in the theatre, in the streets, in paintings and at their exhibitions, in newspaper articles and their illustrations, and by everyone involved in all these experiences.[40] In my examination of physiognomy, I look at the ways in which the display of and participation in cultural experiences such as theatre, painting, literature, photography, and graphic print served as the means not only to communicate ideas but also to develop them.

As should be clear by now, my project asserts that physiognomy, and in fact all forms of knowledge construction and pursuit—scientific, cultural and otherwise—are significant on their own terms. That means, of course, that they need to be approached on their own terms. I have no interest in evaluating the legitimacy or validity of physiognomic applications; indeed, I think that such evaluations have no place in a cultural history of science. Instead, I take as my starting point the interest that my historical actors had in physiognomy, and I seek to understand how they applied it and evaluated its efficacy. In so doing, I take seriously the role that audiences and consumers had in the understanding and development of the practice and thus highlight my broader goal of exploring the relationship between cultural experiences and the construction of scientific knowledge. How did audiences experience the deployment of science and knowledge, and what role did they play in its ongoing and changing presentation?

Few works are devoted to nineteenth-century physiognomic practice, and most of these works concentrate on the ways in which physiognomy was deliberately used in literary or artistic works to communicate character and add depth to stories. Graeme Tytler's detailed study of physiognomy in European literature and Mary Cowling's book on anthropological physiognomy in Victorian artwork were particularly helpful on these points, as was Judith Wechsler's work on French caricature physiognomy.[41] These secondary works guided my research on literary and art history, both of which were integral to the development of physiognomic ideas. Although I draw on the wealth of information in these studies, I am interested more in the practical aspects of physiognomy as it was actually communicated, produced, and used to make judgments and act on their basis. To that end, I have been influenced more by studies dealing with other sciences than by those that chronicle the application of physiognomic ideas in literary and artistic works.

Numerous historians of modern science and cultural historians have demonstrated the sophistication of scientific understanding displayed by nonspecialist audiences.[42] These works have emphasized the important role that audiences play in the communication and development of scientific ideas.[43] This book is strongly informed by Anne Secord's study of working-class botanical networks, *Artisan Naturalists: Science as Popular Culture in Nineteenth-Century England*, as well as the work of other scholars who take seriously the role of communication in the production of scientific knowledge.[44] Alison Winter's *Mesmerized: Powers of Mind in Victorian Britain* demonstrated the wealth of historical insight available by engaging with scientific activities that attracted public attention and contributions.[45] Roger Cooter's pioneering study of phrenology and Roger Darnton's work on mesmerism in France opened up those sciences, which we no longer practice, to historical inquiry and highlighted the roles they played in constructing social and cultural narratives.[46] All these works, especially James Secord's *Victorian Sensation*, highlighted the interplay between the audiences for, and the producers of, scientific knowledge, and in their contents often blurred the distinction between them.[47]

My approach to physiognomy has drawn a great deal from the work of these scholars and has used their guidance to take physiognomy and those who practiced it on their own historical terms. Although I pay particular attention to questions of audiences and their contexts, these audiences were often interchangeable with the producers whose books they were reading, whose images they were viewing, and whose plays they were attending. Rather than drawing a sharp distinction between specialists and nonspecialists, my work is based on the premise that both types of actors contributed equally to the development of the multiple types and applications of physiognomy. In fact, Victorian physiognomy itself made no such distinction; aside from the few works by medical doctors designed for their professional colleagues, most physiognomic writings insisted that all practitioners were potential experts and specialists in its practice. Following my historical material, neither do I.

Chris Otter's recent book *The Victorian Eye: A Political History of Light and Vision in Britain, 1800–1910* has guided me greatly, both in approach and content.[48] Otter's emphasis on the lived experience of perception has inspired me to capture the nitty-gritty of Victorian daily physiognomy and present it in an honest and not overly theorized light. I am indebted to the scholarship of Jennifer Green-Lewis and Jennifer Tucker, whose writings on photography have shaped the framing of this book as I consider how Victorians saw and described the world around them.[49] I have also looked directly to art history scholarship to shape my writing on the changes in images and their audiences, as well as broader questions of viewing practices, artistic trends, and market forces that affected portraiture, caricature, and photography. I hope that this book will find an audience in art historians, particularly those who are interested in the intersection of art and science concerning perception, technology, viewing practices, and representations of notions of the self. Broadly interdisciplinary, my work is framed by questions emerging from the history of science, British cultural history, visual culture, and media studies and communication.

This book is divided into six substantive chapters with strong thematic and chronological connections. These chapters chronicle the establishment of the shared subjectivity of physiognomic communication as it expanded from describing individuals to defining groups. I conclude with some reflections on the relationship between physiognomy and interiority and touch on the physiognomies that are being explored today.

Chapter 1 situates physiognomy as a way to make sense of the city by providing a justification for visual judgment. I establish the ubiquity of physiognomic analyses in daily life and chart its use for jobs, romantic interactions, friendships, leadership roles, and business exchanges. Physiognomy offered a way to mediate the unprecedented volume of interactions. Of course, many urbanites did not wish to be looked at and immediately judged. As a way to avoid being the subject of physiognomic analyses, some Victorians strove for anonymity in clothing and self-presentation, trying to blend in order to avoid standing out and being seen.

Despite the introduction of public lighting and open-boulevard planning schemes, there was a darker side to the city. The urban environment teemed with criminals and slums that filled cavernous corners where physiognomy dared not enter. Urban reformers responded by suggesting widening the streets and opening the alleys to maximize surveillance and policing possibilities. Criminal physiognomy not only provided a technology of safekeeping but also suggested methods of reverse engineering. Pictures and models of criminals, such as those displayed in Madame Tussaud's "Chamber of Horrors," taught Victorians what not to look like. In these lessons we see the self-conscious use and manipulation of physiognomy to avoid either detection or false judgments. The streets became stages for which the actors—that is, pedestrians—had to prepare their costumes carefully. These lessons were well learned by novelists, who used physiognomic descriptions to provide character information, which was in turn applied by their readers to themselves and to those they saw.

Following a detailed cultural exploration of the most prominent physiognomic feature, the nose, the chapter concludes with a case study of Arthur Munby, minor Victorian poet and man-about-town. Munby combined his obsession with working-class women with a keen interest in their physiognomy and used its methods to demonstrate the social superiority of his secret servant wife, Hannah Culwick. In Munby's descriptions, along with those of numerous social commentators and writers, we see the use of physiognomy as a means of objectification, reducing women to parts that are always less than the sum of their whole. This focus on parts rather than the whole allows these commentators to control physiognomy by taking instinct out of the picture, negating overall impressions by focusing only on specific parts and their implications as outlined in learned texts. In describing, Munby and others were defining; they used their physiognomic lenses to focus on those with less social power and prestige. Physiognomy may have been accessible to all, but the reflections of only some were recorded and in turn expanded, forming the framework for future physiognomy and future physiognomists.

Chapter 2 asks, if the streets were self-conscious sites of performance, where was the nature of humanity explored? In an inversion, the stage became a kind of street, a site of interaction between different characters that not only mirrored but also established forms of real human contact. Set against the rise of realism and theatrical historicism, Victorian stage physiognomy developed in conjunction with a new phenomenon: the educated audience. Using sociological theories of audience reception, I analyze the ways in which audiences made sense—or did not—of the character information offered by the actors through makeup, costuming, hairstyle, and body type. Actors experienced tremendous anxiety about the regimentation of their craft in light of expectations of physiognomic and historical accuracy, especially because managers paid particular attention to type in their selections and staging. Physiognomy complicated the job of actors and circumscribed the roles for which they were facially and physically suited. At the same time, the uniformity in costuming and self-styling offered new opportunities for stagecraft and creativity; actors could confidently infuse their characters with the internal personal touch, knowing that the external signs were uniform. The realistic costumes, speaking styles, and scenery allowed audiences to immerse themselves entirely in the fantasy of the play even as, and perhaps because, differential lighting, the use of the curtain, and other architectural innovations created new boundaries between the audience and the stage.

Through an examination of acting manuals and playbooks, as well as theatre reviews and private diaries, I explore the training of actors in the context of physiognomic awareness. On the other side of the stage, I use audience responses to gauge the success or failure of the actors' and managers' attempts to make their roles physiognomically convincing. The faces of actors were newly exposed because of increased lighting technology, which spurred further developments in costuming and makeup that again complicated and expanded the demands on nonverbal communication between audience and actor. Actors were exhorted to study nature in order to perfect their representations of the natural and the real. As we see from the responses of the audience, sometimes, despite their best efforts (or no efforts at all), they did not succeed in their quest.

Chapters 2 and 3 are strongly connected through themes of mimesis, representation, realism, and self-conscious communication of physiognomic types. Chapter 3 takes as its subject drawing and portraiture. Through painting and drawing manuals, exhibition reviews, and close readings of paintings, it examines the ways in which artists considered and selectively applied physiognomic principles to their images. As art ownership became mediated by market forces with the development of the culture-climbing middle classes, painters were no longer supported by a single patron but by exhibitions and sales. The consumer audience for art—like theatrical audiences—brought physiognomic knowledge to bear on their viewing practices, adding a new element to the considerations of the painters. Nineteenth-century painting styles shifted from sycophantic treatments of powerful patrons to biographical and realistic renderings of a broad range of subjects, with increasing pressure on the accurate delineation of character. In consonance with trends established in natural history, drawing became a test of observational skill, and artists were judged accordingly.

This chapter highlights the role that artists, like actors, played in framing the discourse of *physiognomic possibility*. Through their vision, painters and performers were using physiognomy to create, or re-create, people, as well as the physiognomic project, in their image. The "their" is deliberately ambiguous; painters were themselves playing with what they saw and envisioned as ideal depictions, and with what they imputed their sitters to desire in their ideas of themselves. Physiognomic knowledge provided the conditions of possibility by which all contributors to this process—artists, actors, managers, subjects, viewers, and audiences—could engage in these acts of creation. According to modern physiognomic innovator Johann Caspar Lavater, physiognomy illustrated the ways in which human beings were crafted in the image of the divine. According to participants in nineteenth-century English visual culture, it was human beings who were doing the crafting through physiognomy, and they were crafting in the image of themselves.

Portraiture did not exist only in the realm of the fine arts. In fact, most images were viewed and consumed outside the rarefied halls of the annual exhibition of the Royal Academy of Arts. Chapter 4 chronicles the use of physiognomy in caricature and argues that physiognomic codes were used to assign visibility to visually assimilated Jewish and Irish faces. With the help of physiognomic signals, caricaturists developed typical Irish and Jewish faces by assigning difference on the basis of a fantasy of shared visible features. I explore a series of caricatures of Irish and Jewish faces and read these texts against physiognomic monographs and frameworks to chart the training of audiences and their contributions to caricature commonalities. Caricaturists deployed humor and entertainment to calm rising anxieties about immigration and assimilation and invited audiences to share the joke about these imagined means of identification.

With rising political agitation, depictions of Irish people became increasingly monstrous and culminated in explicit ape imagery. These images visually neutralized the threat of the Irish by building caricature cages in which the Irish could be contained. The Jewish depictions deployed a more nuanced set of symbols that eradicated the difference between the wealthy Sephardi (Iberian) communities and the poverty-stricken Ashkenazi (eastern European) recent immigrants. Caricaturists built on and expanded the repertoire of identification symbols of Irish and Jews and established new metonymical signs that came to stand for and even replace physiognomy. For example, the repeated drawings of the "Paddy cap" and the "Jewish nose" became inextricable from the type itself, mapping character onto clothing and costuming symbols. On stage and in images, these symbols were sufficient to establish the identities of the characters in question. Both sets of images increased in circulation and tone in conjunction with the removal of Catholic and Jewish disabilities; as these communities gained more rights, their invisibility represented an even greater threat. Physiognomy offers an important analytic tool to understand these images and their embedded implications, which audiences were increasingly trained to understand, but which remain largely obscure to the historical eye.

Caricature established a means of assigning difference and played an important role in the delineation of group types. Photography built on the trends established by caricature and painting while encountering the limitations of physiognomic messaging. In Chapter 5, I offer a case study of the expansion of physiognomy to include metonymical symbols of clothing, hairstyle, and other forms of self-presentation. Through a close reading of the physiognomic photographs of asylum superintendent Hugh Welch Diamond and their accompanying commentaries by Dr. John Conolly, I argue that physiognomic photographs acted as mediated mirrors through which concepts of self were transformed. By looking at their photographs, patients were forced to encounter gaps between their self-images and the way in which they appeared through Diamond's lens and to undergo an appropriate realignment of their own assessment. For Diamond's patients, looking at their photographs called a new self into being. The self they were encountering, however, was carefully staged by Diamond, who fore-grounded metonymical clothing cues to stand in for the messages of the face. Patients who recovered were literally re-covered as their improve-ments were chronicled by increasing self-care, which was read by Dia-mond and Conolly as physiognomic transformation.

Diamond framed and disseminated his pictures with a very specific set of messages and goals in mind, namely, therapy for his patients, public relations for his asylum, and diagnostic consistency across time and space. Both a doctor and a well-respected photographer, Diamond displayed his photographs to the public in order to allay their fears about asylums and their inhabitants by acting as a guide behind the closed and forbidding doors. He depicted patients who were neither as scary nor as hopeless as many imagined them to be, and he even chronicled cases of cure. In his comments, Diamond focused on the ways in which physiognomy could be used to mark individual patients and their respective maladies. Conolly, by contrast, was interested in group analyses and used physiognomy to discuss the appearance of the mad, broadly construed. In these images, we see multiple uses and meanings of physiognomy deployed simultane-ously: individual and group descriptions, getting and giving information, focusing on specific features and overall impressions, and, of course, cre-ating a common frame of reference. Photography was hailed as the re-demptive technology for claims of physiognomic accuracy because of its mechanical objectivity. In this chapter, I argue that mechanical objectivity was in fact irrelevant to the longevity and efficacy of physiognomy. It was, rather, the subjective nature of its claims that made physiognomy so useful and so trenchant.

Diamond's photographs elucidated both the diagnostic nature of phys-iognomy and the construction of inner space, which are the two major themes of the final substantive chapter. Chapter 6 chronicles the use of physiognomy as a classification technology of large-group types as an attempt to make order in a disordered world. I focus in particular on medicine, phrenology, and, for the bulk of the chapter, the composite photography, anthropology, and fingerprinting efforts of Sir Francis Galton. I finally touch briefly on the attitudes of Charles Darwin about physiognomy and show that although he purported to reject physiognomy's claims, he too was influenced by its language and approach.

Many emerging professional groups, including asylum doctors, phrenologists, and especially anthropologists, tried to use the widespread appeal of physiognomy to attract attention to their own endeavors. I examine the relationship between physiognomy and its too-closely related offspring, phrenology, and show that phrenology was a failed attempt to be the scientific physiognomy. It was the subjective and nonexpert nature of physiognomy that allowed it to flourish even after phrenology's demise. Broadly diagnostic and classificatory, the goals of anthropology in particular overlapped with physiognomy's discourse of ordering human types. Galton built on the work of Diamond and especially Conolly to use photography as a means to access physiognomy, but in a way that entirely eradicated the individual and focused only on large groups. For Galton, like other photographers who came before him, physiognomy was a way to order masses and highlight what was common to these groups. Galton was especially interested in picturing and defining the criminal and the deviant through their shared physiognomic markers. In his use of photography, Galton understood the importance of visuality in the anthropological endeavor and claimed that to look at people was to know them.

The chapter concludes with a move away from physiognomy proper as I turn to other practices requiring the interiority that physiognomy established. I look at Galton's fingerprinting as growing out of the conditions of possibility provided by physiognomy, and I gesture toward psychoanalysis as another practice framed by physiognomic ideas. Much like physiognomy itself, this chapter is both general—elucidating broad themes of group diagnosis and professionalization—and specific, in its use of the case study of Sir Francis Galton. My work here builds on the research and ideas of all the previous chapters and has the broadest historical range, starting in the early nineteenth century and ending at its close. But the story does not end there. Although I do not engage with the more sinister offshoots of physiognomic thought that persisted through the close of World War II and beyond, I am intrigued by recent reinventions of physiognomy, including biological-anthropological researches on hand size, cognitive neurology explorations of face recognition in babies, training courses in facial expression, and racial profiling. I end the book by highlighting some of these manifestations and ask why we are now again interested in penetrating the body with our eyes. What are the stakes for the materialism of the new physiognomy today?

CHAPTER ONE

Pocket Physiognomy

Sense in the City

INCREASINGLY throughout the nineteenth century, London was an extraordinary place to see and (willingly or otherwise) to be seen. Richly sensual, appealing to smell, touch, sound, and especially sight, the streets of London bustled at a pace both exciting and mystifying. The city was becoming increasingly illegible and confusing, its possibilities and dangers mixing as freely as its inhabitants.[1] As part of their attempts to make sense of their city, Londoners read faces as a way to read their surroundings. In a context increasingly obsessed with the sense of sight, the only way for close friends and passers-by alike to hide in plain sight from the gaze of others was through anonymity—in clothing and hairstyle, in manners, and even in face. Dependent on the experiences of both the observer and the observed, physiognomy was a highly subjective modality that depended on visual access to the perceptual field. An important aspect of physiognomy was that even though it was subjective, the rules surrounding it allowed conclusions to be shared, and created a community of physiognomic observers where there might have been only strangers and gawkers.

With the development of new visual technologies such as the panorama and the stereoscope, vision was revealed to be subjective and, therefore, tremendously powerful.[2] The panorama, as Bernard Comment has pointed out, provided a fantasy of dominance over an almost uncontrollable urban landscape and offered inhabitants and visitors (virtual and actual) the comforting sense that the city could be captured and preserved.[3] Physiognomy provided that same reassurance in the context of human interaction by acting as a way to turn visual observation into a source of information and power. One of the most pressing informational needs concerned the people who inhabited this new modernity; to solve this problem, people became pictures, objects, and analytical units—analyzing and to be analyzed.

Recast as physiognomy, visual judgment offered a way for some to ease the crisis of confusion and sensory overstimulation of the city streets.[4] Physiognomic language provided a set of rules by which to make quickly those character judgments that previously had had time and space in which to develop. Pocket physiognomy texts and, more important, instincts, could be referenced when people were walking the city and entering relationships, particularly when they needed to make social decisions and distinctions or to decide whom to trust. Physiognomy was a handy surveillance mechanism that required nothing more than a set of seeing eyes and a quick-and-ready willingness to judge. The more experienced the observer, many believed, the better the judgment, and the more trusted the conclusions. Physiognomic books carried authority largely because of the experience of the observers rather than the rigor of their rules. No one was immune to these analyses; anyone who could be visually discerned could be physiognomically defined.

The physiognomic act—that of observing another—was hardly novel; what was new was the authority that the physiognomic label lent, and the frequency with which it was applied. Physiognomy gave people permission to judge. Although there were communal principles by which observers were guided, physiognomy was an individual action, dependent as much on the history and experience of the observer as on the observed. Few physiognomists took their own subjectivity into account, allowing practitioners to ascribe errors to failures in judgment rather than failures in the system. Often, those whose jobs and even lives depended on assessing others, including kings and generals, had the most finely tuned physiognomic instincts. Nevertheless, even amateurs used physiognomy in their interactions with others and, comparatively, on themselves. Rare was the person who did not reassure himself or herself by a quick glance in a mirror after encountering actual or reproduced criminals and villains.

Vague in the extreme, most physiognomic conclusions hardly referenced principles and philosophies at all. It was in the act of naming observation *physiognomy* that the observed could be imagined to be contained. As a general rule, most analyses were structured around the influential and enduring Platonic principle of *kalokagatheia,* succinctly summarized by Johann Caspar Lavater as "the morally best, the most beautiful. The morally worst, the most deformed."[5] Conclusions easily followed from this principle, based, of course, on the eyes of the beholder.

The urban streets became sites of sight, in which all city inhabitants were both observers and the observed (although some were simply trying to get from point A to point B). In an attempt to read the city and its inhabitants, passers-by developed strategies of making legible the confusing visual document in which they lived and worked. As a way of making meaning, physiognomy was a double-edged sword; although everyone could access its techniques, by the same token, no one was immune from its judgments. To deal with the ubiquity of physiognomic analyses, many urbanites strove for visual anonymity, which led to conformity in patterns of dress and self-presentation. In order to avoid the suspect implications of hiding from the physiognomic gaze, city dwellers hid in plain sight; those who did lurk in the darkness were marked as deviant and criminal, as were those who were visibly different in the light of day. These others provided a reflexive framework by which observers could measure themselves and their own, superior physiognomy.

Many physiognomic observers reduced the observed to specific features and so reduced people to their component parts. By disembodying specific elements of a given person, physiognomic analysts produced a power relationship in which they were whole people and those they were considering were objects, the sum of their parts that was never assembled. Although physiognomic analyses could theoretically be made across class barriers, numerous descriptions underscored the extent to which it was a classifying endeavor. Those with greater social and cultural power were using physiognomy to describe their surveillance of the urban underclass and demonstrating the use of physiognomy to demarcate and objectify groups. Likewise, physiognomy was used to objectify individuals by breaking them into their component parts and analyzing the pieces without summing them into the whole.

The City as Text

There were different strategies for reading what Steven Marcus has called "the illegible city" of the early to mid-nineteenth century.[6] Urban ethnographers such as Friedrich Engels, Henry Mayhew, and Eliza Lynn Linton read their environments through the act of writing, capturing the experience in words rather than pictures.[7] The panorama was a fantastic way to frame and understand the city sights that these writers described. Travel guides and maps, as well as newspaper reports, comic magazines, and other media outlets, offered manageable pieces of the city by unmasking its many treasures. Physiognomy was another, very powerful mechanism to divide the urban mass into its component parts and explain these parts in an accessible way. Anyone with eyes could read people's physiognomy, and the price of admission to the streets was free. In deciphering and decoding, however, these strategies also exposed; under the surveillance of those who were avidly reading the city's inhabitants, there were very few ways to hide.

Merely walking through the streets of London became a physiognomic experience; Victorian urban ethnographies, which were themselves projects of observation, applied physiognomic language to produce easily demarcated types. Works such as journalist and social reformer Henry Mayhew's classic *London Labour and the London Poor* were filled with physiognomic references.[8] For Mayhew, these references identified, classified, and surveyed those city dwellers who had remained largely invisible to their social betters. Refusing to allow their poverty to obscure these urbanites and their experiences, Mayhew highlighted their unique characteristics by using physiognomic language to read, see, and describe his human surroundings. He was a storyteller who built tales from the evidence of his eyes and the dictates of his heart.[9] Mayhew and his audience were engaged in a mutual project of penetrating surfaces and seeing those individuals who had remained invisible by collectively forming a mass (lower) class.

The second page of the first volume of *London Labour* began with a physiognomic analysis of urban wanderers, namely, "the pickpockets—the beggars—the prostitutes—the street-sellers—the street-performers—the cab-men—the coachmen—the watermen—the sailors and such like."[10] Mayhew discussed the appearance of these people and its relationship to their behavior and noted that "in each of the classes above-mentioned, there is a greater development of the animal than of the intellectual or moral nature of man, and that they are all more or less distinguished for their high cheek-bones and protruding jaws."[11] Mayhew illuminated both individual and group characteristics and made it impossible for his subjects to escape his gaze, or the gaze of his readers, by blending into their larger communities.

Similar descriptions peppered this and other works by Mayhew, including *The Criminal Prisons of London* and the explicitly classificatory work *London Characters and the Humorous Side of London Life*.[12] A strong believer in observation as a means to understanding others, Mayhew opened *London Characters* with a series of questions about the city's inhabitants that he set out to answer just by looking at them: "Who are these people who pass to and fro? What lives are theirs? What are their stories? Who are their friends? What is their business?"[13]

Mayhew's questions reflected his curiosity about the urban mass, and his books were an attempt to satisfy that curiosity.[14] In his writings, Mayhew insisted that with careful observation, he could see the differences between those who looked similar on the surface. His subjects, he wrote, "are all so much alike, and yet so widely different; their stories are so wonderfully similar in their broad outlines, and yet so strangely unlike in their minute particulars." From similarities, Mayhew deduced common histories and experiences: "Just as one man's face is like another's, so is the story of his life: no two faces are exactly alike, yet all have many points in common."[15] In searching for distinction, Mayhew reinforced the anonymity of shared experience and, especially, shared class. By focusing on what he claimed were only minute differences in both faces and lives, Mayhew provided the key to escaping attention in the city, namely, finding a community and disappearing within it.

Other writings, such as author and antifeminist Eliza Lynn Linton's more conventional 1855 article "Passing Faces" in the expensive middle-class weekly *Household Words,* took readers on a walk through London and narrated the various types of people to be seen across the social spectrum.[16] In this article, Linton used physiognomic demarcations to demonstrate the range of types inhabiting the city. Linton made explicit the imagical and sensual nature of city observations in "this the strange mass of pathos, poetry, caricature, and beauty which lie heaped up together without order or distinctive heading, and which men endorse as Society and the World." The people Linton saw and described were images, and the streets she inhabited were texts to be seen, tasted, touched, heard, and smelled. She called the city "LIFE, in all its boundless power of joy and suffering—this is the great picture-book to be read in the London streets; these are the wild notes to be listened to."[17]

Linton opened her article with the contention that "we have no need to go abroad to study ethnology." At once cosmopolitan and highly regional, Linton argued that the entire world—or at least the interesting parts of it—was contained in the microcosm of home: "A walk through the streets of London will show us specimens of every human variety known."[18] Some skills were necessary to engage in Linton's project, namely, "a tolerably quick eye, and the educated perception of an artist." Still, even without this education, "those lines are to be seen by all who know how to look for them," or even by those "who understand them when they are before them."[19] Speed remained of the essence in this endeavor because during a "walk through London . . . the passing faces [are] hurrying by."[20]

Linton's physiognomic analyses focused on face shapes and features in her attempt to trace the different races of city dwellers. In her walks, she was struck by the ill effects of both urban life and cultural mixing on the appearance, and thus the character, of her subjects and reflected that "it is perfectly incredible what a large number of ugly people one sees." Extreme ugliness, in Linton's analysis, rendered some of those she saw animals and prompted her to wonder "where they can possibly have come from,—from what invading tribe of savages or monkies. We meet faces that are scarcely human,—positively brutified out of all traces of intelligence by vice, gin, and want of education." Others, although still human, were "the simply ugly faces, with all the lines turned the wrong way, and all the colours in the wrong places."[21]

The ideas on which Linton was drawing again followed those of Plato, Lavater, and all the major physiognomists, that the uglier the person on the outside, the worse the person on the inside. Although Linton's contempt was strongly classed in her discussion, it was spread equally across the poor and the idle rich, including "the men who are called elegant—good lord!—and who maunder through life in a daft state of simpering dilettanteism, but who never thought a man's thought, nor did a man's work, since they were born."[22] Likewise, Linton discussed "equivocal-looking men, who are evidently unsubstantial speculators without capital, and who trade on airy thousands when they want money enough to buy dinner."[23]

In her article, Linton did not explain precisely what organization of features made her subjects appear "equivocal." For Linton, as for others, the language of physiognomy provided the justification for her conclusions. Linton was not working from a particular physiognomic system or set of texts. She conducted her study on the basis of her own intuition and the ideas that she held about what constituted, for example, "acute-looking men."[24] In this way, Linton was applying the most common variant of pocket physiognomy: her conclusions drew on physiognomic theories that had been established in multiple monographs and learned writings but were never referenced in, or related to, the project of daily urban physiognomic readings. Her own instinct was reference enough.

An 1856 *Quarterly Review* article by surgeon and pathologist Sir James Paget succinctly described the pocket physiognomy variant applied by Linton. This article spoke to both the universality of physiognomic practice and the lack of relationship most practitioners had to its underlying principles: "Each man's mental nature may be discerned in his external form. There are few, perhaps, who do not hold such a belief, few who do not often act on it in the ordinary affairs of life, but there are far fewer who could give good reasons for it."[25] Paget argued that physiognomic conviction emerged from consensus rather than from reasoned thought; like Eden Warwick, whom I discuss later in this chapter, Paget thought that sophisticated proofs were unnecessary in the execution of physiognomic judgment. The article later noted that "this general belief is vague, and not intelligent, but so are all general beliefs, and it is their wide diffusion, not their precision, which gives them weight in evidence."[26] In Paget's city, the wide diffusion of physiognomy put the practice in the hands and eyes of everyone. In Paget's exaggerated notion of the city, everyone was watching, and everyone could be judged.

Hiding in the City

Urban ethnographers and city chronicles catalogued the types of people within the city, and under their surveillance, no one was immune from examination. The project of Engels, Mayhew, and Linton (all with different motives) was to prevent the urban underclass from evading detection. Their work provided a model for urban reformers who were attempting to eradicate the invisibility of anonymity associated with the city's poorest inhabitants. To them, hiding was associated with criminal motives and questionable activities. The indistinguishable mass posed a threat to the urban dweller's physiognomic fantasy of visual dominance over the urban landscape.

The problem of dark spaces and their dwellers was compounded by the infrastructure of London, especially in its poorest parts. The 1838 Select Committee on Metropolitan Improvements lamented the refuge of darkness available to London's poorest inhabitants, who were "entirely secluded from the observation and influence of better educated neighbours" and so "exhibited a state of moral degradation deeply to be deplored." To allow greater surveillance of the poor and their inevitable moral improvement through interactions with "more respectable inhabitants," the report suggested that "great streams of public intercourse could be made to pass through the districts in question."[27]

Not only did dark corners protect sinners, argued traveler, member of Parliament, and temperance and antislavery activist James Silk Buckingham, they actually produced them because "such secret haunts" generated a "morose defiance of public decency." These "secret and obscure haunts" were to be eliminated from Buckingham's ideal city, so that "the filthy and immoral" could not be hidden from the "public eye."[28] In Buckingham's vision, the Benthamite panopticon tower would be rendered obsolete; with ample open spaces, the streets would provide the ideal vantage point to observe and to judge. The power of physiognomic judgment was situated in the visually accessible streets of a highly legible city. What Buckingham did not take into account was that physiognomic judgment worked two ways, and the observed were also the observers, drawing on the knowledge of consensus and the legitimacy provided by the masses.

By 1849, when Buckingham proposed his ideal city, a great deal of light had already been shed on the subject, and the subjects, of surveillance. With the introduction of gas illumination on London streets in 1807, observation and performance became constantly possible in public space.[29] As Carolyn Marvin has shown, lighted space expanded opportunities for encounter and power negotiation among different communities, interactions that were themselves highly constructed.[30] These performances were a kind of hiding, beneath which one's true feelings and character could be masked. Self-protection had its cost, however. According to sociologist and historian Richard Sennett, assuming a public face as "a defense against being read by others" required city dwellers to "stop feeling."[31] Urban dwellers were caught between a fear of hiding and a fear of being seen.

Although performance is an important category of my examination, it is not the only one. I do not assume a deliberate self-consciousness for all street experiences and physiognomic judgments. Some Victorians were simply trying to traverse the city unremarked and, in so doing, did not mark what was around them. This attempt at anonymity can be regarded as performative, but it can also be understood simply as walking. Many succeeded in living their daily lives without paying explicit attention to physiognomy, but very few were immune from the social anxiety of fitting in. In the nineteenth century, physiognomy provided a new code for conformity as people became concerned not just with judging others, but with how others were judging them.

Violent street crime decreased significantly and inversely to property crime throughout the nineteenth century, in part because of the introduction of gas street lighting in 1807.[32] Despite the shift away from personal attacks, there were numerous widespread panics about street theft and garroting that fueled a suspicion of lurkers and shadowy forms.[33] Hiding in darkness became equated with immorality, and physiognomy emerged as a form of surveillance of those who ventured into the light. An obvious defense against the ubiquity of physiognomic analyses was to try to blend in by looking like everyone else. Walter Benjamin has argued that the roots of the Victorian detective story lay in the criminal's ability to avoid capture by blending into the urban masses. It was the crowd that provided the context for the two sides of the scrutiny/anonymity coin and its accompanying terrors.[34]

Contemporaneous observers were well aware of the obliterating effect of crowds, particularly on those who grasped the essentials of the average. Artist and engraver to the queen Thomas Woolnoth noted in 1854 that uniformity of expression "has that neutralizing effect upon the mass," rendering those within the group "as undistinguished as if they had no Expression at all." In this uniform mass, distinction became deviance and blurred the line between individuality and abnormality. Woolnoth, like many other upper-class observers, noticed only those among the masses who stood out in a visually arresting way: "What arrests the eye in passing is that more turbulent and depraved condition of face."[35]

Although he was not literally elevated, Woolnoth wrote as though he were on high, a realization of the panopticonization of the streets to which Buckingham and other urban reformers aspired. The mass to which Woolnoth alluded was clearly composed of the working-class poor, observation of whom was his uncontested right. For Woolnoth, like Eliza Lynn Linton, looking at others held a strong degree of reflexivity because they comforted themselves by noting their own physiognomic superiority. The tendency to engage in physiognomic comparisons was exploited by caricaturists and wax modelers, whose impressions of criminal and deviant others were attractive in part because of their power to reassure observers how very different from these representations they themselves were.

Crucial to the effectiveness of the urban physiognomic experience was the speed—unique to this technology—with which it could be applied. Equally important was the instinctual and spontaneous nature of physiognomic identification; conclusions could be and often were drawn unrealized and unprocessed in passing city encounters, only to be expressed and shared later. In the words of artist and critic Lady Elizabeth Rigby Eastlake, "The face is not only the appointed badge of distinction and proof of identity, but it is the sole proof which is instantaneous—an evidence not collected by effort, study, or time, but obtained and apprehended in a moment; and that, as often as not, an unprepared moment."[36]

Woolnoth, among others, cast physiognomy as a specifically urban endeavor, noting that it was "in walking in the streets of the metropolis [that] we have the finest opportunities of enlarging our facial observations."[37] For Woolnoth, physiognomic observation produced a mental archive that he applied to his artistic work. He used the city and its faces as a textbook from which to learn.

In his writings on the artistic uses of physiognomy, Woolnoth emphasized the positive side for those who had physiognomically appealing faces. He noted that the "personal advantages of getting into favour with the physiognomist may be instanced by the necessary protection it affords in terms of excitement and political phrenzy [sic]." Politically charged situations could also be eased through physiognomy. For example, "canvassing for a member, where, should you blunder your interview on the wrong side of the questions, your face might prove your only apology; it might save you the indignity of the door, perhaps allow you a chair, and in some mitigated cases, even forgive your politics."[38]

For some features, the difference between advantage and deviance was a matter of degree rather than kind; what was good in moderation indicated trouble in excess. An article in the *Quarterly Review* offered some programmatic guidelines about the negative implications of the placement of the eyes: "Eyes set too near, or too far asunder, are alike animal in expression and in meaning: the former are like the eyes of apes; the latter like those of oxen, dogs, and horses."[39] Eyes only slightly askew, only very subtly different from the norm, however, hearkened great things:

> It is not very rare to see one eyeball somewhat higher than the other:—if the difference be very slight, it is likely to mark a thinking, considerate man, who looks at every side of a matter. When the eyes sink a little towards their inner angles, they denote warmth of mind directed to realities; when they rise towards them, they denote a similar mind directed to the supersensuous and ideal.[40]

Fitting in facially, either through total uniformity or slight deviation, was one way to blend, but manipulating expressions could be rather unpredictable. A more consistent approach for urban dwellers to achieve uniformity was through adherence to stylistic codes. Dressing in the current mode marked someone as not only fashionable and modern but also able to afford the rapidly changing dicta of consumer society.[41] The range of fashion at any given time was limited; despite the availability of numerous dyes and industrial production mechanisms, only a few colors and patterns were ever in vogue at any one time.[42] With improved public lighting, street clothing became ever more a costume for the urbanite's appearance outside the home, but a costume designed to deflect rather than attract attention.[43]

The right clothes were not always enough to evoke anonymity, nor was the right expression necessarily sufficient. The "Lavater" entry in the eighth edition of the *Encyclopaedia Britannica* commented that "in many places, where the study of human character from the face became an epidemic, the people went masked through the streets."[44] Although the entry is hyperbolic if interpreted literally, it reveals a deep anxiety about revelation beyond people's control. Clothes can be chosen. Faces cannot. Masks, as an 1872 image from *Punch* demonstrated, protected people's identities from the judgments of others and the uncontrollable revelations of oneself (Figure 1.1).

Although actual masks were rare, bonnets were increasingly common, particularly in the 1840s, giving way to thick veils that served the double

AT THE FRENCH PLAY.

HAPPY THOUGHT—INCOGNITO SECURED—BLUSHES CONCEALED—AND SELF-
RESPECT PRESERVED (AT LEAST OUTWARDLY).

Figure 1.1. This 29 June 1872 image from *Punch* illustrates the extent to which masks were seen as a protective feature from the prying eyes of others, even in public settings.

purpose of shielding the face from observation and protecting the skin of those wearing them. Indoors, however, particularly with improved lighting technology, people adopted different strategies of shading themselves. Few middle- and upper-class Victorians, especially women, were seen in full light beyond the first blush of youth; they dimmed their oil lamps and gaslights, dressed in the dark, and kept their houses in semilight. Aside from physiognomic revelations, full light would uncover the truths of age and fading beauty and the artifice that attempted to hide them.[45]

The repressed nature of Victorian street clothes stands in sharp contrast to the elaborate outfits worn by upper-class Georgians. In the eighteenth century, clothing provided more transparent clues to status and class than did the affordable vestments of the industrialized and imperialized nineteenth century. As Simon Gunn has shown, the ready abundance of cheap material and affordable ready-made suits and hoops paradoxically made clothing and self-presentation ever more significant guides to people's identity and character.[46] The very excesses of Georgian style provided their own form of protection for the educated and physiognomically aware.[47] Given the more democratic nature of nineteenth-century public people reading, it was best to avoid standing out, either by overadherence to trends or, equally, by ignoring them completely. An 1845 article in the *London Journal,* a cheap periodical aimed at self-improving working- and middle-class women, counseled its readers that "no one should dress in a manner to render himself conspicuous: attire should be good but 'quiet.'" Attention could also be drawn by ignoring stylistic codes, so the article emphasized that "a due regard to *fashion* should be observed, because if you happen to be far behind the march of improvement, you become singular—an appearance we have before recommended you to avoid."[48] Fashionable was one thing; unusual was an entirely separate, and undesirable, matter.

Blending into both the right crowd and the right class was not only a matter of money or even a matter of access to the right accessories. According to Richard Sennett, the most important key to "passing" unremarked was knowing the codes of behavior. Far more important than being of a certain class was looking like you were, which entailed knowing the rules of the game and especially the rules of fashion.[49] This closed system, of course, ensured that only those in the know would know who belonged and who did not. If one was unaware of the rules, one could not judge others by their strictures. By contrast, those who were aware of the rules possessed the ability to judge not only others but themselves, and to use physiognomic techniques to establish their own superiority over the criminals and deviants.

Judging Faces: Criminal Classification

Despite the best attempts of urban reformers, the city maintained endless dark corners and pockets. These acted as places for people to hide, centers of criminal activity, and poverty-stricken neighborhoods rife with disease and death. In addition to being a place of excitements, new experiences, and sensory challenges, London was dark, dangerous, and defiant. Pocket physiognomy was a lantern illuminating opaque surfaces and exposing endless depths. Even as the nineteenth century became more democratic in education, religious diversity, dress, and social standing, the class codes of performance and presentation were all the more entrenched. Almost anyone who stood out in an undesirable way was suspect, and many guidebooks, caricatures, diary entries, and newspaper headlines were devoted to the identification of these deviants and likely criminals. In using physiognomy to identify criminals, every individual was lawyer, judge, and jury, whose courts were private homes, places of business, and, especially, the streets of the city.

Christopher Lane has argued that the Victorian era was a time of hatred and misanthropy, masked by necessarily rigorously demarcated forms of civility and etiquette.[50] The city exacerbated the experience of human suspicion and made the need for accessible techniques of quick evaluation of others all the more pressing. People were watching. The evaluators, however, were also the evaluated—with physiognomic technology, no one was in total control. An important skill in this climate was the ability to identify deviants and, equally, to distinguish oneself from them. These skills offered protection from being attacked and, ideally, from being suspected; knowledge of criminal faces provided a framework for comparative physiognomic analysis against which innocents could be favorably judged.

Madame Tussaud's, the famous wax museum, provided examples of criminals with which visitors could compare themselves. In 1855, the "Chamber of Horrors" exhibit, dedicated to displaying famous criminals and offering patrons the opportunity to experience the settings of their crimes, changed its name to the "Chamber of Comparative Physiology." In a typically satirical yet substantive comment, *Punch* explained the switch as a nod to changes in public sensibility, "a recognition of an improvement in the popular taste, to which the horrible no longer affords any attraction, and which instead of that, demands the scientific." The voyeuristic draw of such an exhibit no longer lay in its shock value but in its prophylactic and protective power. Patrons "now go to the Baker

Street Waxworks, not to gape with morbid interest at [murderers] COUR-VOISIER and DANIEL GOOD, but for the purpose of studying the lineaments of those villains, with a view to proper precaution against gentlemen of similar aspect."[51] (These comments call to mind the modern "Bodyworlds" exhibit, with its similar blending of macabre voyeurism and outreach and education.)

Protective the exhibit might have been, but it was also prescriptive. According to *Punch,* the newly named chamber was diagnostic and pedagogical, teaching careful patrons what criminals looked like and whom to avoid. No one was safe from the surveillance of these Madame Tussaud visitors. Criminal look-alikes could be found anywhere, especially by those with faulty physiognomic judgment: "Neither the writer of this, nor any of his readers, would like to have a resemblance discovered between themselves and RUSH by any would-be LAVATER of their acquaintance, who had been pursuing his researches in the Chamber of Comparative Physiognomy."[52]

The exhibit was also reflexive. Not only were people comparing the models with others but also, with the safe reassurance of obvious distinction, with themselves. A blurb advertising a new exhibit in the chamber highlighted the mixed results of the comparative aspect of physiognomic modeling: "Comparative Physiognomy is the physiognomy of such brutes as the murderer YOUNGMAN in contrast with our noble selves. It is a pleasing study at least to those whose physiognomy differs from that of such gentlemen as the murderer YOUNGMAN."[53] (It was not as pleasant for those who might have had a resemblance to Youngman or the notorious killer James Bloomfield Rush.)

On the matter of criminals, urbanites were urged to follow their gut feelings. One of the most user friendly of the pocket and employment physiognomy guides, *The Pocket Lavater,* provided verbal and visual examples by which to recognize criminals. It warned against "the salient angles of the nose, the projection and sharpness of the chin," which "indicate an astute, enterprising, and crafty character" (Figure 1.2). More important than these details, however, was the instinctive reaction of readers and observers to this type of face, which they "cannot regard without repugnance, and in which it is impossible to confide."[54]

In her anonymous 1851 *Quarterly Review* article on physiognomy, Lady Elizabeth Eastlake emphasized the importance of urban physiognomy as a means of criminal identification, asking, "What else but a power rapid and unerring as this could preserve society from the most bewildering confusions and fatal mistakes?" She argued that with the help of astute

Figure 1.2. According to *The Pocket Lavater,* this face was immediately recognizable as belonging to a crafty and possibly criminal character. Johann Caspar Lavater, *The Pocket Lavater* (New Haven: Baldwin and Treadway, 1801), Plate 28. (Reprinted with permission from Widener Library, Harvard College Library, Phil 6021.2.53.)

acquaintances, the physiognomy of the falsely accused would prove their salvation, and, likewise, the face of murderers would ultimately condemn them:

> The stranger in a foreign land, who, from a concurrence of these and other coincidences, stands charged with the crime of another, looks round, and joyfully discovering the face of one who has seen his face before—and that perhaps but once—knows that he is safe. The wretch whose mask fell off in the murderous onset—he looks round too, and recognising with sicken-

ing sincerity the eye that met his, though but for a moment, feels that he is detected.[55]

Mistakes could be made, and criminal faces could seem to mislead, but Charles Dickens argued that the errors lay in the eyes of the beholder rather than in the faces of the violators. In his 1856 *Household Words* article detailing his observations of a poison trial, Dickens insisted that despite some impressions to the contrary, "Nature never writes a bad hand." Rather, "Her writing, as it may be read in the human countenance, is invariably legible, if we come at all trained to the reading of it. Some little weighting and comparing are necessary." Superficial observations could be wrong, so "it is not enough in turning our eyes on the demon in the Dock, to say he has a fresh colour, or a high head, or a bluff manner, or what not, and therefore he does not look like a murderer, and we are surprised and shaken." In fact, "The physiognomy and conformation of the Poisoner whose trial occasions these remarks, were exactly in accordance with his deeds; and every guilty consciousness he had gone on storing up in his mind, had set its mark upon him."[56] Although instinct contributed to physiognomy, skills could be honed over time to avoid errors and misapprehensions.

Ideally, physiognomy could also be used to identify not only those criminals already in the city but also those trying to enter. In 1826, the *Mirror of Literature, Amusement and Instruction,* a cheap weekly miscellany, lamented that physiognomy was not applied currently to immigration procedures as it had been by judges like Lycurgus to protect England from undesirable residents.[57] As people were streaming into the country and especially the cities, the fantasy of physiognomic identification presented a tantalizing way to keep others out: "What a pity it is, he is not now in existence, that he might be stationed at the Cinque Port of Dover, there musing, at intervals, over 'Lavater's Physiognomy,' to enable him to discriminate between good and bad."[58]

Urban Classification

Pocket physiognomy texts and anecdotes read as obsessed with social class. Through the burgeoning commercial market and the increasing accessibility of basic and higher education, participation in the knowledge industry—from science to literature to industrial development—encompassed an ever-greater group of people and led to the development of new kinds of cultural spaces and communities.[59] Pocket physiognomy, in particular, was a technology available to everyone and applied by and to all. The gift of instinct and the skills of observation were, according to

Eastlake, defined by random bestowment, unlinked to class or education: "The characteristic of instinct is that it is not taught, because not possible to be taught, by any study or observation of our own, but given to us, or stimulated within us, as the name also bespeaks, independent of all knowledge."[60] As scary as the random distribution of this power was, it was preferable to the alternative of having no way to tell people apart at a moment's glance. Eastlake insisted that the countenance held "the tremendous responsibility . . . in the social economy of this world, as the great medium of recognition between man and man."[61]

Even if the pocket physiognomic instinct was framed as class blind, the practice itself was not. The ability to penetrate the rules governing the display of class was of considerable use in the increasingly democratic urban metropolis. The *Quarterly Review* suggested that physiognomy was particularly revelatory of class status, exposing individuals and identifying larger groups. In a discussion of hands, the article commented on those "whose chief feature is a coarseness, and, as it were, a want of finish" that "symboblise a rough, unfinished mind, a mind lowly developed, obtuse intelligence, slow resolution, dullness of feelings." These particular hands "are found especially among the common people."[62] Likewise with feet; the "elemental foot . . . coarse, plumb, and clumsy; too flat-soled; short, broad, and fleshy . . . [can be] commonly found in conjunction with elemental hands, and have the same import; they are the feet of the mass."[63]

The *Quarterly Review* was again echoing the words of Eliza Lynn Linton, who emphasized the extent to which physiognomic observation was a class-ifying project: "Now to their social condition as their histories, [is] stamped on them as legibly as arms are painted on a carriage panel."[64] Lady Elizabeth Eastlake proved particularly adept at deciphering these stamps, although she suggested that reading these clues was "a lower kind of physiognomy" that "proceed[ed] from external circumstances" as distinct from unchanging "natural physiognomy." Among those environmental markers were those provided by the sun, which "is not only a colourer of the skin, but an inexorable contractor of the features." For the attentive, "A husbandman and a sailor may be recognised by that sneer of the whole countenance with which the eyes habitually try to shield themselves from intense light. The same is seen, but in far greater exaggeration, in the face of the dweller in tents." Similarly, "The Arab of the Desert [has] a knit brow, small contracted eye, and nostrils drawn up at a sharp angle; signs which are less attributable to any national physiognomy than to the two fires—the glowing sun above and dazzling sand below—between which he spends his days."[65]

Eastlake was careful to note that although physiognomic conclusions were based on principles and systems, they were often drawn instinctively and immediately and, with varying degrees of success, by everyone. These conclusions were not always well articulated, expressed as they were in "the unstudied language of the common people." Upon being asked "as to the look of an individual—what he or she is like— . . . they will answer for 'he's a hard-looking man,' or 'a stupid-looking fellow,' or 'she's a bright-looking girl.'" These descriptions, Eastlake made clear, emerged from their recollection of "something indicative of that inner man wherein lies the true distinctness from every other." However, features were rarely specified because "the unalienable, unalterable features are not dwelt upon, because not in one case out of a thousand remembered."[66] The anonymity of the masses did not preclude physiognomic readings entirely, but they were often rendered as impressions rather than detailed descriptions.

Many did refer to specific features, however, as I discuss later in this chapter. As we have already seen, bodies were broken down into individual parts, including hands, feet, eyes, and especially noses. The emphasis on these specific features was a move on the part of physiognomic advocates to underscore the extent to which their readings were in fact based on faces and bodies rather than on external markers such as clothing and carriage. In their disembodied language, however, is a hint of protesting too much that is particularly acute among those with greater power recording their observations of those with less power, including the rich writing about the poor, and men writing about women. By reducing their subjects to their component parts, they made these people objects akin to wax figures and models who could be dissected, verbally, at will. Physiognomy became a way to express power differentials precisely when society was becoming increasingly democratic.

As I have noted, even as clothing and occupational codes created more social mobility, these symbols became increasingly entrenched, and the most minute differences became infused with meaning. The upper classes "graciously" absorbed the middle classes following the Reform Act of 1832, recognizing the importance of engaging with those who had a powerful share in shaping political realities.[67] In so doing, they deliberately designed the interaction as one of guidance and deference in which the middle classes eagerly emulated rather than overtook their betters. Within the socially mobile structure, subtle signs of hierarchy, from street labels to social clubs, from seating arrangements to visiting protocols, rigidly marked the distinctions even as they seemed to become more penetrable.[68]

Overall, as an 1854 article in the highbrow cultural journal the *Athenaeum* expressed, along with the improvement of people's stations came a corresponding improvement in their faces. Extending the absorption of the middle classes to an acceptance of their appearance, the *Athenaeum* noted that "we believe that in the present day a better type of physiognomy is beginning to appear:—the face grows more oval, the forehead higher and fuller, the lips smaller and firmer, the nose nobler and straighter." The improvement in features reflected a "refinement of manners [that] is already perceptible on the national features."[69] Modernity and the urban experience meant not only an increase in interaction between the best and worst elements but also that the best elements were becoming better.

This refinement appeared across the classes, but to varying and identifiable degrees. Nevertheless, conflicts did arise between facial physiognomy and other external markers of class. The diaries of Victorian minor poet and man-about-town Arthur Munby contained many examples of working women whose physiognomies indicated internal traits that raised them above their stations. Munby was particularly sensitive to this phenomenon as a man powerfully obsessed with working women. His commitment extended to marrying one; in 1873, almost twenty years into his clandestine affair with servant Hannah Culwick, the two were married at the church of St. James in Clerkenwell. The relationship remained a secret, although Munby made reference to Hannah in his writing. Hannah refused to leave the service of others and continued to refer to Munby as "Massa," using his first name only once in their association.[70]

Munby recorded a number of instances in which the physiognomy of working women offered a contradiction to their profession. He was particularly attentive to specific body parts, reveling in the objectification of working women as he championed their cause. Recalling his first meeting with Hannah fifty years earlier, he recorded that she had been "a robust hardworking peasant lass, with the marks of labour and servitude upon her everywhere; yet endowed with a grace and beauty, an obvious intelligence, that would have become a lady of the highest."[71] Hannah was everything Munby had ever wished for, despite (or because of) their difference in class: "Such a combination I had dreamt of and sought for; but I have never seen it, save in her." It was the contrast in their stations, he believed, that strengthened them both: "And from that day to this, my love for her, and hers for me, has been in each of us a passion and a power that has stimulated and ennobled life, even through the very contrast of our lives."[72]

According to Munby's diaries, his impression of Hannah's refinement was shared by others, including strangers on the bus. He wrote of such an encounter told to him by Hannah which occurred when she was traveling in 1860:

> She told me, in her simple way, of the "odd things" an elderly gentleman had said to her in the omnibus as she came. He looked hard at her, asked her some indifferent questions, and then said bluntly "I supposed you are very low?" (He could see her bare hands, poor thing, & her common clothes!) "Yes Sir" she answered meekly, unwounded by the words, "I am a maid of all work." "Ah, I thought so," said he "but you have better blood in you than you know of." She stared, scarce understanding, and he went on "I can see by your profile that you have good blood in you. Has nobody belonging to you ever been better off than you are?" "No Sir" she answered "I never knew of anything but what I am." "H'm—perhaps", said the old gentleman; "but that profile doesn't belong to your class in life—you have blood in you, I tell you!"[73]

The gentleman on the bus was struck, according to Munby, by the discord between Hannah's station, as marked by her clothes and hands, and her noble, if undescribed, physiognomic profile. Munby's retelling of the story emphasized specific—and disembodied—body parts, particularly Hannah's hands, and the messages they communicated simply by being exposed. In so doing, he expanded the physiognomic framework to include clothing or, in the case of Hannah's hands, lack thereof. These messages were underscored by his photographs, many of which focused on Hannah's hands in the context of her entire body or were of her hands alone (Figure 1.3).

Unlike many city encounters, this gentleman had ample time to observe Hannah over the time of the journey and was judging her as much by her bearing as by her face and clothes. The surveillance practiced by the gentleman was atypical in duration but common enough in principle. People were always looking at one another and drawing conclusions from what they saw. In this case, the message was a puzzling one, full of contradictions between the clues of Eastlake's "lower kind of physiognomy" and its "natural" counterpart. It is likely that Hannah, under the tutelage of Munby, had begun to assume the carriage of those of her lover's station rather than her own. However, because she maintained her position in service undetected for the duration of her relationship with Munby, she clearly managed to assume the necessary posture and appearance of a servant when operating in that role. This was no small matter; employers paid careful attention to the physiognomy of those who worked for and with them.

Figure 1.3. These three images, all taken by Arthur Munby over the course of his relationship with Hannah Culwick, were designed to display Hannah's "servant hands." The bottom two highlighted the contrast between Hannah's noble profile and her lowly appendages. (Reprinted with permission from Trinity College Library, Cambridge.)

Notes on Noses: A Case Study in Judgment

The most famous example of a professional physiognomic reading that almost changed history was made by the captain of the *Beagle*, Robert FitzRoy. Charles Darwin was meant to accompany FitzRoy on the *Beagle*'s projected two-year scientific tour as a sort of captain's companion.[74] Upon meeting his prospective naturalist, FitzRoy expressed grave doubts about Darwin's suitability for the role. In particular, FitzRoy, an avid physiognomist, was initially concerned that Darwin's nose was too short to allow for the resolve necessary to see the journey through. Darwin wrote of FitzRoy's concerns in his autobiography, long after they had been overcome:

> Afterwards on becoming very intimate with Fitz-Roy, I heard that I had run a very narrow risk of being rejected, on account of the shape of my nose! He was an ardent disciple of Lavater, and was convinced that he could judge a man's character by the outline of his features; and he doubted whether anyone with my nose could possess sufficient energy and determination for the voyage. But I think he was afterwards well-satisfied that my nose had spoken falsely.[75]

Darwin, whose well-known physiognomic skepticism I discuss in Chapter 6, demonstrated how physiognomy could mislead and force prospective employers and possible friends into making the wrong decisions. It is possible, however, that, in the inverse of Dickens's warning about overly generous assumptions, the false reading lay in FitzRoy's judgment rather than in Darwin's nose. Physiognomy was not only about knowing the rules and, indeed, was often not about knowing the rules at all. The young and nervous FitzRoy did not yet have the good judgment that characterized good leaders and good physiognomists, a lack that almost cost him a sailing companion and a prominent role in history. (It is worth noting, however, that Darwin had a very difficult time with the journey and suffered debilitating seasickness.)

Literary critic and essayist William Hazlitt argued that the best physiognomists were the ones most skilled in human interaction. Kings, in particular, Hazlitt wrote, had the greatest facility for face reading because of their long practice in detecting deception and sycophancy: "It has been suggested (and not without reason), that the difficulty of trusting to the professions of those who surround them, is one circumstance that renders Kings such expert physiognomists, the language of the countenance being the only one they have left to decipher the thoughts of others." Their own experience at "disguises which are practised to prevent the emotions of the mind from appearing in the face, only render[s] [kings] more acute and discriminating observers."[76] Unlike many other writers, Hazlitt recognized the complex factors brought to bear in making visual judgments; physiognomic readings drew not just on the face of the observed but also on the experience and history of the observer.

Like kings, politicians developed physiognomic savvy and often used the ambiguous messages of the face for their own ends. In his biography of Lord George Bentinck, first published in 1852, Benjamin Disraeli, the future prime minister, wrote a lengthy description of the physiognomy of Sir Robert Peel, who held the position of prime minister of Britain from 1841 to 1846. Disraeli opened with praise, commenting that "Sir Robert Peel was a very good-looking man. He was tall, and though of latter years he had become portly, had to the last a comely presence . . . The expression of the brow might even be said to amount to beauty." When Disraeli focused on specific parts of the face, however, the tone quickly changed: "The rest of the features did not, however, sustain this impression. The eye was not good; it was sly, and he had an awkward habit of looking askance. He had the fatal defect also of a long upper lip, and his mouth was compressed."[77] Disraeli claimed that the harmony of Peel's face was an illusion that was not sustained by careful observation. By breaking Peel down feature by feature, Disraeli asserted his own power as a complete human being over the collection of poor features that constituted Peel.

In this passage, Disraeli intimated that the few positive aspects of Peel's countenance were belied by the rest of his face. The goodness implied by the beauty of his brow was subordinate to a sly eye and a miserly mouth. On balance, Disraeli suggested that the ugly and the bad outweighed the beautiful and the good in Peel. Even those unschooled in physiognomic principles could easily recognize Disraeli's true intentions in this literary portrait.

Like kings and ministers, military generals have employed physiognomic techniques throughout history, according to an 1866 article in the middle- and upper-class literary and political journal the *Dublin University Magazine:* "Napoleon is said to have chosen his ablest servants from the length of their noses; Caesar, on the contrary, wished to be surrounded with sleek men over whom authority might be established."[78] Physiognomy was not limited to "such exceptional instances," however; even less lofty personages, including "employers and employed, masters and pupils, husbands and wives, daily perform a vast amount of physiognomical observation, the results of which exercise no small influence on their proceedings."[79]

These "unexceptional" people, lacking the experience of kings and generals, may have resorted to *The Pocket Lavater,* attributed to Lavater and drawn from his original writings in significantly abridged form.[80] Simple drawings were laid on the quarto-sized pages, with the facing pages providing an analysis of that generalized type.

Later in the century, many readers turned to a more tongue-in-cheek treatment of pocket physiognomy. One text simplified the complicated and often-contradictory claims of the academic monographs by focusing on only one feature, the nose. The widely read and enduring *Notes on Notes,* originally written by George Jabet under the pseudonym Eden Warwick as *Nasology; or, Hints towards a Classification of Noses,* first was published in 1848. Jabet explicitly situated his book in contrast to polite and academic physiognomy texts, departing from the trend of building one's system on the foundations of others that characterized early nineteenth-century physiognomic monographs.[81] He wrote at the outset that "the only circumstance which can attach any value to our observations is, that they are entirely original, and wholly unbiased by the theories of any other writers of physiognomy."[82] Jabet emphasized the lack of connection his ideas had to any others because "in order to do this with any accuracy, it was absolutely necessary still to keep the mind unacquainted with the system of any other writers." This strategy of intellectual isolation, Jabet wrote, would prevent the work from "unconsciously imbib[ing] preconceptions and hints which would render its independent researches open to the suspicions of bias."[83]

A pocket book geared to the masses, Jabet's text was designed to be different from those systems and texts that called for prior knowledge of any sort. Instead, Jabet provided simple conclusions based only on the evidence of his own eyes and accessible to the eyes and minds of his readers. Rather than engaging "with much show of learning, on the influence of the Mind on the Body," Jabet "felt strongly how unfitting it would be to offer such mere personal observations as *proofs,* that we have carefully refrained from admitting any example which is not open to the observation of almost everyone."[84]

Jabet did not just avoid scientific proofs; he explicitly condemned them as agents of filthy lucre rather than purveyors of ideas. According to Jabet, "Every effort is made in scientific works to impress the material and sordid money-getting uses of science as its only true end, and the highest relation it bears to humanity." He listed geology, a science engaged in using surface artifacts to penetrate depths (much like physiognomy), as the archetypal example of science for financial gain:

> Read any tract on the uses of geology, and is there a word of high hope that the addition which recent discoveries in this department have made to knowledge will assist in raising and elevating the mind, or throw a new light upon the mysteries of nature? Not a word: but it is carefully detailed how an acquaintance with the order of stratified rocks will facilitate the discovery of minerals, or the boring of Artesian wells.[85]

Jabet conceded that in his system "the proofs are thought insufficient in number."[86] In a clever and deliberate rhetorical twist, Jabet turned his lack of evidence to his own pecuniary advantage by framing his book as the only truly practical system of physiognomy and one accessible to all readers (and purchasers). Jabet empowered readers to gather their own evidence and, equally, to use this evidence as part of a mounting proof of the efficacy of physiognomy that was based largely on consensus, so that "physiognomy, or the form which mind gives to the features, is universally recognized."[87] In Jabet's model, the experience of the individual physiognomist was of paramount importance, be that person a king, a minister, or a more humble observer.

Individuals could make mistakes, although Jabet instituted damage control by acknowledging that among the six distinct categories of noses were few perfect types because "there are infinite crosses and intermixtures."[88] Perhaps FitzRoy's error lay in wrongly breaking down the components of Darwin's particular nose. A mixed nose indicated "a compound character; and it is only in the rather rare instance of a perfect Nose of any of the classes that we find a character correspondingly strongly developed."[89] The six "classes," in Jabet's words, were the following:

Class I. THE ROMAN, or Aquiline Nose
J II. THE GREEK, or Straight Nose
J III. THE COGITATIVE, or Wide-nostrilled Nose
J IV. THE JEWISH, or Hawk Nose
J V. THE SNUB Nose, and
J VI. THE CELESTIAL, or Turn-up Nose[90]

Jabet continued by explaining the implications of these noses and offering a basic visual sketch and a number of historical examples of each one. Each nose had its positive and negative associated traits; the Greek nose boasted by Petrarch, Byron, Shelley, Rubens, and Voltaire, while indicating a cultured mind, also showed a lack of energy for that which was not immediately enjoyable:

THE GREEK, or Straight Nose, is perfectly straight; any deviation from the right line must be strictly noticed. If the deviation tend [*sic*] to convexity, it approaches the Roman Nose, and the character is improved by an accession of energy; on the other hand, when the deviation is towards concavity, it partakes of the "Celestial," and the character is weakened. It should be fine and well-chiselled, but not sharp. It indicates Refinement of character, Love for the fine arts and *belles-lettres*, Astuteness, craft and a preference for indirect, rather than direct action. Its owner is not without some energy in pursuit of that which is agreeable to his tastes; but, unlike the owner of the Roman Nose, he cannot exert himself in *opposition* to his tastes. When associated with the Roman Nose, and distended slightly at the end by the Cogitative, it indicates the most useful and intellectual of character; and is the highest and most beautiful form which the organ can assume.[91]

That an entire book was devoted to the reading of noses was not surprising. The expression "plain as the nose on your face" refers even today to the obvious and visible nature of noses. They protrude from the face and are thus the first appendages to reach the sun (and get correspondingly marked by burns); likewise, they are often the first feature to reach an observer's eyes. When decisions were being made quickly and on the basis of fleeting impressions, noses often provided the strongest and longest-lasting pieces of evidence. An 1862 article in *Temple Bar*, a low-cost literary and educational magazine, exclaimed that "if we are to look in the face for the strongest, highest, and most perfect expression of character . . . that feature is . . . THE NOSE . . . The nose is the central feature, and the face would not be a face without it."[92]

Like Jabet, *Punch* too collapsed physiognomic deductions to the evidence of the nose, noting in 1849 that "we can comprehend physiognomy, which affects to get a scent of one's disposition from one's nose, and to say whether he will succeed in life with a hook, or be snubbed by Fortune with a snub."[93] Likewise, a writer for the *Athenaeum* underscored the importance of noses in particular, caustically commenting that on this front, Lavater was perhaps too generous in his reading of faces, including his own: "'*Non cuique datum est habere nasum*' (it is not given to every one to have a nose), says Lavater plaintively, forgetting that to some the gods grant too much nose, as *he* might have seen in a moment in the looking glass."[94]

The *Anthropological Review*, however, felt that Jabet's book fell into a common physiognomic trap by reducing the complexity of the human face to one of its parts and, consequently, reducing the humanness of the subject: "One of the most common causes of the failure of those who

profess skill in physiognomy, is in the attempt to trace the entire character in a single feature, to the neglect of others. Of this we have an example in an interesting work entitled *Notes on Noses.*" The nose was a rich
physiognomic source, but, the *Review* emphasized, misleading if taken
on its own because "the nose has surely much physiognomic significance;
but it is unwise to take it apart from the other features, except for the
purpose of analysis."[95]

These sentiments echoed those of Eastlake, who, despite a lengthy discussion of the implications of various nose types, constructed a thought
experiment to warn against judging by one feature alone: "To prove also
the inefficiency of one single feature to tell the face, or rather to identify
the individual, we have only to try the common trick of placing a person
behind a curtain, and exhibiting one feature of his face through a hole in
it." In all but the most exceptional cases, "No one, unless it were stamped
with some salient peculiarity, would be able to decide to whom it belonged."[96] Although Eastlake's experiment focused on the eyes, she was
quick to clarify that "the nose or the mouth taken singly would be equally
irrecognisable."[97] Here Eastlake was arguing for considering the entire
person, including all features, clothing, and bearing, when making physiognomic decisions.

For some, however, the nose was not just distinctive on the face but
was more informative than other features. According to an anecdote recorded by Munby (of the clandestine servant marriage) in 1859, the nose,
or its absence, could actually bar an applicant from service employment.
He described a missionary visit that he paid to Mary Anne Bell, whose
nose had been eaten away by cancer, leaving a hole in her face. Mary Anne
was about to get a new nose, and with it, a new job. Munby wrote that
their "conversation was amusingly peculiar" as he asked her about her
future prospects:

> "Well Mary, your face looks quite nice now"—"Yes Sir it's a deal better, if
> only I get a nose put on"—"And when you've got a nose, what will you do?"
> "Well Sir, when I've got my nose, I think I shall go into service." "How? But
> wont [*sic*] they find out that you've got a false nose?" "No sir, I expect not—
> they wont see the joining. My nose will be fastened on with a hood, and I can
> take it off when I like!"[98]

Munby was interested in how Mary had done without her nose for four
years and asked her if "you don't feel the want of it after all?" She responded that it mattered for appearance and appearance only: "Oh no
Sir, it's only the look!" The look, however, was very important at this
time. Despite her casual dismissal, Munby recorded his sense that "she is

very sensitive about it however, & looks forward with pride and joy to the possession of a nose; I hope her project may succeed."[99]

No more is written of this incident, and it is possible that it was the sheer shock of Mary Anne's noselessness that might have prevented her from working as a servant. It is likely, however, that Mary Anne's potential employers would have been put off by the implications of sexual immorality associated with no nose. As Sander Gilman has argued, noselessness carried particular negative resonances as a visual marker of the ravages of syphilis.[100] Munby's obsession with noseless and other deformed women was a kind of fetish; their disfigurement acted as a form of titillation and sexual taboo.[101] Their misshapen and absent body parts made it easy for Munby to dehumanize these working-class women by focusing on their components rather than on their whole. For Munby, physiognomy was an objectification technology that allowed him access to a forbidden and highly exciting realm of bodily desire and disfigurement.

Mary Anne Bell might have been able to dissociate herself from the taint of syphilis by recounting the story of her struggle with the cancer that ravaged her nose, mouth, and throat. Her incomplete face would still have been a barrier to employment; without her real nose, prospective employers could not accurately judge her physiognomy. The novelist Maria Edgeworth wrote in a letter in 1802, "Isabella of Aragon, *or* Lord Chesterfield, or both, call a good countenance the best letter of recommendation."[102] If the prosthetic remained undetected, Mary Anne's nose would provide a part of the necessary character reference (which, by the mid-nineteenth century, was called simply a "character") needed to get a job in service. If her nose was obviously fake, Mary Anne's prospective employers would be unable to trust any evidence, physiognomic or otherwise, that she offered about her character.

As the article "Noses: A Chapter out of Lavater" emphasized, "The change of this one feature is all that is necessary for the most effectual disguise. A false nose is as delusive as an entire mask."[103] Here the physiognomic act was not just one of observation but also one of relationship building. The legacy of Lavater lingered in the stakes for suspected manipulation. In this case, Mary Anne's new nose was not good enough; when Munby visited her a year later, she was reduced to sewing garments from home, unable to find work in public.[104]

Jabet's case study focused on the most prominent facial feature, the one that provided the easiest and quickest evidence for the eyes. In a move that inverted the attempts of writers like Linton, Mayhew, and Engels to use people as texts to read the city, Jabet used actual texts to provide the clues to reading people. Jabet drew directly from literature and emphasized that authors and illustrators were among the best observers of human types. Novels provided some of the richest and most accurate physiognomic examples; even "without being professed Nasologists," authors "unconsciously verified our hypothesis, and associated Nose with character."[105]

One novel in particular provided powerful evidence for *Nasology*. Jabet identified both the text and the illustrations of Dickens's *Oliver Twist* as examples of the relationship between nose and character. Despite Jabet's claims that physiognomy was universally accessible, he underscored the reliability of his sources on the basis of their intelligence and observational experience: "The inimitable Dickens, and his equally clever illustrator [George] Cruikshank, both of whom owe their power to their correct observation and delineating of character, afford many well-known examples." *Twist*, Jabet claimed, was such strong support for *Nasology* that the system could have been founded on the novel. Most strikingly, Jabet drew on the authority of Dickens and Cruikshank as individuals, artists, and physiognomic experts: "Had the hypothesis been founded on *Oliver Twist* and its illustrations, it could not have been more strikingly substantiated by them—than it is—thus proving that if we err, we err in company with observers of more than common accuracy, and whose observations have been verified by the applauses of all."[106]

Jabet outlined how he mapped his system onto Dickens's words and Cruikshank's illustrations. He discussed the noses of many of the novel's characters and their implications, including those of "the shrewd penetrative Jew with his hawk-nose; the mild, but high-minded Oliver Twist, with his fine Greek Nose; the Artful Dodger and his brother-pals with the characteristic Snubs and Celestials."[107]

For Jabet, literary evidence was not just a legitimate but an indispensable source; as those who described and chronicled human behavior, authors had the greatest knowledge of human nature. Books provided another source of power over the urban landscape by offering insight into the experiences of the city and its inhabitants that could be applied to daily life. The works of scientists and learned authorities were, to Jabet, worse than irrelevant: they were actually corrupt. They were also not as helpful as the texts of writers and illustrators, whose project was to translate and make legible the experiences and characters of the people about whom they were writing. The work of Dickens and Cruikshank was the inverted counterpart to Linton, Mayhew, and Engles, and Jabet was the one who connected these ways of reading the city and its inhabitants.

The fastest-growing city of its time, London was not just the largest city in the world but the largest in the history of the world.[108] Inhabitants of this urban metropolis spanned the spectrum from slums to mansions, with everything in between. Despite the almost insurmountable divide between these extremes, all city inhabitants had something in common: they had to make sense of the sights, sounds, and demands of this new type of way of living. The experience of the nineteenth-century city was unprecedented.

Likewise, the nineteenth-century spaces of social interaction were unprecedented; the rich and the poor and everyone in between literally rubbed shoulders in the hustle and bustle of the city streets.[109] The proximity of neighbors, the frequency of passers-by, and the fleeting nature of contact with others necessitated a shift in the way in which people evaluated one another.[110]

Pocket physiognomy provided a solution to the challenges of urban interaction; according to an article in the prestigious and expensive literary criticism magazine the *Quarterly Review*, physiognomy could "teach men how they may, with little trouble, ascertain the characters of their neighbours."[111] Physiognomy was widely accepted as an urban survival technique, and the article emphasized "the nearly universal assent to . . . the practice of judging all men by their personal appearance."[112] Equally important was the speed with which these judgments were reached, because "we are no sooner presented to any one we never saw before, but we are immediately struck with the idea of a proud, a reserved, an affable, or a good-natured man." For these judgments, visual observation was the only technique required; no talking or interactions were necessary: "Upon our first going into a company of strangers, our benevolence or aversion, awe or contempt, rises naturally towards several particular persons before we have heard them speak a single word, or so much as know who they are."[113]

Physiognomy gave urban inhabitants a quick and accessible way to read the city and those within it. The techniques and models offered by wax museums, newspaper reports, and, especially, the evidence of people's eyes in seeking out the different and the deviant gave them a standard by which to judge others and, equally, themselves. Eager to avoid eyes that might be less kind on their own faces, urbanites chose to hide in the anonymous mass through conformity in clothing and self-fashioning; anyone who stood out was suspect. Criminality became marked not only by illegal and dangerous actions but also by the refusal to be identified and therefore judged. Judgment, however, lay in the eyes of the beholder, and not everyone was equally adept. Mistakes were made, and opportunities were lost. Employers, kings, and generals often developed a high-tuned physiognomic instinct, but even the most humble seers could exert power over others through a physiognomic analysis that focused only on specific features. Those physiognomists who reduced others to their eyes, their hands, and especially their noses precluded the possibility that people might be greater than the sum of their parts.

CHAPTER TWO

Performing Physiognomy

Imitating Art and Life

I F EVERYONE ON THE STREETS OF LONDON was part of an anonymous mass, where was humanity revealed? Sometimes things are what they appear to be. In that sense, the nineteenth-century British theatre was precisely that: a stage on which human types were explored and presented. But sometimes things are the opposite of how they appear. In that way too, the British stage was not just exploring but also manipulating character, using the principles of physiognomy to bring traits into being where they had not existed before. The nineteenth-century British stage was in a state of flux, struggling to balance the use of its space as one of aspirational middle-class respectability with older traditions of raucous entertainment and audience participation. It was an arena in which actors answered calls for truth to nature through their execution of their roles, adhering to trends in realism across media and in historical accuracy on stage.

As part of their project and mandate to make the theatre a realistic site of human interaction and exploration, actors and managers worked together on the visual representation of character through clothing, props, makeup, and prosthetics. In the theatre space, managers, actors, and audiences played. They played with character and its representation, and they played with expectations thereof. They played, but the project was quite serious. For actors, the game was to persuade audiences to see beneath physiognomically variant surfaces to sophisticated portrayals of character depth. At stake were audience and critical attention and approbation, as well as adherence to the codes of the acting craft. In an attempt to standardize the exterior, managers and actors adhered to a kind of physiognomic camouflage of regimented costumes, makeup, and hair-styles that created the right appearance while helping call characters into being. When the normalization was (deliberately) breached, actors aimed to play with audiences, challenging and even subverting expectations to underscore the skills of excavating and executing human exploration.

Managers did not leave the process of physiognomic adherence and normalization entirely up to the strengths of camouflage techniques. Although actors had long specialized in certain kinds of roles and had often played to type, there was a shift in the early nineteenth century to explicit category selection that foreshadowed later innovations in typecasting and experiments in casting against type. Although explicit typecasting has been historiographically located in the late nineteenth and early twentieth centuries with the advent of film and the emergence of the position of casting director, a physiognomic approach to stage history situates it earlier, with developments in nineteenth-century theatrical realism and historicism.[1] Managers, like their audiences, were looking at faces, and actors were looking at tricks and techniques to make those faces look right, as determined by acting manuals and teaching texts, which called for actors to study faces scientifically.

Typing moved to the forefront of the actor-manager's decisions in the early nineteenth century, and this change caused a shift in importance from props to faces and types and established a new set of theatrical communicative codes. The newly prominent rhetoric of physiognomy and scientific naturalism created the imperative to explore humanity and its visual correlates on stage. To help this process or at times challenge it, actors deployed a range of techniques to improve their physiognomic adherence to their roles. As we shall see through an analysis of prompt-books, training manuals, and theatrical reviews, the widespread use of exterior physiognomic cues, including makeup and prosthetics, complicated the relationship between the actors and the audience, between the fantasy and the reality of the production. The actors were not cast because they embodied the characters of their roles (as demonstrated by their physiognomy) but rather because they could appear to do so, often with some artificial help. If these interventions were done well, they would be invisible to audiences, who, as Jonathan Rose has shown, would submit entirely to the fantasy of the experience on the basis of its apparent reality. This submission was also a process, and a slow one; audiences were used to being part of the show and only gradually adjusted to sitting silently in their seats.[2]

And the audience? It was, and not simply, looking. It was thinking, making decisions, learning, and moving with and sometimes against the actors and what they were trying to communicate. Audiences, for their part, wanted to be able to make sense of the offerings on stage through accurate setting and staging, through physiognomically appropriate portrayals of character and realistic scenery and sets. And, quite simply, they wanted to be able to see. They wanted clearly lit faces on a clearly lit stage. Also, while seeing, theatregoers wanted to make their own decisions about the appropriateness of the actors and the quality of the performances. Physiognomy was one of many analytical factors that audiences used to judge the production as they negotiated their readings of the performance and its coded meanings.[3] It was also the one that actors were least able to change, so instead they expanded the purview of what kinds of things offered physiognomically meaningful messages by infusing props, costumes, body types, and hairstyles with physiognomic import and communicative power.

The Victorian theatre, a site of entertainment, was also a site of exploration, education, and experience, an unfolding story of how to be middle class and have refined tastes, of how to share cultural space, and of how that cultural space changed. The stage offered models of the expression of character and ways of reading that expression in a bounded space. Physiognomy was, and newly, part of the story, which started with eighteenth-century Continental theories of theatrical realism and historicism and moved through early nineteenth-century developments in scenery, lighting technology, costuming, and ideas of gesture and bodily training.[4] The story quickened during the 1820s and 1830s as notions of physiognomy came to bear on actors, managers, and audiences alike as they worked together to construct a new, and newly respectable, theatrical experience. The story tensed up over the anxieties of the actors, who had to balance the appropriate portrayal of the surface with the revelations of the depths as they honed their art in a newly naturalistic environment.

By the 1860s, part of the story ended with the falling of the curtain, with the construction of the fourth wall, and with the no-longer-porous boundary between actors and audience. With the refinement of realism, the audience had permission to immerse themselves fully in the fantasy of the production by removing themselves from its execution.

Physiognomy was both explicitly and subtly part of the story of the realistic stage. Managers, actors, and audiences had stakes in physiognomic principles, which dictated that character could be seen in the face. But can we call all manifestations of self-presentation physiognomy? Is every costuming decision, every makeup application, every hairstyle, every bodily adjustment, a physiognomically motivated move? In that formulation, makeup, clothing, and even props, normalize the exteriors of the actors in order to guide audiences to pay attention to the depths. To the historical eye, costuming and other techniques of standardizing character seem to undermine physiognomic dictates even as they adhere to them, by exposing the manipulability of these forms of analysis and judgment. But theatre demanded that audiences immerse themselves in a fantasy of which manipulation was an integral part, and in which it was an integral part of physiognomically communicating character.

Actors had mixed feelings about these manipulations even as they studied their application and contributed to their development. Critics also trod carefully in the shift to realism and its implications for stagecraft, even as they evaluated actors and their productions by the new criteria. But what of the most elusive group of all, the educated, class-conscious, increasingly sophisticated and demanding stakeholders and ticket holders, the audience? How did they respond to the normalizing physiognomic regime, and to what extent did they push back?

Listening to the Audience: A Historical Experiment in Response Theory

The audience—or, rather, the multiple kinds of audiences and audience members, with their varied opinions, assumptions, and experiences—is not and, despite the claims of the Frankfurt school, never has been a passive and unthinking entity.[5] As sociological theories of audience reception have shown, audiences make active decisions about how they respond to media and what they choose to understand and accept.[6] In order to understand how nineteenth-century audiences negotiated theatrical physiognomy, I interrogate traditional historical evidence, including reviews, diary entries, promptbooks, and playbills, through the possibilities outlined in cultural theorist Stuart Hall's powerful and now-classic encoding/decoding model.[7] Hall's model insists on the possibility of active audience interpretation through what he identified as the bounded framework within which material is presented. The infrastructure of the presentation and the modes of production encode the material on the basis of the knowledge frameworks of those designing the presentation; interpretation is not, in his formulation, limitless.

According to Hall, audiences, operating under what might be different knowledge frameworks and relationships than the producers of cultural material, negotiate what they see in three possible ways. In the context of the nineteenth-century stage, the "dominant/hegemonic" audience reading accepted and reproduced the preferred or seemingly transparent messages shared by actors and managers. Viewers were entertained through the realism of the production, accepted the invitation to immerse themselves in the experience, and concluded that the characters and their presentations of type were convincing and successful. The "negotiated" reading was the result of some audience modification of the message; although these viewers broadly accepted the preferred reading, they resisted certain aspects that came into conflict with their own understanding, background, or framework. For example, as I explore later in this chapter, an elderly woman might see an old witch in *Macbeth* as an attractive, rather than ugly, manifestation of evil. The third kind of reading, "oppositional" or "counterhegemonic," involved understanding the dominant reading and rejecting it to come to a different conclusion.

For Hall, these understandings and rejections were based largely on the social positions of the various actors, but I extend the model to deal with varying levels of skill of actors and managers, as well as the knowledge base and expectations of the audience. Umberto Eco has argued that decoding is socially contingent because audiences may use different tools and understandings to decode material than those used to encode it and thus create variant and unanticipated (in his formulation, "aberrant") readings. "Open texts" are more likely to lead to aberrant decodings than "closed texts"; mass media, in which I include nineteenth-century theatre for the purposes of this analysis, fall in the latter category.[8]

In all three readings, the active participation of the educated nineteenth-century audience was framed by their relationship to realism and physiognomy. Although a preferred reading of a play rested in part on consensus about what constituted a convincing presentation, negotiated and contested responses were still executed under a contained set of boundaries. Critical audiences who doubted the success of actors' realistic and physiognomic presentations were still operating within the framework of these theatrical techniques. Audience experiences were bounded by the shared physiognomic language, and it was within the increasingly important analytical frameworks of contextual accuracy and realistic presentation that they evaluated the quality of the show. These viewer assumptions and reactions in turn inspired the ways in which managers and actors coded their messages.

The reason to go to the theatre was, ostensibly, to be entertained. But—and this is a very Victorian sort of idea—it was also to learn: about other audience members and the ways in which they interacted, about history and the ways in which it was enacted, and about character and the ways in which it was acted. These lessons all came from different sources and could be understood in a variety of ways. They were not always successful, or, to put it another way, audiences did not always (want to) learn what actors thought they were teaching. Actors were not always good at their jobs of convincingly executing their roles. Sometimes they simply misaimed and misfired their interpretations, at least from the perspective of those who were watching. Audience members sometimes pushed back against the coding of character through physiognomy, which in turn prompted actors and managers to learn from their viewers how to go about exploring and exposing humanity on stage.

A number of conditions of possibility were in place on respectable stages that facilitated communication and learning between audience members and theatrical producers.[9] The audience had to be educated or, at the very least, educable. The actors had to have an investment in exploring character and presenting information to their viewers. Also, there had to be an environment in which the realistic communication of character constantly was in play. Like many other media, the nineteenth-century theatre was experimenting with ideas of realism, both in implementation and transgression.[10] Certainly, for a culture obsessed with the hierarchy of humanity, a confined space in which types were being paraded and organized was seductive.[11] So too was the opportunity to push against a normalizing physiognomic regime as audiences made their own judgments about whether the actors got it right or wrong.

The relationship between nineteenth-century actors and their audiences was an unstable and sometimes rocky one because everyone was negotiating new and shifting terrain. Along with the nature of theatrical productions and what they represented, theatregoers themselves were changing.[12] In dramatic contrast to the rowdy and bawdy experience of the eighteenth century, in which those seated in the pit were in many senses part of the show, the nineteenth-century audience was becoming sedate. Gone, or at least going, was the expectation that the audience would answer, jeering and hooting and even throwing orange peels and nuts onto the stage. Going, even, were those very seats as mainstream theatres renovated and did away with the stalls and the cheaper accommodation, in part to upgrade the status of the theatre and in part to protect the actors from flying food.[13] The always already empowered audience shifted from aggressive to subtle participation in the show, quietly decoding rather than loudly defaming. It took managers and actors a while to figure out how to understand what their audiences were seeing and understanding.

Managers and the Realism of Types

The theatre experience works because actors and audiences communally engage in the creation of a fictional world; as Aristotle wrote, the role of the actor is to conform to the rules of this world, and the role of the audience is to willingly suspend disbelief about its existence.[14] One of the rules to which the actors had to adhere in the nineteenth century was physiognomic fidelity to their characters.[15] How, then, could actors make themselves stand out under a visually normalizing physiognomic regime? Critics judged performers on the basis of their successful creation of encompassing worlds, done in part through convincing character representation and expression. To achieve these goals, actors heeded calls to study human types, seeking texts and models that demonstrated the expression of character. As realistic presentations replaced bombastic exhortations, aspiring and successful players became anxious that they were mere puppets on a string, devoid of individuality of expression. Part of the actors' concern was that they were playing to shallow surface emotions at the expense of deeper feelings and allowing audiences to avoid more thoughtful encounters with what they were seeing.[16] Such concerns echoed criticisms leveled at a variety of Victorian media, including sensation literature, Pre-Raphaelite painting, and, as Catherine Hall has argued, history writing.[17]

Actors were supported and guided in their endeavors by training texts, costume guides, and promptbooks. They usually did not have to manipulate themselves to heroic extremes because managers carefully considered appearance and type when they built their shows. The ideas behind typecasting—the use of an aesthetically and socially appropriate actor for a role—were, like visual judgment, new neither to the nineteenth-century stage nor the twentieth-century screen. They were, however, subordinate to the actors' (personally owned) props and costumes in determining suitability for a role during the late eighteenth and early nineteenth centuries. Combined with growing physiognomic awareness, nineteenth-century realism resulted in changes in how roles were assigned. It was only in the late nineteenth century that the modern notion of "casting" developed; it became fully realized in the early twentieth century with the development of cinema. Before this transition, the actor-manager alone chose his players or, often, his troupe of actors. With the formalization of the theatrical profession and its widening range of jobs throughout the nineteenth century, others, including directors and producers, became involved in the selection process. Still another set of new professionals had stakes in these decisions. Costume designers, lighting designers, makeup artists, limelight operators, and effects supervisors all had to work with who and what was at hand. The existence of the actors as theatrical canvases was not new; these professions were.[18]

Victorian realism is a complicated and multifaceted phenomenon that swept across a range of mimetic media, including literature, reporting, painting (as I discuss in the next chapter), and, of course, theatre.[19] Caroline Levine has argued that Victorian realism had its basis in models of scientific experimentation.[20] By extending the term backward to early nineteenth-century theatre, I situate realism as a gradual process with roots in the 1820s and 1830s and with strong connections to positivism and materialism. This move widens the purview of realism and helps explain the relationship between physiognomy and acting trends. In particular, exploring stage realism in conjunction with physiognomy offers a new perspective on the history of typecasting. With the turn to realism, the demands on the nature of the copy changed. Levine's analysis limits the scope of realism to a specific aesthetic project originating with John Ruskin's call to test representations against one's own experience. She contrasted this usage with a wider definition that includes all attempts at mimesis.[21] Although I acknowledge the technical history of the term, I use "realism" in its broader instantiation and cluster Victorian calls for truth in representation under this rubric. Ruskinian realism was but one manifestation of the Victorian obsession with classification expressed through realism.

On the stage, the early nineteenth century saw an increasing commitment to historical realism and costuming accuracy.[22] Audiences demanded knowledge about the characters they were watching, a transparency unavailable to them in their increasingly anonymous urbanized daily lives. Historical accuracy provided some measure of believability and opportunity for judgment, a desire first exploited in depth and with great care by actor-manager Charles Kean in his Shakespearean productions of the 1830s. Kean, a Fellow of the Society of Antiquaries, spared no expense in costumes, scenery, sets, and backdrops. His playbills were detailed and almost academic in their historical expositions. To the frustration of his cast, he was often guided by historical fidelity over theatrical expediency and sometimes garnered critical reviews for the tastelessness of his settings and costumes.[23] For Kean, the stage was a site of reenactment as much as an opportunity for entertainment, and he saw his job as bringing the past to the present as truly as possible.[24] A teacher explicitly engaged in knowledge acquisition and production, Kean used the theatre to learn and to teach. As Kean built his sets and costumes, he also built codes of communication that he set out to train his audience to understand and, ideally, appreciate. As an experiment in entertainment, its success was initially uneven and eventually resoundingly successful.[25]

Kean was among the first British actor-managers to embrace Continental theories of theatrical historicism. These notions extended to forms of acting and rhetorical style as the vogue shifted away from the exaggerated gestures and voice work of the eighteenth century. This transition was broadly welcomed, although as the century progressed, some critics were concerned that it had gone too far. In (using Hall's terms) a negotiated response to these changes, one anonymous critic wrote in 1872 that "the present style of acting is very unexciting. We are told it is natural." Natural, the critic continued, was an improvement over the absurd mechanisms of some former actors, but the critic feared losing drama along with embellishment: "Mr. Thackeray always seemed to think that the natural was the *ne plus ultra* of art. To that view we may demur. The unnatural, the ranting, the bombastic, no good taste admires. That mouthing, grandiose style of the early part of this century is dead. But while we revolt against the old, stilted school of those days . . . there is no reason why the grand and lofty in acting should be ignored as a delusion and a mockery." Naturalism in fact detracted from certain plays and roles by robbing them of their grandeur and power: "How absurd, in fact, is what is called 'the natural mode' of speaking in *Hamlet* and *Macbeth*. It is obviously an incongruity."[26] Actors, also active participants in the communication process, often agreed with this assessment; in the words of theatre giant Sir Henry Irving, naturalism and its attendant regimentation were "destructive of the real spirit of the actor's art."[27]

As Gillen D'Arcy Wood has shown, naturalism on stage and in works of art stirred up strong negative reactions and oppositional readings among the educated elite.[28] As much a protest against the expansion of audiences as against styles of representation, these objections anticipated the criticisms leveled by the Frankfurt school, describing realistic trends as inartistic coping mechanisms designed to deal with the mass marketing of visual culture.[29] Actors experienced similar concerns, fearing the removal of individual skill in a more mechanistic and rule-oriented style of performance. These fears echoed broader cultural concerns about the loss of individuality and artisanal skill in the automated age.[30] Physiognomic awareness both heightened the problem of automation and offered a solution by leading actors and managers to think about faces and bodies in new ways. To meet these challenges, actors attempted—successfully or otherwise—to deploy a kind of physiognomic camouflage that drew attention inward by satisfying outward expectations. Exterior normalization worked in conjunction with realism to create the space for actors truly to explore character and its representation on stage.

Theatrical realism and historicism opened the curtains on a kind of fantasy not previously possible. Attempts—physiognomic, historical, and contextual—to make theatre more accurate and aesthetically lifelike blurred the boundary between playing and deceiving. With changes in costuming, makeup, gesture, and acting techniques, this always leaky border was disintegrating. Unlike earlier productions, where the line between fact and fiction was firmly drawn, greater realism urged the audience to immerse itself in the experience on the basis of its believability. This tendency was heightened by improvements in special effects with lighting and sets and, as the century progressed, by changes in theatre architecture. Design and infrastructural innovations strongly bound the codes of the production in an attempt to guide the audience's experience. As viewers became more passive participants in the show, the production itself became an increasingly closed text with a tightly controlled range of readings.

In 1843, the Haymarket Theatre dispensed with the ancient apron and proscenium doors, robbing actors of easy entrances and exits. In their place, theatres began to rely more heavily on the curtain to signal dramatic shifts. By 1850, "curtain" meant the end of an act, and a new scene would always have a rising curtain.[31] Around the same time, "sky pieces" were replaced with proper ceilings and theatre boxes; these architectural innovations combined to make clear the previously blurry distinction between actors and audience encouraged by audience participation in the stage—or private—dramas.[32] The installation of a curtain, along with differential lighting between audience and stage (used for momentary effect from the 1830s but not made permanent until 1876), represented the heavy hand of the installation of a more metaphorical division between audience and actors. As the theatrical fourth wall dividing actors and audiences became entrenched, those on stage conversely were given license to make the experience ever more real for the audience. It was only by underscoring the fantasy that theatre could resemble reality.

Lighting effects played a dramatic role in the development of theatre and of audience perception of the actors. As Wolfgang Schivelbusch has pointed out, late eighteenth-century actors were caught in a communication and illumination dilemma: the distortions of footlighting wreaked havoc with facial nuance, but the paltry overhead lighting robbed many actors of their more subtle tools. The (unsuccessful) actress and writer Madame Marie Jeanne Riccoboni explained in justification of clustering of actors on the forestage that "the face contributes to the total expression. There are moments when a glance, or a slight inclination of the head, can be very meaningful . . . But if the actors are more than three paces from the lights, nobody can see their faces."[33] Gas lighting compounded these difficulties by showering the actors with what was often too much light and robbing them of the opportunity for subtlety.[34]

Actors and the Study and Creation of Character

Along with the transformation to time- and place-appropriate presentation, nineteenth-century actors became more sophisticated in their use of themselves. In order to succeed and excel, actors turned to study and observation to fashion themselves and their accoutrements, changing their faces, bodies, hair, and costumes to fit their roles physiognomically. But the process was far from seamless because actors and audiences alike complicated the message and its reception. In addition to the anxiety that stage realism provoked about automation, actors and managers were concerned that their knowledge would prove inadequate to the demands of historical costuming and styling. Playwright and novelist J. R. Planché reflected these fears in 1842 when he wrote about actor-managers' desperate attempts to "acquire sufficient knowledge of costume [in order] to avoid committing such errors as disgraced the works of many of their greatest predecessors."[35]

Players participated in the physiognomically normalizing regime partly as a way to subvert its limiting effects on their craft. But that was easier said than done; in order to present character-appropriate physiognomic features, actors first had to figure out what they were and then how to achieve them. Actors had to embark on their own learning projects in order to succeed on stage. As the theatre became a more socially acceptable profession, the growing number of acting manuals, as well as managers' notes and critical feedback, were full of physiognomic advice designed to prevent overenthusiastic aspirants from attempting to exceed their limitations.[36] Actor-teacher Henry Siddons told his readers that even though "Lavater is a book which I have not ready at hand . . . if you happen to have the book, I beseech you to read what is there said concerning attitudes."[37] He urged his disciples to study physiognomy as they would natural history, for if "an amateur in natural history is able to imprint the shape of many thousands of plants and insects in his mind," then "we may with reason conclude, that a collection of physiognomies, collected and classed with the same industry, is a scheme equally possible, and that a new art would result from the attempt, not less important in its kind."[38] Like Kean, Siddons explicitly framed the theatre as a site of knowledge acquisition and knowledge production and charged actors and audiences alike to use the opportunity to learn, as well as to participate in entertainment. Siddons underscored the effectiveness of physiognomy as an acting technique and, equally, the possibilities for innovation with its application, provided the actors studied diligently. Rather than signaling the end of creativity, naturalism and its requirement for physiognomic awareness provided the opportunity for a new kind of acting, in which the fusion of science and the stage would create a new kind of art.

Built by artifice or naturally born, the physiognomy of the actors mattered a great deal—so much so, in fact, that despite the dedication of a player to study and innovation, and regardless of his or her skill in various cosmetic and prosthetic techniques, manuals warned actors against straying too far from their own physiognomic boundaries. Siddons cautioned in his training manual that "he whose visage is not adapted to laughter, will surely never acquire the science by rule and lessons."[39] Attempting to do so could have disastrous consequences: "There are some men who cannot vary the traits of their faces, without offering us a disgusting appearance of the upper lip, or a wretched set of ugly teeth." To avoid these ugly and inartistic results, Siddons again urged actors to engage in observation, but here he had them turn their physiognomically educated eyes on themselves: "I would exhort the comedian to study not only the effect of the passions, but also their operations on his own face, that he may be able to distinguish those which became, as well as those which disfigure it."[40]

Should an actor's physiognomy be limited, Siddons counseled that "it would be wise to quit the stage entirely, where the first grand requisite, an expressive countenance, is wanting."[41] This aspirant not only would be a bad and unpleasant actor but also would fail to achieve some of the broader goals of the theatre at this time, including offering audiences the opportunity to probe the relationship between face and character and the chance to learn from the experience. Such an actor would be ineffective, either because his inappropriate face would distract audiences from his performance or because his inexpressive countenance would fail to allow him to evoke the necessary depths of emotion and communication.

Siddons was not alone in his calls for actors to study and, in so doing, assess their own potential. A figure far better known, nineteenth-century British actor and playwright Dion Boucicault, advised his audience in a public address to pay attention to how they looked and to think about the best roles not only for their desires but also for their faces. Actors had poorer judgment than nature: "Nature knows best." Boucicault then listed specific features and their ideal roles: "If you happen to have a short, sharp face, a hard voice, an angular figure, you are suited for the intellectual characters of the drama, such as Hamlet and so forth." For those with more gentle appearances (and, consequently, gentle dispositions), other roles would suit better: "If you are of a soft, passionate nature—if you have a soft voice and that sort of sensuous disposition which seems to lubricate your entire form, your limbs, so that your movements are gentle and softer than others, then this character is fitted for a Romeo or an Othello."[42]

Even the most skilled performers—including Dion Boucicault and, as we shall see, Sir Henry Irving—were limited by their physiognomies and types; similarly, even mediocre actors could succeed professionally if they learned (through study and art) how to assume character-appropriate appearances. At the very least, audiences would be guided to understand certain traits of these characters, and this would remove one burden from less accomplished actors. Only actors who looked right for their roles could focus on offering performances that were astounding rather than adequate.

Audiences, actors, and managers were demanding increased attention to the accurate presentation of the exterior. This included all aspects of appearance, such as, in decreasing order of difficulty of manipulation, features, age, body, hair, and costumes. Hair could easily be changed to powerful effect; an anonymous writer identified only as "An Old Stager" listed a variety of wigs as indispensable props for anyone hoping to secure employment on stage.[43] He advised aspiring thespians that "*Crape Hair* is decidedly the *best* imitation of *Moustache, Whiskers &c.* and can be easily attached to the face with liquid glue, or a solution of powdered gum and water."[44] (No advice is given on how to remove said moustache. In fact, there was almost no guidance on makeup and prosthesis removal.) Hair was not only simple to change but also very powerful; hairstyles left lingering impressions that drew attention away from the less malleable facial features while still producing a meaningful physiognomic effect. Noses were also easily altered by a wide array of prosthetics developed to assist syphilis and cancer patients. As Sander Gilman has chronicled, noses were often changed on and off stage in an attempt to change character or at least perception of character.[45]

In the 1834 production of *Man-Fred*, a burlesque show (and satire of Lord Byron's 1816 gothic classic *Manfred*) by Gilbert à Beckett, the costume list specified that the character of Man-Fred should have long black hair.[46] This, along with his carefully described costume of a shabby genteel striped waistcoat, hinted that he was a master chimney sweep suffering from the new child-protection laws regulating his trade.[47] Man-Fred's appearance was a pivotal element in the plot; as the frontispiece drawing by George Cruikshank illustrating act 1, scene 3, demonstrates, the liminal position occupied by Man-Fred was a source of confusion not just for audiences but also for characters in the play (Figure 2.1). In the

Figure 2.1. This frontispiece from Gilbert à Beckett's 1834 play *Man-Fred* shows the confusion caused by the title character, whose clothing and hair communicated important character information to anyone who saw him. (Reprinted with permission from The Harvard Theatre Collection, Houghton Library.)

caption beneath the illustration, the lines spoken by the character City Charley read:

> An't that a man up there? How queer he looks!
> He's not respectable, that's my belief
> Yet he don't look exactly like a thief.[48]

In the play itself, City Charley continued:

> His dangerous position makes me stare;
> I wonder how the deuce he got up there
> He looks so so, because his coat is seedy
> A decent person, probably, but needy.[49]

In *Man-Fred,* clothes and hair gave important, if ambiguous, character information. Man-Fred's costume framed a wide but bounded range of possible meanings; it was up to the actor and the action to clarify the code. Here the communicative power of clothing was deployed to sustain possibility and leave space for the actor to produce the preferred reading. The play challenged audiences to understand that costumes were limited in their reliability and transparency, and it urged them to devote the bulk of their interpretive attention to the dialogue and expressions of the actors.

The bodies that the costumes adorned were also sources of useful information. Aspiring players were advised by their teachers to pay careful attention to both the movements and the shape of their bodies. Like the manipulation of expression, the actor's detailed study of the human form had to work in conjunction with the material at hand. The primary "requisite for the stage," according to one manual, was "a good figure," followed closely by "good education—a good voice—and good sense."[50] Or, as Irving said, "The force of an actor depends, *of course,* on his physique; and it is necessary, therefore, that a good deal of attention should be given to bodily training."[51] A rigorous and professional training regimen would aid agility and grace, as well as giving the actor a more commanding presence on the stage. However, the goal of these new interventions was not to have uniformity, because physiques of all kinds were required. Irving continued by noting that "it is clear that the physique of actors must vary; there can be no military standard of proportions on the stage."[52] Irving maintained his commitment to diversity among actors while at the same time remaining resolute in the need for correspondence between the physicality of the actor and the nature of his or her role. Stage presence had always been an important aspect of the actor's craft, but Irving's attention to different kinds of physiques and the types they represented shows a concern that presence alone was not enough; just as there were different characters, so too there had to be different bodies.

In ancient Greek theatre, the problem of individual variation among actors was eliminated or at least regulated by the use of elaborate masks that covered the entire head, including the hair. In this way, the exclusively male actors could play a variety of characters, including women and young and old men, regardless of their own limitations of age, expression, and facial features. A man with the most cunning lips could play a simpleton, and the most impishly eared player could easily perform the role of a grave old man. As Henry Siddons pointed out, these masks offered other advantages as well: "A performer did not then suffer so materially from those ravages which the hand of time will inevitably make upon the finest set of features. As long as the organs of utterance were unimpaired, the wrinkles of age were but slight impediments to the efforts of an accomplished actor, even in the trying task of sustaining and supporting characters of vigorous juvenility."[53]

The physiognomic markers of a given player were rendered irrelevant through an explicit normalizing regime. By the nineteenth century, such straightforward and puppetlike means of hiding the face were no longer acceptable in full-scale dramatic productions. This change was lamented by English essayist and artist Max Beerbohm at the end of the nineteenth century in his satirical diatribe against stage makeup: "Wise were the Greeks in making plain masks for their mummers to play in, and dunces we not to have done the same!"[54] Physiognomic camouflage emerged as a new kind of theatrical masking technology. It was a trickier method than masks, but with a higher payoff.

Without the luxury or limitations of masks, actors had to devise different methods to represent various emotions and character types in ways that were meaningful and comprehensible to their audiences. Some techniques had long histories, including the representation of aging over time. Others, especially more subtle character nuances, required innovation, particularly with the advent of artificial light. With improved lighting technology, audiences could see more.[55] Following the first installation of gas lighting in the East London Theatre at Wellclose Square in 1816, rapid expressions were discovered. With the pressures of realism on them and the exposure of light in front of them, physiognomy offered actors a means to negotiate these new challenges. For actors, unlike city dwellers in the streets, hiding in plain sight through anonymity was not an option. Physiognomically camouflaged actors had to stand out from the inside.

Creative and innovative actors used the combination of powerful lighting and physiognomic ideas to challenge audience members to be more critical viewers and participants. Among the opportunities afforded by exposed physiognomy was the opportunity to play against type. This strategy, similar to those adopted by many novelists, deliberately challenged the assumptions of audiences to surprise them and complicate their expectations. Much like Fanny Burney's beautiful but soulless sister in her 1796 novel *Camilla* (discussed in the Introduction of this book), architect and dramatist George Wightwick, along with famed actress (and mother of Henry) Sarah Siddons, established new conventions for the women in *Macbeth*. Victorian diarist Caroline Fox recorded her conversation with Wightwick, noting that "one of his grand objects in these Shakespeare studies is to correct the impression of character made by actors and actresses." As a result of impressions, "Lady Macbeth is always conceived as a magnificent unapproachable woman—in fact, as Mrs. Siddons." Reading the role in a different way, "he, and Mrs. Siddons too, think she was small, delicate, almost fragile, with the quickest, sharpest of ferret eyes, as such is the ordinary build of women greatly gifted for intrigue." Witches ought also to be cast in a different way, because "witches too, and specifically Hecate, should be wild, unearthly beings, not ugly old women: Hecate the palest of ghosts, with a little spirit to do her bidding."[56] Exposure of character on stage revealed what different types of people were supposed to look like and thereby reaffirmed and created physiognomic assumptions. Theatre managers, like novelists, sometimes used these set ideas to challenge audiences by casting against type. When done well by actors as skilled as Sarah Siddons, these counterintuitive presentations forced audiences to acknowledge and sometimes even challenge their own assumptions and enlisted their participation in character development on stage.

Regardless of Siddons's and Wightwick's plan, casting the "ugly old women" as witches would have posed challenges in the absence of actual ugly women. The marks of age hold almost universal visual meaning but, as the writer identified as "An Old Stager" pointed out, were uniquely difficult to achieve: "The art of making up to represent old age is a study in itself; nothing that we could write would convey any instruction! This can only be acquired by a study of the play of the muscles and the most common contractions or furrows of age."[57] It was only through study of the effects of age on character and appearance that an actor could master their representation. Acting required a kind of education about how to study character and how to apply these lessons successfully to one's own body, face, and mind. With mastery of a certain type of appearance, an actor could dwell successfully in mediocrity, relying on the visual codes rather than on acting skill.

Once cosmeticized, the acting of age was itself among the easier and more strategic parts for which an aspiring and not especially talented player could develop expertise. The Old Stager urged women in particular to develop this type of role, given the dearth of young female actors willing to take on aged parts: "Indubitably, the greatest opening is in the *Old Woman,* a line, unfortunately, almost extinct. Nor let any young lady, from motives of vanity, reject our advice, for possessed of average talent, she must, in a few years, derive wealth and distinction from this branch of the profession."[58] Even mere adequacy in the execution of the elderly could yield theatrical success.

Taking into account the limitations of bodily adjustment, makeup advice abounded about how to make actors look older or younger, kinder or more harsh, honest or untrustworthy. This more superficial advice, however, was usually extended only to men; as the Old Stager noted, "The Ladies in general are so *au fait* at improving their charms, that nay advice from us, must seem ridiculous."[59]

Audiences and Critics Speak Back

Women's makeup mastery, however, did not always hold true. In an 1860 letter, Twynihoe William Erle, a theatrical scene painter, described the female lead in a farce at the Royal Marylebone as "an afflictingly vulgar, as well as drearily ugly, woman, rouged to such a pitch that her cheeks glowed like a couple of chemists bottles." Her behavior did not match her appearance, Erle recounted, much to the confusion of her audience, who struggled to frame the preferred reading within clashing codes. The contradiction in her face and her role undermined her acting abilities to the point of rendering them irrelevant and making it impossible for the audience to pay attention to anything but the faulty surface: "She evidently, however, to judge from the coquettishness of her demeanour, felt comfortably satisfied that she looked very ravishing, but her own opinion and that of the spectator could not fail to be diametrically opposed, and indeed hopelessly irreconcilable on this point."[60] Part of the problem was the actress's lack of skill in makeup application under the new and brighter gas lights.[61] The greater problem, however, was that the actress was simply wrong for the role. Her appearance did not match her role, and this rendered any skill she might have had as an actor beside the point.

Erle's reaction to casting against type was specifically physical and physiognomic. He criticized not only the face of this actress but also the nonverbal techniques and signs that writers and actors applied to convey physiognomic information. According to Erle, these methods included makeup, costumes, props, and symbols inscribed on the body, particularly "a dagger, a key, a ring, a phial, a strawberry mark on somebody's arm, and a parchment." These techniques were tired dramatic shorthands on which the resolution rested, whose overuse undermined their believability and showed a lack of respect for the sophistication of the audience. Erle wrote that "according to novelists and playwrights, 'rightful heirs' monopolise all the strawberry marks granted by Providence to humanity, while ordinary individuals are never so distinguished."[62] Erle objected not only to the lack of originality in using birthmarks and daggers as dramatic proof but also to the disconnect between these techniques and reality. Although these signs were physiognomically communicative, they taught Erle nothing that he could apply to his own examinations of humanity. In his oppositional reading of these signs as meaningless, Erle acknowledged and then rejected the intentions of the playwrights and managers and signaled their failure to produce a preferred response.

Looking through Earle's eyes, we see that the intended or preferred effect of makeup and other physiognomic markers was not always achieved. Despite the best, if at times unsuccessful, efforts of actors to engage with and adhere to the rules of nature, communication could not be controlled. Sometimes actors did their jobs poorly. Sometimes the fault lay with the playwrights or managers. Physiognomic rules as applied by actors did not always match the knowledge and understanding of the audience. Although nonverbal communication was a highly significant aspect of stagecraft, it was also a very risky one.

To avoid the pitfalls of poor physiognomic choices, the rules of acting became ever more regimented, in conjunction with the nineteenth-century professionalization of the theatre. Many actors responded to naturalistic techniques with concern that they were easily replaceable by others with equal or even greater knowledge of the rules. These fears were hardly unfounded; in his London theatre journal, written from 1851 to 1866, literature professor, writer, and physician Henry Morley sometimes gave the advantage to mechanical players over the real thing. He well understood the nineteenth-century vogue for puppet shows and commented in his journal that "puppets have at various times, therefore, and in various countries, had a larger following than one might have thought fairly due to the merits of wooden actors in the abstract. Wooden actors in the concrete (flesh and blood) have been so much worse."[63]

Perhaps. Puppets always looked the part. Puppets were consistent and reliable, and, especially in the repeating stories and behaviors modeled by Punch-and-Judy shows, audiences knew exactly what they were getting with puppets.[64] They were getting entertainment they could count on. What they were not getting was the opportunity to examine character, to be challenged, and to learn something new about what motivated people and how they behaved. In this most closed of texts, there was little scope for negotiation of the readings. Not everyone wanted to be educated and engaged while they were being entertained.

Although the objects themselves were occasionally critiqued, the appearance of puppets was not subjected to the same kind of scrutiny as that of live actors. Critics and audiences paid careful attention to the relationship between an actor's face and his or her role. Morley often expressed either pleasure or dissatisfaction with the attention (or lack thereof) paid by theatre managers to their players' physiognomies. For example, about the play *Two Loves and a Life,* he commented that "Mr. Howe is not enough of the ruffian in Dirk Hatteraick. He looks rather an honest fellow."[65] Playing a ruffian, Howe was betrayed by his honest face, and rather than using that contradiction to his benefit, he let the impression of his honesty stand. He failed to take advantage of the opportunity afforded by the stage to explore character. Although Howe may have been a good actor, his general demeanor and appearance controlled the impression that he left with his audience and ultimately rendered his presentation ineffective. Howe might have used the contradictions between his face and his role to complicate his presentation and surprise his audience. Instead, he disappointed them.

In a review in the *Times* of London in 1824, the writer praised the well-known actor (and father of Charles) Edmund Kean for his "excellence," including "an accurate conception of his author— . . . a physiognomy speakingly expressive, and a voice of great flexibility and sweetness." These attributes constituted "so many of the elements of good acting combined."[66] "Physiognomy" was used to refer to Kean's face, but not his face alone; this slippage indicates how strong the connection was between appearance and character. Looking at a face meant knowing that person, as face and physiognomy became interchangeable language for both the surface appearance and what lay beneath.

Other attempts at physiognomic fidelity were less successful. In an 1826 review, William Farren was taken to task for his inappropriate portrayal of Sir Peregrine Quixote in James Kenney's *The Green Room,* for it was "apparently written with an eye to the physiognomy of Mr. Liston" (Figure 2.2).[67] Roles were designed for specific actors who best suited the characters; should the role be played by another, the pitfalls, particularly in self-presentation, were obvious. The character and the actor became collapsed, and this heightened the stakes for adherence to visual codes. Farren failed to convince his audience that he too could play the role designed for Liston, either because he did not camouflage successfully or because his execution contradicted his appearance. As the trend toward actor-specific roles increased, some parts became almost untouchable by anyone but their original actors or those who looked and acted a great deal like them. The Gilbert and Sullivan company created a number of roles, and even types of roles, to suit the strengths and styles of its emerging stars. The "patter baritone," for example, emerged entirely around George Grossmith, and subsequent plays were written with this part designed exclusively for him.[68]

Different people tend to look different from one another. However, nineteenth-century actors had to really look the part and, in some sense, try to look the same as, or at least similar to, those who had successfully played the roles before them. Physiognomic mandates had actors and audiences paying attention to faces in an explicitly character-driven way.

Figure 2.2.   William Farren (left) and John Liston (right) often played in similar roles, which led to critical comparisons and discussions of their physiognomic fitness for the parts in question. (© National Portrait Gallery, London.)

In a new training process, actors had to study their characters in all senses of the word: they had to learn about their roles and the likely appearance of these characters, and they had to learn about themselves and how they appeared to others. The labeling of appearance as a scientific form of revelation changed the stakes for the presentation of the actors, especially because appearance was increasingly obvious with improvements in lighting technology.

Training and Learning on Both Sides of the Curtain

If an aspiring actress were to perfect the makeup and external appearance of the *Old Woman* as prescribed by the Old Stager, would her work then be done? Was presentation an end in itself? A necessary but partial part of the process of bringing the character into being? A timely but ultimately unimportant camouflage that served to stop audiences from being distracted? All of the above? Perhaps perfection in character presentation was possible only when exterior and interior executions were paired; appearance was meaningless without bringing the character to life. Perhaps makeup was not enough, but, for some, it just about sufficed.

Even with the increase of rules about physical appearance and its acting correlates, actors were getting mixed messages. There was tremendous anxiety among the increasingly professionalized playing community that they would be perceived as mere puppets, woodenly repeating lines and fooling audiences with visual tricks. Although they were exhorted to study others and apply these lessons to themselves, they were warned against following rules too rigidly and thereby failing to bring something of themselves to the stage. Henry Siddons objected that acting manuals and rules "would render that player a mere *pedant,* who should follow them to the letter."[69] Siddons wrote that "the best digested rules, the finest picture galleries in the world will not exempt him from the necessity of *thinking* for *himself.*"[70] Another manual contended that "to suppose, for instance, that nothing more is required in a due personation [*sic*] of *Othello's* jealousy, than a certain exact arrangement of the arms, wrists, fingers, etc. is to suppose a gross and grievous absurdity, as unjust towards the essayist, as injurious to the actor."[71] The best actors knew well how to apply the rules and also when to judiciously moderate or even abandon them. Like all forms of physiognomy, stage physiognomy relied on personal judgment above all.

Sir Henry Irving balanced the competing trends toward regimentation and individuality with deft rhetorical skill, combining the importance of accurate characterization with the talents of the particular player in question. In one of his guides for aspiring actors, he emphasized that the better the presentation of character, the better the actor. Again, Irving guided his readers toward the study of physiognomy and character, which would better equip them to work within and around the rules and, in so doing, avoid automatic presentations and audience confusion: "Here the actor who has no real grip of the character, but simply recites the speeches with a certain grace and intelligence, will be untrue. The more intent he is upon the words, and less on the ideas that dictated them, the more likely he is to lay himself open to the charge of mechanical interpretation."[72]

This was a particularly important lesson for those seeking to enter the craft, whom Irving presented as touchingly naïve in their perception of the skills required for the profession: "In common with other actors, I receive letters from young people, many of whom are very earnest in their ambition to adopt the dramatic culting, but not sufficiently alive to the fact that success does not depend on a few lessons in declamation."[73] Irving emphasized the importance of appearance precisely in order to draw attention inward to the actor himself or herself. Normalizing appearance in broad and occasionally less broad strokes made the difference lie in the individual player.

The theory of physiognomic camouflage supported by Irving and others was expressed in the highly detailed clothing notes found in nineteenth-century promptbooks. For example, according to the costuming list from an 1835 production of *A Dream at Sea* by John Baldwin Buckstone, the demands were incredibly elaborate and detailed, far beyond what many costume outlines would be like today.[74] This level of detail and uniformity had increased steadily from the mid-eighteenth through the mid-nineteenth century.[75] The increase provided a method for actors to normalize external appearance by placing great importance on its proper execution while leaving space for individual variation in the acting itself. Clothing bound the message and supplied practical and symbolic structure for the play while providing much room for interpretation and engagement on both sides of the stage. Richard Sennett has chronicled the inverse relationship between Victorian street and stage costumes: stage costumes revealed truth while street costumes hid it.[76] While in Sennett's formulation, the audience of passers-by were passive participants in this process, here we see that they were active both in the theatre and outside it.

Even within the framework established by clothing, makeup, and diligent study, capturing character could be challenging, particularly for certain kinds of roles. Much like nineteenth-century society at large, the hierarchy of parts and of the difficulty associated with playing them was strongly classed (with old women, unsurprisingly, well toward the bottom). In a different take on the presentation of a role, Charles William Smith wrote about gentlemen in his mid-Victorian acting guide, "The requisites to *personate this character completely* are many, and difficult to attain."[77] He went on to list the necessary attributes, many of which required a refined upbringing or years of study. Likewise with heroes and fine ladies: in these cases, makeup and costuming would be insufficient because the actor actually had to be fine to act fine. These roles demanded the greatest physiognomic fidelity and extended the purview of the term from features and birth station to life experience. Much could be faked by a talented player or a good study, but birth and breeding would tell in the body and in the face.[78] For the face to speak, the audience had to be listening. Smith's treatise was predicated on an audience that was able to make class distinctions, and it underscored the ways in which theatrical experiences were a training process and a space of shared knowledge.

Unlike other types of roles, upper-class characters could not, according to Smith, be brought into being by donning the right clothes and accoutrements.[79] Smith was pushing against the egalitarianizing instinct of the acting craft and the theatrical profession, which insisted that with the right training and fashioning, all classes could be fairly represented, and that all classes could enjoy the experience. Here Smith's contention that life experience and social station were immediately obvious spoke to an anxiety that this might not be so, and that, in fact, assuming the right clothes and gestures would indeed allow an actor to assume the characteristics of a gentleman. As the century progressed and acting became a more respectable occupation, the concern about class divisions became more acute. With the increased likelihood that an actual gentleman (or an approximation thereof) was playing one on stage, many insisted that any other class of actor would immediately stand out as inadequate. This trend mirrors Victorian society at large; even as class (and, as I discuss in Chapter 4, race and religion) barriers became more permeable, there was a great deal of insistence on their rigidity.[80] Indeed, Smith complained, "There have been almost *as few gentlemen* on stage as *heroes*."[81] For Smith, in the case of class, physiognomic camouflage was just that—a veneer that could not adequately mask the lack that lay beneath.

Fortunately, according to Irving, by the late nineteenth century there was an unprecedented crop of qualified actors to play upper-class roles because "the dramatic art is steadily growing in credit with the educated classes. It is drawing more requites from those classes. The enthusiasm for our calling has never reached a higher pitch." The limitation became not one of volume but one of skill because, although "there is quite an extraordinary number of ladies who want to become actresses," unfortunately, "the cardinal difficulty in the way is not the social deterioration which some people think they would incur, but simply their inability to act."[82] The accoutrements of the stage, including costume and makeup, could do only so much in the eyes of the audience and the masters of the craft. In one way, Smith and Irving were in agreement: normalizing the exterior was just not good enough.

Julie Codell has argued that Victorian notions of propriety placed tremendous restraints on behavior and the expression of emotion. Physiognomy, in her formulation, became a necessary device through which these hidden feelings could be accessed by others.[83] It was this very repression, however, that made physiognomy so hard to read in daily life. Victorians engaged in most of their physiognomic exploration of humanity not on the streets but in the theatre. The streets were anonymous, and the stage was alive.

The turn to spectacle in daily life moved in consonance with a spectacular turn to realism on the stage. With the possibilities for exploring, for playing, and especially for learning and producing knowledge opened up by realism, came a number of challenges and burdens. Increasingly educated audiences were interested in productions that looked right, and increasingly educated actors and managers had to learn how to make them so. In addition to changes in sets and scenery, the actors themselves had to look and act differently. They had to look the part. To do so, they had to learn their parts—their characters—in a whole new way. Following the dictates of acting manuals, managers' guidelines, and critical and audience feedback, actors turned to study and observation of human types to learn how to bring their characters into being.

Actors could bring many techniques to bear in the project of producing realistic roles, including speech styles, bodily training, makeup, hairstyling, and costuming, but there was only so much they could do with the bodies and faces they had. Managers became particularly careful in their selection of actors for roles, paying attention to face and body type in an early model of typecasting. Who actors were and how they appeared grew in importance and became a significant factor in the evaluation of how they acted. Audiences and critics were sensitive to physiognomic nuance. They praised appropriate presentations and damned those who fell outside the physiognomic parameters of their parts. To circumvent such judgments, actors approached exterior styling as a kind of camouflage that standardized the exterior and drew attention to the performance itself, a performance aided by assuming or already inhabiting the right look. With the introduction of gas lights, faces became more visible, and this allowed actors to draw on additional physiognomic cues while at the same time it presented greater challenges in matching their appearance to their roles.

Despite the best efforts of actors and managers to please their paying viewership, audiences brought their own, sometimes unpredictable expectations to the theatre. Audience response theory shows that theatrical viewers were far from passive participants in the experience and negotiated their reactions on the basis of their own contexts, as well as the ways in which the material was framed. Physiognomic realism formed an important part of audience analysis as viewers chose to accept, challenge, or negotiate with the preferred reading of the show.

Successful actors both adhered to and worked against audience expectations, occasionally playing against type to produce new effects and reactions. Educated and culturally aspirational audiences placed considerable pressures on the performers, who developed a series of rules to guide them through the new theatrical frontier. These rules urged actors to turn to study and nature in their self-presentation, but, like all physiognomic endeavors, they emphasized the importance of instinct and individuality. Many actors feared failure in negotiating the balance between the two, which would render them another casualty of the automated age, little different from puppets on a string.

The realistic theatre of the Victorian age had a most unrealistic effect on representational reproduction. As the theatre became less fantastic, the lines between actors and audience and between fantasy and fact were more firmly drawn. The stage became a site of exploration as actors investigated ways to communicate character and expose and make visible the nature of their characters. The theatrical fourth wall, represented by a rising curtain and differential lighting, created the conditions of possibility for a more believable theatrical experience. Accompanying this process was a great deal of anxiety on the part of actors that the increase in rules decreased their creative contributions. They responded by using their skills to standardize the realism of their presentations.

Because acting was always a mimetic endeavor, actors, like painters, were trained in the skills of communication through the copy; at the same time, they strove, through artistry, to mark their representations as unique. Writer Samuel Taylor Coleridge, in an 1814 letter to actor Charles Mathews, highlighted this challenge in his distinction between the imitation and the copy: "A great Actor, comic or tragic, is not to be a mere *Copy*, a *facsimile,* but an *imitation* of Nature. Now an *Imitation* differs from a Copy in this, that it of necessity implies & demands *difference*—whereas a copy aims at *identity.*"[84] Imitation, to Coleridge, implied artistic effect; copy was mere deception to convince viewers that they were seeing reality.

The move to social realism was not limited to the canvas. In fact, Lucy Hartley has argued that Pre-Raphaelite painting principles were in continuity with, and possibly drew from, acting manuals that dictated greater adherence to life.[85] Gillen D'Arcy Wood has demonstrated that portraiture and the stage were linked by both increasing realism and the production of mimetic art.[86] With respect to physiognomic codes, artists and actors faced many of the same challenges. Comic artist William Hogarth, mentor to the great Georgian actor David Garrick, described his work as a theatrical endeavor: "My picture was my stage, and men and women my players, who were by means of certain actions and expression to exhibit a dumb show."[87] In the next chapter, I explore the relationship of portrait painters to their subjects in life and on canvas as they too responded to pressures of physiognomic accuracy. Painters had to balance the dangers of unflattering physiognomic messages against mimetic fidelity. Complicating this delicate dance were scientific understandings of perception and vision, set against the increasing prominence of pictures as pedagogical biological tools. Drawing and painting people became a test not just of artistic but also of observational skill. Artists were subject to the demands of a new market sensibility that dictated whom and how they drew.

CHAPTER THREE

Portrait Physiognomy

Communicating Character

Painters always make ladies out prettier than they are, or they
wouldn't get any custom.

—Charles Dickens, *Oliver Twist*

FOR EARLY NINETEENTH-CENTURY natural historians,
the ability to draw was a test of their ability to observe.[1] As
Anne Secord has shown, drawing encouraged a scientific way of
seeing, and specimens acted as the point of comparison against which
an individual's skills were judged. Pictures could often convey information that words did not, and thus provided an invaluable pedagogical tool. Pictures were also pleasurable and proved a useful way to excite and entice students and audiences. But because of their ability to
excite not just reason but also passion in an unpredictable and often-
untrained group of observers, pictures of botanical specimens were also
dangerous.[2]

Both the production and the viewing of pictures were activities mediated through scientific notions of perception. Scholars, most notably
Charlotte Klonk, have explored these links through landscape painting
in the first two decades of the nineteenth century, as artists moved from
the picturesque model to a more direct record of the way they saw nature. Klonk named this new representational strategy, which privileged
observation and description, "phenomenalism."[3] Lacking an artistic language to express this approach, painters turned to scientific texts to describe their projects. In this chapter, through an exploration of artist-
training manuals, critical evaluations, and artists' commentaries, I extend
Secord's and Klonk's analyses to portrait painters, who developed their
own observational and perceptual skills to produce biographical paintings. In order to communicate not just appearance but also character and
experience, artists leaned heavily on physiognomic principles, applying,

and in so doing developing, new physiognomically meaningful signs on their canvases.

In Britain, artistic audiences, participants, and purchasers expanded rapidly throughout the first half of the nineteenth century to include the middle classes. Drawing and painting became activities for interested amateurs as well as skilled professionals, sparking a wide industry devoted to art as a leisure activity. The presence of physiognomy in portraiture varied according to the skill of the artist; amateur guidebooks emphasized the difficulty of executing meaningful faces and advised their readers to avoid the attempt without serious study and observation. For the experts, mastery of faces and their corresponding characters was not just expected but required; to this end, knowledge of physiognomy was a prerequisite to artistic and commercial success. As the patronage model based on commissioned works was replaced by public exhibitions and sales, success was mediated by the willingness of audiences to buy the art. In this context, although the goal was entertainment rather than education, part of the pleasure was in the nature of the representations and the ability of the artist to tell a story. Like plants, drawing of people was also a test of observation.

In the noneducational context of art exhibitions, pictures—and pleasure—were not dangerous to anyone but the artist, who could be punished by a nonpurchasing audience who did not like what they saw. As Chris Otter has chronicled, the act of seeing was changing through numerous developments in optical research.[4] This research complicated notions of vision but also aided spectacle wearers to see one another and, in the words of Victorian man of science Sir David Brewster, "enjoy the beautiful in nature or in art."[5] The status of this vision was the source of numerous Victorian debates about the universality of perception set against a cultivated and educated artistic spectatorship. While Victorian biologist Thomas Huxley argued that sight was "altogether mechanical," artists and critics such as John Ruskin and Philip Hamerton insisted that vision would always remain subjective. Ruskin wrote at length about sight as a spiritual phenomenon that differed with each person.[6] Hamerton lyrically expressed that "no two men ever saw the same rainbow."[7] Artists were subject to the vision of their audiences, who, by the middle of the nineteenth century, expected biographical stories, realistic depictions, and entertaining images. Physiognomy and, according to painter Ford Madox Brown, expression, provided a shared language for artists and audiences alike to communicate and test these criteria.[8]

Amateur and professional artists and audiences amassed and produced physiognomic knowledge through their studies of drawing manuals and critics' reviews, which themselves were often influenced by physiognomic monographs. Audiences, in conjunction with artists, helped form new physiognomic conventions that infused portraits with meaningful biographical information. With the developing format of the public art exhibition, artists faced a new set of intellectual and artistic considerations and had to cater not to one patron, but to a wide range of middle- and upper-class viewers. Rather than painting for an individual patron and his or her family, nineteenth-century British artists often produced their portraits for an exhibition audience.[9] These portraits demanded a new set of considerations for the imagination and understanding of a wide and commercially powerful audience who might or might not purchase a painting on the spot.

History of Art and Physiognomy

Physiognomy has always been of special interest to portrait painters, who have drawn on its principles in their representations. Many art instructors turned to physiognomy as part of their lessons, particularly in the Middle Ages and the early modern period, when formalized physiognomy was the purview of the learned and elite: philosophers, clergy, and especially artists. Of particular note were sixteenth-century Italian magus and natural philosopher Giambattista della Porta, who applied the principles of animal analogies to humans in pictorial form, and seventeenth-century French artist and instructor Charles Le Brun. Le Brun developed and expanded della Porta's approach into sophisticated and integrated images, explicitly referencing physiognomy in the lectures he gave at the Académie royale de peinture et de sculpture, which he cofounded on the basis of the Italian model.[10]

Johann Caspar Lavater widened the audience for physiognomy in the late eighteenth century from a select group to a more general elite, as well as, eventually, transcending class and social boundaries. The presence of physiognomy in portraiture was of particular interest to Lavater; he was deeply involved in the execution of all his own portraits, insisting on a type of representation that he saw as consistent with his physiognomic truth. Dissatisfied with the painting of himself by J. H. Wilhelm Tischbein in 1781 and the engraving based on it for his book by "L," likely the artist Johann Heinrich Lips, Lavater complained that the image conveyed too much wisdom and not enough poetic expression.[11] To Lavater, every angle, every line, and every proportional measure in a portrait carried tremendous meaning for personal representation. Inaccurate renderings, for better or for worse, were, to Lavater, nothing short of falsifications of the truth of someone's character.[12]

In his original writings, Lavater directed many of his comments explicitly to artists. An entire section titled "On Portrait Painting" pointed out the improvements that knowledge of physiognomy would add to representations of people.[13] Like botanists and other natural historians, Lavater recognized the importance of pictures as models from which others could learn the principles of his science. Lavater also acknowledged the crippling effects of poor representations on the development and dissemination of accurate physiognomic knowledge: "One of the greatest obstacles to physiognomy is the actual, incredible, imperfection of this art. There is generally a defect of eye, or hand of the painter."[14]

Many painters heeded Lavater's call to study physiognomy and incorporate it into their portraits, both to enhance their representations and to provide evidence for further study of the practice. I am not claiming that all nineteenth-century artists read Lavater or other physiognomic texts. Rather, because physiognomic ideas were deeply interwoven into representational culture, artistic manuals and artists engaged with physiognomic ideas even without explicitly naming them, often drawing on the shared scientific, artistic, and physiognomic language of observation and perception. These references can be decoded when they are viewed with a physiognomically informed historical eye. Although the relationship between physiognomy and portraiture was long-standing, the strengthened ties between perception and painting lent authority to the realism claims of Victorian portrait painters. With new demands for truth in representation, physiognomy offered a way to infuse portraits with biographical information about their subjects and make meaning that could be shared and communicated within a well-known observational and artistic framework.

Prominent Georgian caricature artist James Gillray was an early adherent of Lavater's notion of physiognomy as a revelatory artistic technology. However, Gillray differed with Lavater and later Victorian realists over his ideas about the necessity for strict fidelity to appearance in the project of visually representing truth. In scores of images, Gillray presented exaggerated and caricatured features in order to emphasize the physiognomic messages that might not have been obvious to the casual observer. A different type of portrait artist, the caricaturist had license to distort in order to reveal; invisibility through anonymity was impossible to sustain under the caricaturist's pen. In his most explicit application of physiognomy, the 1798 etching and engraving "DOUBLÛRES of Characters; or, Striking Resemblances in Physiognomy" (Figure 3.1), Gillray made little recourse to exaggeration and caricature and only subtly emphasized traits in order to excavate biographical and physiognomic meaning.[15] In this picture, Gillray contended that fine clothing and titles disguised what was in fact readily apparent to the keen and skilled observer. Immediately following the title of the work is the Lavaterian quote "If you would know Men's Hearts, Look in their Faces."

In this image, produced initially for the *Anti-Jacobin Review*, Gillray accused a number of prominent Whigs of duplicity and ulterior motives.[16] Lurking behind each man was his true physiognomic face. Without significantly altering the appearance of the subjects, Gillray portrayed them in the worst possible light. Images of the seven men, namely, Charles Fox, Richard Brinsley Sheridan, the Duke of Norfolk, George Tierney, Sir Francis Burdett, Lord Derby, and the Duke of Bedford, had a caption beneath them for each of their two faces. For example, Fox was both "The Patron of Liberty" and "The Arch Fiend." The second caption, according to Gillray's depiction, was always a more accurate title than the first. Gillray was using his skills as an artist and an observer to enhance the physiognomic messages already present, demonstrating the power of pictures to convey information that the originals could not. Like botanical reproductions, Gillray's classificatory pictures gave both plea-

Figure 3.1. James Gillray, "DOUBLÛRES of Characters; or, Striking Resemblances in Physiognomy," 1798. Gillray exploited the techniques of character and physiognomy to reveal the hidden characters of prominent politicians. (Reprinted with permission from Yale University, Harvey Cushing/John Hay Whitney Medical Library.)

sure and knowledge and called on his viewers to pay attention to minutiae in order to develop appreciation for differences.[17]

In addition to caricature and physiognomic portraiture, there were other ways to turn people inside out visually. In a sequence of lithographs in 1830, the artist George Spratt constructed composites of people through the tools of their trades, offering an alternative artistic way of determining personal characteristics through the features of the body (Figure 3.2).[18] In "The Entomologist" a man is built from bugs, while, in a more explicit commentary on physiognomy, "The Physiognomist" is a person composed of a series of faces lecturing to another series of faces sitting in the audience.[19] Gently mocking, these images use humor to challenge the possibility of actually seeing what people are made of through transparent external clues.

Like caricature, composites had the license of humor to distort and exaggerate, with their own set of communicative conventions that identified and assigned identity to its subjects. As I discussed in Chapter 1, illustrators such as George Cruikshank and Hablot Knight Browne combined the techniques of caricature and portraiture to communicate visually what written descriptions could not. Like painted portraits, illustration acted as a source for physiognomic study and helped develop the principles of this pursuit.[20] I explore the power of physiognomic caricature in the next chapter and look at the ways in which it assigned visibility to invisible groups of people. Portrait painters, however, were working under a different set of demands, particularly as calls for realism in representation became louder and more influential. These artists had to learn how to communicate internal character and lived experience while adhering strictly to the viewed external appearance. Instruction manuals had to figure out how to teach these skills. Physiognomic techniques provided at least part of the solution.

Framing the Picture: Physiognomy and Art Instruction

Physiognomic manipulation was a long-standing technique to flatter great rulers with generous depictions of mastery and strength. Painters had to juggle the potential pleasure of their patrons and their own artistic integrity, all the while ensuring that their representations were identifiable and recognizable to others. According to writer and scholar (and parent of future prime minister Benjamin Disraeli) Isaac D'Israeli, Charles Le Brun paid rather too much attention to his patron, thereby detracting from Le Brun's own physiognomic accuracy. In a self-reflective painting, "Le Brun, the great French artist, painted himself holding in his hand the portrait of his earliest patron." The prop was highly revelatory because "in this accompaniment the Artist may be said to have portrayed the features of his soul. If genius has too often complained of its patrons, has it not also often over-valued their protection?"[21] D'Israeli noted the tendency of artists to flatter their patrons, which distortion, he argued, did a great disservice: "It is to be regretted that men of genius have not been careful to transmit their own portraits to their admirers; it forms a part of their character; a false delicacy has interfered." D'Israeli offered a list

Figure 3.2. George Spratt's 1830 lithographs "The Entomologist" *(left)* and "The Physiognomist" *(right)* demonstrate that people are the sum of their parts. In contrast to a traditional physiognomic approach, Spratt displayed the different ways in which the exterior could mark hidden interior characteristics. ("The Entomologist" reprinted with permission from James Secord. "The Physiognomist" reprinted with permission from Yale University, Harvey Cushing/John Hay Whitney Medical Library.)

of such debased likenesses, including "Goldsmith," who "was a short thick man, with wan features and a vulgar appearance, but looks tall and fashionable in a bag-wig." Likewise, "Bayle's portrait does not resemble him, as one of his friends writes. Rousseau, in his Montero cap, is in the same predicament. Winkelmann's portrait does not preserve the striking physiognomy of the man, and in the last edition a new one is substituted."[22] One notable exception to the sycophancy trend was the portraits of King Philip IV by Diego de Velázquez. Apparently in accordance with the wishes of the king, Velázquez's final two portraits of Philip IV were brutally realistic, devoid of the symbols of rule in both figure and background.[23]

By the late eighteenth century, the expectations of the portrait painter changed from those of a flatterer to those of a biographer.[24] Consonant with the increased interest in classification and naturalistic representation,

pictures of specimens became sources of scientific information. The art of painting—portrait or landscape—was inadequate without the science of perception and observation. Artists were increasingly expected to show the truth of character and experience in the faces of their sitters. But faces were hard, for many reasons. Artistic mastery of faces and their expressions was achieved only by the late fifteenth century, and even through the seventeenth century, superior skill in this area was worthy of remark and discussion.[25]

In their depiction of faces, portrait artists were drawing on the long and dynamic history of character presentation in portraiture. Often—but not always—explicitly reliant on physiognomic techniques, this relationship dates to antiquity and was continually refined by artist-teachers and their disciples.[26] Artist and critic Lady Elizabeth Rigby Eastlake noted her debt to ancient techniques in an anonymous article that emphasized the role of the arts in providing physiognomic data: "In that philosophy of the fine arts which the Greeks have left us we alone find the rudiments of a true study of physiognomy."[27]

Literary critic and essayist William Hazlitt, himself an aspiring artist, suggested that the portraits of a superior artist such as satirist William Hogarth should not be viewed only for pleasure but also should be studied as data about the nature of humanity. Hogarth acquired these data through study and preparation: "The merit of his [Hogarth's] pictures does not depend on the nature of the subject, but on the knowledge displayed of it, on the number of ideas they excite, on the fund of thought and observation contained in them." Like botanical illustrations, these pictures were models "to be studied as works of science as well as of amusement; they satisfy our love of truth; they fill up the void in the mind; they form a series of plates in natural history, the history of our own species." Providing the ideal and elusive balance between exciting pleasure and exciting rationality, these unique pedagogical images "stimulate the faculties as well as soothe them."[28]

Isaac D'Israeli expressed similar sentiments about pictures of the great and the good, emphasizing their power to stimulate and teach: "What is more agreeable to the curiosity of the mind and the eye than the portraits of great characters?" D'Israeli turned to other thinkers to emphasize his point, noting that "Lord Orford preferred an interesting portrait to either landscape or historical painting. 'A landscape, however excellent in its distributions of wood, and water, and buildings, leaves not one trace in the memory . . . But a real portrait is truth itself, and calls up so many collateral ideas as to fill an intelligent mind more than any other species.' "[29]

An article in the *Cornhill Magazine,* a shilling weekly that offered critical articles and serialized literature, echoed Hazlitt's, Eastlake's, and D'Israeli's views on the valuable role played by portraiture in the observation and classification of human types through physiognomy: "To sustain and to verify such [physiognomic] generalisations as these, portraiture is absolutely essential." Without physiognomically nuanced representations, advanced physiognomic study was impossible, as evidenced by the failures of the past: "Nothing is more curious than to see the straits to which the older physiognomists, who had no portraits at hand, were driven in order to satisfy the natural craving of the human mind for generalisation of some sort."[30]

By the turn of the nineteenth century, the ability to communicate character became the mark of a good portrait painter; excellent representations were distinguished not just by mimetic accuracy but by biographical depth. To deal with the challenge of nuanced faces, manuals guided painters to hone their skills of observation and treated subjects as specimens to be accurately recorded. Like all specimens, human models needed to be displayed in such a way as to elicit the most useful—or most flattering—classificatory information. Painters' training guides abounded with advice about the best representation of difficult sitters whose external ugliness was, predictably, mirrored by an equally challenging internal set of characteristics. Largely directed toward amateur and beginning painters, manuals often counseled readers to avoid faces and their characters as much as possible until they mastered the skills of observation necessary for physiognomic representation. Advanced texts provided more exact advice and used more explicit physiognomic language, as did professional artists and critics.

The anonymous and widely read manual *The Draughtsman's Assistant* (later discovered to be written by Carington Bowles) advised the beginning artist to avoid the difficulties of expressing character "before he has made a thorough Proficiency in the earlier and more practicable branches." The representation of character was both the hardest to achieve and "by far the most difficult Part the Pupil has to learn," requiring great artistic and observational skills: "In drawing a Likeness, great Care is necessary to express the Passions in the liveliest Manner, and this is done by minding the Disposition of every Feature, with peculiar Nicety." The guide counseled patience in the pursuit of what it called artistic "Perfection," urging artists to study and develop their skills, avoiding "too hasty Strides," and instead to "ascend progressively the necessary Steps which lead towards it."[31] It was only through the honing of physiognomic observation over time that artists could truly master accurate representation, which included the capture of character on canvas.

James Merigot, in his 1821 art manual for amateurs, echoed this manual by suggesting that aside from the truly exceptional, artists should avoid expression and character altogether. For fear of causing offense to sitters, Merigot advised students that although "the human countenance may be said to be the theatre on which the soul acts . . . we have to represent the human countenance devoid of expression, reduced to a state of insensibility."[32] By erasing the possibility of communicating character, the artist could not be blamed for accidental insalubrious biographical representations. The ideal, of course, would be to capture the soul, but most would fall short and should not, without diligent study and repeated practice, even make the attempt.

An 1824 guide to portrait painting underscored the importance of study and preparation in the all-important aspect of character, noting that a "perfect knowledge of the expression of the countenance of a sitter is of the first importance, for, however correctly the various parts or features may be painted, it will be but an insipid, uninteresting performance, if destitute of that individuality of character and feeling which will be found on close observation to be peculiar to almost every subject that comes under the notice of the artists." Drawing was indeed a test of observation; for a portrait to be truly good, an artist had to capture the individuality and character that was apparent only through careful looking. Part of this process was the display of the subject, for "on the placing of a sitter depends much of the success of the endeavour to obtain a faithful and agreeable portrait," which placing, if done poorly or thoughtlessly, could draw attention to that which most people would like to keep hidden. In particular, "In portraiture nothing should be more carefully avoided than caricature" because "no man would wish to be known by his deformities."[33]

For those subjects for whom accurate representation would be insalubrious, artists were advised on techniques to display their specimens, or sitters, to the best possible advantage. Some of the problems presented by an unappealing subject could be finessed through a specific type of advance preparation, as an 1844 manual on miniature painting suggested: "Before the student commences the drawing, he should well study the character of the face which he is to depict, that he may place the sitter in that position which will best display the features."[34] The writer was careful to emphasize the role of the painter in making staging decisions and empowered the artist with physiognomic autonomy: "Obliquity of vision and particular marks in the face must be attended to before the sketch is made, and heightened or softened according to the judgement of the painter."[35] The sitter and the artist were working together to produce a kind of truth that could only emerge though images, a truth that combined the observation and execution of the artist with the experience and dynamism of the subject.

The author of this text, artist and illustrator Nathaniel Whittock, a prolific writer of instruction books, gave a number of examples of portraits in which artists made physiognomic decisions in their work.[36] Whittock made clear, however, that in the age of biography, there was a limit to artistic autonomy. Artists must remain true to the spirit of their sitters, which could be accessed only by proper study and observation. In one of his analyses, Whittock noted that "No. 2 is an outline of the justly celebrated William Penn, the founder of the State of Pennsylvania in the United States of America. What artist would think of painting this just and pious man in a light frivolous position?"[37] This question was predicated on knowledge of Penn's character and life experience, without which a good representation would be impossible. According to Whittock, the role of the artist was to communicate this knowledge through the painting, and the burden of observation and understanding was placed first on the artist and only then on his or her audience.

In his commentary on a portrait of the head of the Reverend Laurence Sterne, Whittock discussed the artist's decision to highlight Sterne's whimsical rather than his ecclesiastical side: "Who that looks on this arch waggish face would think it was that of a reverend divine?" This decision, according to Whittock, was based on the artist's sense that Sterne's humorous writing defined him more than his religious identity: "The painter, feeling that the reverend gentleman was better known and appreciated as a humorous writer than as a clergyman, took no pains to represent the dignity and solidarity of the latter character, but directed his attention to the delineation of the witty author of Tristram Shandy and the Sentimental Journey."[38] In addition to underscoring the power of the artist to communicate character, Whittock expressed total confidence that the aspect of a "reverend divine" would appear totally different from that of a "witty author." In either case, the artist needed to express biographical information, but he had to decide which aspects of the biography to highlight.

The anonymous author of the 1847 guide *The Manual of Oil-Painting for Young Artists and Amateurs* echoed the advice of Whittock's text that artists should prepare for portraits by advance study of the faces of their subjects. In its approach to defects and unflattering features, this text was more explicit in guiding painters to manipulate not only their sitters but also the paintings themselves. Unsightly features, if deemed unimportant to the true character of the subject, should be excluded, while "if there be defects which cannot be omitted, you are to mollify them; let them be there, but in their proper insignificance."[39] In so doing, the artist would produce both a painting more acceptable to the sitter and a more accurate representation by making defects appropriately inconspicuous.

In order to render such defects insignificant, the manual counseled painters on techniques designed to bring the best physiognomic aspects of their sitters into being, because "every individual has one aspect more favourable than another, and which is called forth by the state of the mind, as being in repose or in excitement." These techniques required advance preparation and study: "An artist should ascertain this [favorable aspect], in some way or other, previously to his work." In order to bring forth this aspect, "the painter [must] pen a conversation with him that shall pleasantly excite his faculties." Once the faculties of the subject were indeed rendered pleasant, the artist was to "study the play of the features, and bear in mind what is most agreeable and striking, that it may be recalled when no longer apparent, or be strengthened by accidental renewal."[40]

This excerpt provides insight into how physiognomic ideas were understood, and how they changed through the interplay between readers, writers, and practitioners. The manual suggested that through their painting, artists could actually change the appearance of their sitters. Artists create their subjects in many ways; here reality followed representation because painters produced features in their sitters that would match those expressed in their portraits.

Thomas Woolnoth, historical engraver to the queen, attempted in his 1852 treatise to "unite mental with linear Portraiture, in confirmation of physiognomical rule."[41] Artists, Woolnoth contended, had the potential to be the best physiognomists if they troubled to apply the powers of observation on which their craft rested. He argued that the challenges of executing the face were tied to a lack of physiognomic practice, and he called on artists to develop their observational skills because "our powers of recognition are greatly weakened for want of simple exercise."[42]

Woolnoth, like many other artists and instructors, suggested that the key to communicating character on canvas was familiarity with the sitter, which could be achieved through advance preparation of observation and relationship building. Such a relationship, he recognized, might not be feasible, in which case artists would have to rely exclusively on physiognomic principles and skills to aid their art: "As it is of necessity . . . a variety of cases must be attended with uncertainty or conjecture, from partial or total ignorance of the character itself, still the mental impression will be there, which renders it the more necessary that the ideal formation should be the result of some knowledge of the individual." Lacking such knowledge in advance, artists should rely on "the closest observation," following which "the positive lines of physiognomy may be safely consulted."[43]

Many of the British artist manuals that I examined only gestured to a concern with the reactions of the sitters to the physiognomic messages of their portraits. By the nineteenth century, the British networks of artistic support were mediated through the commercial market rather than operating under the patronage model that persisted in France.[44] The rules were changing for British artists, and manuals helped them adjust to a different kind of audience. Along with professional painters and critics, amateurs and the artistically ignorant participated in these networks through the purchase of art manuals, the production of their own work, and, increasingly, attendance and acquisition at public exhibitions.

My examination of artists' manuals was made easier by the abundance of training texts in nineteenth-century Britain. Print was relatively cheap, and books abounded correspondingly. But this is only part of the story. Literacy did not become almost universal in Britain until the second half of the nineteenth century. Rather, the increased interest in artistic manuals represented growing attempts by the middle and lower classes to participate in those forms of culture that had formerly indicated elite status. This type of imitation extended beyond practices of spectatorship; for those who could afford it, participation in artistic culture meant not just viewing but also buying art. Aspirants to cultural sophistication used training manuals to produce art and to learn about its production. In learning about portraiture, readers were also learning about physiognomy as understood by the manuals they read and the artists they viewed.

Painting became a source of widespread entertainment that extended beyond the wealthy patrons of the past.[45] This trend increased as the fine arts became associated with nonartistic institutions, including schools, shops, the theatre, and private purchase by the nonelite. Patrons and supporters of the arts extended through the middle classes, as did artistic practice. Teaching manuals changed their focus correspondingly, with, as we have seen, an increased emphasis on basic skills for amateurs that prevented them from attempting too much, too soon.

New forms of middle-class commercialism coalesced with the growing accessibility of knowledge and cultural participation in the nineteenth century.[46] The well-respected intellectual periodical the *Fortnightly Review* lamented in 1855 that although art used to be "indulged in as a luxury or a whim, by a selected and exclusive caste . . . it is now the province of the prosperous middle class."[47] This new audience for art became an audience for artistic physiognomy, which combined with the physiognomic ideas they were already applying and producing from other social and cultural spheres.

With the emergence of the professional and industrial middle class, there was a rising demand for leisure activity in the domestic space. The constituency of refined amateurism in the artistic realm, which had always been the purview of upper-class women, increased accordingly. In short, these ladies, young and old, needed something to do, so they turned to drawing and painting, long-standing marks of educated skill that could be placed in direct opposition to masculine business duties and professional training.[48] As Ann Bermingham has demonstrated, the first half of the nineteenth century saw unprecedented growth in artistic amateurism.[49] She has charted the increasing feminization of nonprofessional pursuits and has argued that women became the major consumers of amateur art supplies.[50] These supplies were readily available because the culture of artistic exhibitions and commercial artistic ventures generated widespread interest.[51]

However, as the culture of amateurism increased, the quality of professional instruction in the Royal Academy School deteriorated to such an extent that by 1830, it became a subject of concern in Parliament.[52] Equally telling, if not more so, was the frustration of art critics with the increasingly commercial, and correspondingly constrained, nature of the Royal Academy's annual exhibitions. With the rise in middle-class patronage, the works that were in most demand were those best suited, both in size and subject matter, to be hung in dining rooms and boudoirs.[53] As Helene E. Roberts has shown, critics bemoaned the exhibitions, complaining that they allowed commercial appeal to outweigh artistic merit by giving the most prominent space to works that sold the best.[54]

Fraser's Magazine complained about the Royal Academy Exhibition of 1855 that attendees were more interested in socializing than in viewing art: "How many go thither because it is the fashion, and how many because they care for art, may be estimated by the scanty attendance between eight and ten o'clock—the time when the pictures really can be examined." This estimation suggested that "it is not too much to say that four-fifths of the men come to look, not at the pictures, but at the fair owners of the bonnets."[55] These new attendees at art shows brought a great deal of social enthusiasm, but rather less artistic knowledge, to their spectating experience. Art manuals and periodical reviews served as an important guide for the art-hungry and status-hungry viewer, for whom "some slight acquaintance with the pictures is . . . essential [if he] aspires to the high aim of making himself agreeable in society."[56] With their influence over purchases, these guides acted as important commercial arbiters for painters. Many critics were deeply engaged in the question of how commercial concerns skewed quality while simultaneously recognizing that they, in part, created and were sustaining the problem.[57]

In this way, the changing scope of patronage and purchase significantly affected the type of art that was being produced. Similarly, with their focus on amateur and middle-class audiences as both artists and patrons, writers of art manuals paid careful attention to the insecure sensibilities of the artistically uninitiated.[58] Unsurprisingly, amateurs followed in the steps of their professional teachers and mentors. In fact, professional artists found major employment opportunities as drawing masters, private teachers, and manual writers. These commercial ventures helped create the nineteenth-century art industry, in which art books featured prominently. There were many ways of learning how to draw.

Although successful artists were often subject to the vagaries of taste and fashion, the demands on them had usually originated from one powerful and wealthy patron. As the market for art changed in the nineteenth century, artists had to consider a mass audience that spread across a wide social spectrum, and whose demands varied accordingly. Victorians were consistent, however, in their desire for biographical portraits produced through highly developed skills of perception and observation. Like other inhabitants of the city, artists were recorders of human life and daily interaction, which they in turn represented on their canvases. Unlike writers such as Eliza Lynn Linton and Henry Mayhew, these documenters of the urban experience and its inhabitants were communicating visually, infusing their representations with physiognomic imagery rather than physiognomic language. Visual artists particularly depended on the understanding of their audience to express their ideas. They could not, through their medium, expand and explain the meaning of their work in language, and this inability led to unpredictable results. As Charlotte Klonk and Kate Flint have chronicled, according to the Victorians, different people (especially in an artistic context) saw differently.[59]

Seeing and Spectating: The Viewers' Perspective

The decreasing skill and quality of the art had no effect on attendance at the Royal Academy's yearly exhibition. Throughout the first half of the nineteenth century, attendance at this event and other art shows continued to increase steadily and, some would say, indiscriminately.[60] Noticeable in midcentury exhibitions was the prominence of narrative paintings, particularly historical portraits and so-called modern-life social realist works. Families in hard times were a particularly well-represented theme around the 1850s; as I discuss in Chapter 5, artists used the symbols established at this time to represent the physiognomy of fallen women overwhelmed by desperation and despair. Rather than representing only the wealthy, portrait artists were interested in people from all social classes, a trend reflected in caricature in graphic print, fine arts paintings, and, as the century progressed, photographic studies.

Despite the careful guidance of training manuals, sometimes artists got it wrong. For paintings to be considered realistic, exhibition audiences—a new category of viewer—had to be convinced that these representations were consonant with their own experiences of the world. Although artists may have been particularly gifted and trained observers, audiences were visually and physiognomically savvy, and this led critics to evaluate art, in part, on artists' ability to communicate character through physiognomic conventions. One 1854 reviewer at the Royal Academy's annual show praised an artist specifically for physiognomic fidelity: "One of the best paintings in the Academy for physiognomical character, not intense, but varied and appropriate, is Mr. G. B. O'Neill's *A Jury*."[61] Other artists were not as lucky.

Victorian critical commentary on paintings paid particular attention to the anatomical and psychological renderings of their subjects. Art historian Mary Cowling has contended that the level of analysis in the nineteenth century was far more sophisticated than that of current criticism. In *The Artist as Anthropologist,* Cowling demonstrated the extent to which critics examined paintings on the strength of their physiognomic and phrenological effectiveness and even, at times, their accuracy.[62] One critic for the highbrow *Athenaeum* objected to artist Henry O'Neil's *Before Waterloo,* commenting on the unlikelihood "that so many English folks of this class in question have ever been assembled with so little that was beautiful or noble in their features."[63] Whether deliberately or not, this classifying comment was as much about the physiognomic likelihood as it was about the skill of O'Neil's depiction.

Like the art manuals, the professionally focused *Art Journal* suggested that artists could avoid poor depictions by acquiring physiognomic knowledge through careful study: "Artists often fail in delineating a character, because they are ignorant of the facial attributes which indicate the temper, feeling, or disposition they desire to portray. They have not . . . studied physiognomy; hence their failure."[64] In turn, writers and reviewers of polite and professional physiognomy articles and monographs often referred to artists as sources of expertise and inspiration. Lady Elizabeth Eastlake's article in the *Quarterly Review* compiled an impressive list of physiognomic supporters that included not just specific artists but also the entire profession. According to Sir James Paget, portrait artists were physiognomists by definition: "To conclude our list of authorities we might bring in the whole body of artists; for the whole application of the fine arts to the representation of men is based on the principle that the minds of those who are represented may be indicated by their forms."[65] This broad categorization echoed an earlier article in the same journal by Elizabeth Eastlake, which argued for the long historical connection between physiognomy and art: "[For] theories of physiognomy . . . it is to the first artists in the world that we are indebted for the only safe basis on which they stand."[66]

In that same article, Eastlake discussed the importance of physiognomic knowledge for both the artist and the observer, underscoring her claim that the representation of nuances of expression was the sign of true portrait mastery: "And it is only in the highest masters of the art of portrait-painting that we can find those intricate shades and grades—those crossings and blending of character, in which, upon close examination, the physiognomical identity of the individual, as well as of the passion, is found to lie." Proper viewership, like great painting, could be found only among a limited community of the properly trained and educated because "the human face . . . [is] like other pictures, it can only be fully enjoyed and understood by the cultivated eye.[67] Perception, according to Eastlake, was not an empirical and predictable phenomenon; some—the "cultivated"—saw better than others.

From the Painters' Perspective

Portrait artists were observers, which, particularly in the nineteenth century, meant that artists—good ones—were also physiognomists. Starting with landscape painting at the early 1800s, visual reproductions became subject to the calls for truth in representation that eventually coalesced as the realism movements of midcentury. In portraiture, realism required pictures that were both mimetically accurate and communicative of character and biography. By the 1830s, criticism of romantic painters, such as J. M. W. Turner, became particularly harsh and sparked a shift among commercially and aesthetically minded artists toward subjects of smaller scope with detailed execution.[68] These changes in painting combined with some romantic techniques to find prominent expression in the works of the Pre-Raphaelite Brotherhood (PRB) and its followers. Committed to what they called "truth to nature," these artists drew attention to prominent social issues, following the model of "modern-life" or "social realist" pictures of such painters as Richard Redgrave and William Powell Firth.[69]

For the delineation of character to have meaning, not only the artists but also their audiences had to understand what was being conveyed. Physiognomy was a very powerful communication tool, especially when deliberately applied to add nuance and depth to portraits and other paintings. When physiognomy was used to illustrate images of urban decay and industrial poverty, it caused these paintings to resonate with viewers by highlighting the human element in a way that matched their own fantasies of city life. One of the best-known social realist paintings, Firth's *Derby Day* (1858), was a painstaking and detailed panorama of human social types, filled with multiple narrative incidents. This mass of interacting people had been ordered with an eye to middle-class satisfaction. Although it featured petty crime and mild destruction, the scene, like many of Firth's paintings, was designed to conform to the ways in which Victorians wished to see themselves.[70]

Relying on physiognomic principles, Firth used *Derby Day* to order the urban disorder while being careful to represent a believable and varied range of types. In so doing, Firth effectively used the reality effect to portray just enough reality to be interesting, but not enough to be alienating or overly challenging. Firth's careful combination of physiognomic realism and pleasant poverty established the framework for later trends in social picturesque photography. All his types conformed to appropriate physiognomic expectations, lending his painting believability and his subjects a lifelike aspect that made the image come alive for critics and other viewers.[71] One of the most widely reviewed paintings of its time, *Derby Day* impressed viewers with the way in which it made the anonymous crowds of urban London seem to possess characters, biographies, and life experiences. Firth, a self-proclaimed physiognomist, expended great care in the selection of his models; their faces (and their characters) had to match the messages of his paintings.[72]

The PRB emerged in the late 1840s to communicate what its members conceived to be more honest portrayals of their subjects, eschewing sophisticated trickery in their representation of serious and inspiring topics.[73] Grittier in their evocation of pathos than the sanitized social scenes of Firth, their paintings drew on the discourse of reality while emphasizing the technical skills of the painters in their details. Self-defined realist painters, including the PRB, were often more explicit than the carefully worded art manuals about their engagement with physiognomy as a way to communicate character. Midcentury realist painters, such as

Edward Hicks, John Callcott Horsley, Dante Gabriel Rossetti, and Holman Hunt, wrote explicitly about the role of physiognomy in their artistic techniques.[74] Like Firth, Ford Madox Brown, who was closely associated with the PRB, focused on the depictions of groups and their common physiognomic traits to "delineate types, and not individuals."[75]

Artist Henry O'Neil, in his Royal Academy lectures on painting, acknowledged his use of physiognomy even as he decried its accuracy: "I often find myself attracted or repelled by persons to whom I ascribe a character wholly derived from a perusal of their features; and truth obliges me to confess that my first impressions have too frequently been unjust."[76] Nevertheless, to O'Neil, representation of character was the most important aspect of portrait painting, and his work reveals great attention paid to physiognomy and especially pathognomy. One laudatory reviewer commented on his 1858 *Eastward Ho* that the "classes of life, the ages, and the stations of the different leave-takers are admirably expressed and contrasted."[77] O'Neil's conflicted physiognomic commitments caused him to direct students to "studying character" and to emphasize that the "simplest form in which the artist can delineate the character of mankind is Portraiture."[78] Portraits thereby became sources of information about character and classification of the original specimens, O'Neil's "mankind."

Both artists and actors not only adhered to but also developed the growing body of physiognomic conventions and principles and expanded the range of physiognomically meaningful signs. Artists relied on physiognomy for two purposes: to get information about their subjects through observation and advance preparation and to give information about their subjects to portrait viewers, who were demanding not only mimetic accuracy in representation but also biographical detail. Like other natural history specimens, human subjects acted as sources of classificatory knowledge, and artists were scientists whose job was to produce pedagogically useful copies of the original. Artists were also entertainers whose livelihood depended on the pleasure—expressed through purchasing—of their audience. In the nineteenth century, with increased demands for realism that, in the fine arts, inspired the social realists and the Pre-Raphaelite Brotherhood, this pleasure depended in large part on making portraits come alive through the communication of character.

Portrait artists used features to tell a story about their subjects. To do so, they were trained to hone their powers of observation, as well as the perceptual skills of their audiences. The former could be trained, while the latter were left somewhat to chance. Given the challenges of executing faces with nuance and depth, instruction manuals guided the growing field of artistic amateurs in techniques to fake the face if it could not be altogether avoided. In these beginners' guides, written to meet the demands of the middle classes eager to join the cultural elite, physiognomic language was often subtle. Along with advice to be patient and practice the many skills required in drawing and painting, physiognomic guidance was couched in the oft-repeated injunction to readers to develop their powers of observation. Professional artists, especially the social realists and those who followed, were often much more explicit in their reliance—willingly or otherwise—on physiognomic techniques.

All painters, however, had to consider the reaction of their sitters and were advised about the best ways to manipulate features to portray them in the best possible light. Artists were creators, making physiognomic decisions about who their subjects were and how they should be viewed by others. This power of painting and the painter knowingly to manipulate sitters was a significant advantage over the developing art of photography. Upon being asked by Queen Victoria if photography would contribute to the demise of his profession, well-known painter of miniature portraits Alfred Chalon replied, "Ah, non, Madame, photographie can't flatèré."[79]

Performance and portrait physiognomy developed the power of self-conscious physiognomic application and manipulation to convey information about both individuals and generalized types. The use of physiognomy on stage and on canvas emerged out of the turn to realism because physiognomy offered an answer to the demands for truth in representation. Like other specimens, pictures of people demonstrated the power of images to convey information that words could not. Caricature, not strictly bound by the need for mimetic accuracy, combined physiognomic techniques with humor and satire, distorting in order to reveal what was not obvious through plain sight.

Unlike painted portraits, caricature was devoted as much to the production and representation of group traits as individual features, using physiognomy to produce conventions about the identification of communities. It is important to remember that these processes did not follow one another in strict sequence; they were messy and constantly in flux and often happened in conjunction with one another. Although physiognomic fashioning flourished on the stage and in portraits, it also hit the political arena and the papers, busily demarcating the faces of, for example, the Irish and the Jews.

These two examples are not chosen at random. The stage Irishman and the stage Jew were prevalent stock characters throughout the nineteenth century. Unlike more obviously different foreigners in London, including Africans and Indians, the Irish and the Jews represented a particular physiognomic conundrum because although they were obviously distinct from Anglo-Saxon English, at least in the British imagination, they were not always visibly so. In the next chapter, I examine two case studies in which physiognomic ideas were combined with artistic renderings to self-consciously create Irish and Jewish facial types. These fictional imaginaries played an important role in emerging nationalistic ideas about what it meant to be English in the context of a growing empire. Rather than focusing on an individual Irishman or an individual Jew, caricatures and political discussions showed what *all* Irish and what *all* Jews looked like, dressed like, and spoke like.

The representations of Irishness and Jewishness were shared across media, in literature, in painting, in photography, and especially on the stage.[80] In many guides to acting, actors were instructed in techniques to play people of various nationalities and, in particular, how to mix makeup to create dark skin. However, it was the stage Irishman who was the most ubiquitous type. So common was this role that actor-teacher Henry Siddons could comment about playwright Richard Cumberland that *his* "specimen of Hibernian whimsicality . . . defies all competition in characters of humorous Irishmen."[81] Caricatures contributed to the growing set of about what exactly it meant to be Irish or Jewish, and how exactly these outsiders could be identified. Often humorous, occasionally satirical, and sometimes kind, these caricatures gave a visible face to the invisible other. As I show in the next chapter, they did so by using physiognomic signs.

CHAPTER FOUR

Caricature Physiognomy

Imaging Communities

LASSICAL AND MEDIEVAL SCHOLARS used the study of the face to denote both individual and group traits. In so doing, they created verbal images that acted as shortcuts to cue a set of associations and understandings.[1] The connection between art and identification was strengthened with the late eighteenth-century physiognomic revival. In Britain, imperial expansion further spurred the imperative to produce transportable means of visual diagnosis and differentiation. One of the major points of access to physiognomy for the British public was the ability to imagine national physiognomies and, through these, national identity.[2] In this chapter, I examine the power of the scientific rhetoric of physiognomy in the development of visual and cultural practices. Although physiognomy mapped easily onto visual imagery across the empire, a more complicated area of inquiry deals with the use of physiognomy to assign difference when it was not immediately apparent. The simianization of Irish Catholics and the standardization of Jewish depictions in British graphic print in the first half of the nineteenth century were processes informed by anthropological, evolutionary, amusement, and especially physiognomic principles. These systems worked together in the invention of recognizable and universal Irish and Jewish faces.[3]

Physiognomy and physiognomists were promiscuous in their choice of subject matter, but some kinds of people received special attention. Irish Catholics and Jewish immigrants to London offered tantalizing possibilities as physiognomic subjects. Through physiognomic readings and visual representations, Irish and Jewish faces could be constructed and then, in turn, deconstructed. Equally important, and what made the Irish and the

Jews stand out in the crowds of white immigrants, was that they were, in the British imagination, entertaining. The happy-go-lucky Irish (unlike the dour Scots) and the old Jewish peddler with the hybrid English dialect were funny.[4]

Physiognomy married science with entertainment and solved a number of problems through a nifty visual trick.[5] Rising fears about Irish Catholic political agitation, increasing Jewish political power, and the seemingly undetectable racial difference of both were calmed by visually caging the Irish and visually combining different Jewish communities. The Irish Catholics and the Jews had a great deal in common as English outcasts; both groups immigrated in waves because of difficulties in their native countries, both formed strong communities in their new homes, and both had religious allegiances that caused them to act in ways different from those of the Anglican English. Caricature physiognomy initially focused on specific Irish Catholic and Jewish individuals, but as the century progressed, it began to follow in the tradition of missionary and explorer David Livingstone, using what Conor Cruise O'Brien has called the "pejorative singular" to act as racial exemplars for an entire group.[6] Despite multiple social, cultural, religious, and geographic distinctions, all Irish Catholics were turned into Irish apes, and all Jews (Sephardim of Iberian descent and Ashkenazim of eastern European descent) became only Ashkenazim.[7]

Rhetoric and representation are to be found in many forms, including, as scholars have discussed, imagination.[8] Ideas of British nationalism and English superiority were aided not only by imagining but also by imaging and, in particular, imaging groups.[9] In Britain in the nineteenth century, envisioning nations was called for as a technique to make sense both of empire writ large and of empire as it was manifested in one's country, city, neighborhood, and street.[10] With the proliferation of printed material in the form of magazines, newspapers, and graphic print, by the early nineteenth century, visual images were a significant part of communication and imagination.[11] Physiognomy was an important mechanism in this process because it provided a set of rules to justify visual judgments. By inviting viewers to share the joke, caricaturists enrolled participation in the process of typing and used entertainment to produce shared subjective conclusions. Dancing on the edge of the grotesque, caricaturists combined the monstrous and the ridiculous and invited both humor and horror from their viewers.[12] Caricatures were not all negative, but the positive representations—which themselves were often simplistic and patronizing—were not as much fun.[13] The logic of visible racial physiognomy allowed the English to demarcate the various constituents of the globe, and particularly those of the global British Empire, merely at a glance.

The anxiety about population growth, in conjunction with immigration into London and other major cities, fueled the tremendous attention paid in Britain to national physiognomies.[14] The anonymity of the thronging streets, as I discussed in Chapter 1, put additional pressure on visual identification and social classification. Physiognomy texts, as well as periodical literature, novels, and especially visual material, devoted at least a portion of their systems to individual identification and, increasingly, large-group distinctions. But these examples were the easy and speedy kind. Visual difference on the basis of color could be immediately assigned to Africans and Indians, two major constituents of the British Empire.[15] For the Irish and the Jews, whose racial uniformity was ambiguous at best, the demarcation of difference took more time and creativity. Through the use of caricature and captions, the Irish and the Jews were made different by combining the rhetoric of objective physiognomy with the subjective modality of visual humor and entertainment. The power of visual images lay precisely in this synthesis, which inverted the Victorian obsession with mechanically objective identification technologies by allowing observers, with the aid of physiognomic cues, to draw their own conclusions.

By the middle of the nineteenth century, with the rise of anthropological examinations of race, much attention was focused on the notion of Irish prognathism (projecting jaws denoting a close relationship to apes) and Jewish blood. As Dermot Quinn has chronicled, the experiences of the Jews and the Irish in England share many similarities, both in their own internal dynamics and in the ways in which they were treated by others.[16] Both groups occupied a liminal space with respect to the English, differing in points of religion but sharing skin color. Neither the Irish nor the Jews (like the less amusing and more religiously similar Scots and Welsh) could be seen by the English, and thus visually identified, in quite the same way as the Africans or Indians. As a *Household Words* article commented in 1855, "Few people dream of tracing out the Jewish ancestor . . . though the Hebrew sign is distinctly marked in the very midst of blue eyes, fair skin, and flaxen hair." Worryingly, "People seldom judge of races excepting by colour."[17] And it got scarier as the century progressed and the Irish and the Jews agitated for and received increased political voices and access to British educational and professional institutions. With the Catholic Emancipation Act of 1828 (passed in 1829), Catholics could enter Parliament, vote in parliamentary elections, hold municipal office, obtain naval commissions, be called to the bar, and matriculate at Oxbridge. These rights were extended to Jews more gradually between 1830 and 1871. As voting representatives, the Irish, with their allegiance to Rome over Britain, could not be trusted. So too with the Jews, who failed to recognize the highest power of the Savior and Son of God.

It is important to emphasize here that the distortions of Irish and Jewish physiognomic markers were not in and of themselves imagined to be real. The British viewing public did not believe that caricature images were literal representations of actual faces and bodies. Nor did it matter; the physiognomic project was not about redirecting the way people saw, but rather about systematizing and sanctioning what they were doing. Representations of Irish and Jews deliberately ignored the very meaningful differences of class, culture, and religious practice within the groups and subsumed all distinctions under a fiction of racial uniformity.[18] By ignoring internal differences, visual representations rendered meaningless the class and cultural overlaps between the English and these groups by categorizing them as racially distinct. In many cases, visual depictions of the Irish and the Jews reproduced culture, but these cultural factors were labeled racial through physiognomic references.[19] By reading images of the Irish and the Jews in particular, we can chart the construction of difference through a racial imaginary.

My chronological scope in this chapter is ordered by the political agitations and achievements about Irish nationalism and famine relief and the removal of Jewish disabilities in the first half of the nineteenth century.[20] Because of this focus, there is almost no discussion of the waves of eastern European Jewish immigration toward the end of the nineteenth century.[21] Both temporal and thematic considerations have resulted in the exclusion of the most prominent and politically successful Victorian of Jewish background, Benjamin Disraeli. Although this chapter focuses on emblematic individuals and groups, Disraeli was in many ways unique, and although depictions of him played on Jewish themes, they often focused on him and his specific situation rather than on Jews generally.[22]

As Irish and Jewish histories took their separate paths throughout their respective struggles for religious and social equality, so too did their visual and textual depictions. In written texts, learned physiognomy manuals, and especially caricature representations, the Jews were poorer and less linguistically sophisticated as they became increasingly collapsed into recent immigrants rather than long-standing Jewish residents of Britain. Portrayals of the Irish became more aggressive and monstrous as Irish religious and political distinctions, and indeed individual distinctions at all, were ignored in favor of agitators for the repeal of repressive anti-Catholic laws.

Physiognomy provides an important analytic tool in examining these caricatures, designed to be both entertaining and informative, because it was a significant aspect of why pictures were meaningful to nineteenth-century audiences. By reading images with the aid of physiognomy, modern viewers can begin to decode the embedded, very powerful messages that connect them. These images built on one another to produce a shared language and set of visual shorthands that developed over time. By making Irish and Jewish physiognomy uniform across the groups and distinct from other groups, they made the invisible foreigner visible, visualizable, and reducible to the lowest common denominator. The differences between the Protestant and Catholic, as well as the Ulster Loyalist and the Home-Rule Irish, were visually eradicated; likewise, the distinctions between the long-settled, largely Iberian Jewish communities and the more recent eastern European immigrants disappeared in the British imagery and thus in the British imaginary.

A Strange Sort of Foreigner

In the eyes of the British in England, the Irish and the Jew were odd sorts of outsiders. Apparently religiously, nationally, and racially distinct, they occupied a boundary zone between being assimilable and remaining culturally separate.[23] The English had no explicit taboos on intermarriage with Irish or Jews, unlike with Africans or lower-caste Indians; likewise, both the Irish and the Jews occupied imperial positions of administrative and legislative importance that would never have been allotted to the colonial locals.[24] Resented by other Londoners, the Irish and the Jews were accused of taking jobs and financial opportunities from the "real" English.[25] Cast as religiously different and physically powerful laborers, Irish Catholics looked relatively similar to and usually spoke the same language as their English conquerors.[26] These similarities spurred the English to demarcate clear differences between themselves and their neighbors in pictures and the printed word.

The Jews, on the other hand, were not a specifically colonized people, and therein lay one of the conundrums of their existence: were they a race or a religion? Throughout the nineteenth century, as interest in anthropology developed, the idea of a Jewish race became entrenched. Conversion to or from Judaism did not include or exempt the converts from their original physiognomic designations.[27] It was precisely this undetected assimilation that led to increasingly explicit typologies of Jews in English caricature and to creation of a visual dam against the tide of intermarriage and the spread of contaminated blood.[28] Like the Irish, the Jews were religiously and racially different; again like the Irish, these differences were made visually explicit through physiognomic symbols and fashion clues as the nineteenth century progressed.

The Irish Catholics and the Jews differed in their relationship with the English in at least one important regard: shared history. In 1830, during the parliamentary debate about whether to allow Jews to take seats in Parliament, the chancellor of the exchequer pointed out that "there was this difference between the Jews and the Catholics—that the Catholics had shed their blood for us—they had fought our battles both by sea and land—they had swelled the force of our fleets and our armies, and there was a good reason why we should not make enemies of those who had served us, and who amounted to seven million people." Because of the ambiguous affiliation of the Jewish people with respect to their host country, it was unclear where their allegiance lay, whereas the Irish—despite repeated repeal agitation—had shared battles and shed blood alongside their Anglican neighbors. Unlike the Irish, "the Jews had not fought our battles—they had not served in our armies and navy, and they did not amount, it was stated by a writer of their own nation, to more than 27,000 persons." Therefore, the chancellor continued, unlike the Irish Catholics, for whom religion had been removed as a political barrier in the Catholic Emancipation Act, "the arguments which applied to the Roman Catholics seemed . . . therefore, to have no application to the Jews. The relief given to the one was no precedent for granting the claims of the other." He winningly concluded by saying that his opinion reflected that of the English at large, for "as he did not wish to oppose the general religious feelings of the country, he should oppose the Motion."[29] The message was clear: Jews had their own allegiances and were not to be trusted as having the best interests of Britain at heart.

Jews were not alone in their power to contaminate the English and the British. A great defender, although not a great admirer, of the poverty-stricken inhabitants of England, Friedrich Engels devoted a great deal of attention to Irish immigrants to England in his early study *The Condition of the Working Class in England*. Engels was writing this work, first published in German in 1845, as the London slums began to teem with Irish people fleeing the famine.[30] In his analysis, Engels quoted Thomas Carlyle directly to demonstrate that although the Irish could live harder, they threatened to bring the English down with them: "That the condition of the lower multitude of English labourers approximates more and more to that of the Irish, competing with them in all the markets: that whatsoever labour, to which mere strength with little skill will suffice, is to be done, will not be done at the English price, but at an approximation to the Irish price."[31]

With the confusing caveat that "if we except his exaggerated and one-sided condemnation of the Irish national character, Carlyle is perfectly right," Engels echoed the concerns of Carlyle about the damaging effect the unmotivated Irish were having on their English neighbors. He began his analysis by assuring the reader that the true English could easily and swiftly be distinguished from the Irish immigrant, both geographically and visually, because "whenever a district is distinguished for especial filth and especial ruinousness, the explorer may safely count upon meeting chiefly those Celtic faces which one recognizes at the first glance as different from the Saxon physiognomy of the native, and the singing, aspirate brogue which the Irishman never loses."[32]

Caricature Cages: From Irish Monster to Irish Ape

The richness and variety of Irish culture and the distinctions in Irish religious and social groupings were not always flattened into the single representation of a strong ape-man so lyrically rendered by Engels and others.[33] The process by which the Irish became simianized in caricature was linked to political developments in Irish agitation over time.[34] The Irish became apes as a means of justifying imperial rule, which served the simultaneous goal of calming growing evolutionary fears. By placing the Irish in metaphorical cages by likening them to animals, the English entertainingly assured their dominance over this growing threat. At the same time, like the now-dependent imperial creatures behind bars in English zoos, the image of the Irish apes assured their captors that this dominance was well justified.[35]

The 1800 Act of Union with Ireland was implemented in 1801. Before the act was passed, caricaturists such as James Gillray devoted some of their artistic attention to representing the Irish as inferior brutes who required strong rule and careful control. In the print *United Irishmen upon Duty,* drawn weeks after the 1798 rising of the United Irishmen, the rebellious force was shown to be motivated by destruction and violence rather than moral or political imperatives (Figure 4.1).[36] There are early hints of the direction that Irish caricature would take in the nineteenth century: the threatening and pillaging Irish all had coarse lips and flaring nostrils, as well as protruding foreheads and chins. The man pushing the wheelbarrow was particularly apelike, with a hunched posture, shapeless legs, and disproportionately large head. Unlike later images, however, this picture emphasized differences between the Irish, representing both the United Irishmen aggressors and their hapless Irish victims. Although both groups shared some traits, the distinctions between them in behavior and physiognomy were significant to Gillray and his audience.

All these markers were symbols that Gillray's audience was learning to read as Lavaterian physiognomy became widely and explicitly practiced in the late eighteenth century. The foreheads, posture, and lips were particularly significant, both on their own physiognomic terms and in contradistinction to the English. This image has political and physiognomic context and must be read with reference to both. In addition to thinking about the United Irish uprising, audiences might have considered Johann Caspar Lavater's physiognomy text, the most widely read physiognomy writing of the time. Lavater wrote that (unlike the Irish) "Englishmen have the shortest, and best arched foreheads, that is to say, they are arched only upwards; and, towards the eyebrows, either gently decline, or are rectilinear. They very seldom have pointed, but often round full, medullary noses." Other English physiognomic virtues included "large, well-defined, beautifully curved lips; they have also a round, full chin; but they

Figure 4.1.   James Gillray, *United Irishmen upon Duty,* 1798. This print showed early hints of the simianization and animalization of the Irish agitators. (© The Trustees of the British Museum.)

are peculiarly distinguished by the eyebrows and eyes, which are strong, open, liberal, and steadfast."[37]

Although Lavater did not address the Irish explicitly, he did deal with the significance of the features common to all the rioters in Gillray's print. Of foreheads, he commented that "projecting [means] imbecility, immaturity, weakness, stupidity."[38] Moving down the face, he noted that such a person had "thick, black, strong eyebrows, which decline downwards, and appear to lie close upon the eye, shading deep large eyes." One with a "conspicuously bony forehead" could think only of violence and aggression and should be treated gently and at a distance. These types were "only to be consulted for advice when revenge is sought, or the brutal desire of doing injury to others entertained—in other respects they are to be treated in as yielding a manner as possible, and that yielding as much as possible concealed."[39] The lower half of Gillray's uprising faces conformed to Lavater's description that "very fleshy lips must ever have to contend with sensuality and indolence."[40] Even the chins expressed rebellious and aggressive tendencies; according to Lavater, "A long, broad, thick chin . . . is only found in rude, harsh, proud, and violent persons."[41]

Although not all viewers would have read Lavater or made direct connections between Gillray's print and the relevant textual passages, the clues in the former (Lavater's writings) reminded audiences of the principles of the latter (Gillray's print). At this time, print viewing was often a communal activity in coffeehouses and in front of shop windows. Audiences discussed the images, and nonreaders benefited from the insights of their literate companions. Artists and audiences created and participated in a common visual language, developed over time through shared discourse. This bond was important in the relationship between fellow viewers, as well as between the producers and the consumers of the images.

The primary population that responded to the Act of Union (1800) by emigration was the Irish gentry, of whom there were few images after their early nineteenth-century assimilation. The representations of these Irish, largely composed of Anglican landowners, were gently mocking rather than aggressive and dropped off rapidly in frequency as they ceased either to innovate (by creating difference) or to entertain.[42] They soon disappeared as the dominant notions of the Irish as Catholic and rebellious overtook all other depictions.[43] An uprising in Dublin in 1803 and the Battle of Garragh between Catholic Ribbonmen and Orangemen in 1813 represented a sea change in Irish responses to English power and Catholic responses to Anglican oppression, respectively. Drawing on the two facets of this energy, in 1823 Daniel O'Connell formed the Catholic Association to campaign for Catholic emancipation. This organization was perceived to be fairly benign and successfully achieved its goal with the Catholic Emancipation Act in 1829.

Now the Irish had rights—limited rights—which sparked a more serious effort to agitate for autonomy and self-rule.[44] July 1829 saw major riots in Belfast. Suddenly, it seemed to the English, the monster had been unleashed. In visual imagery, the monster was created. Between 1828 and 1832, a period of only four years, the number of prints and drawings about Ireland and the Irish skyrocketed.[45] Starting around this time, images of the Irish narrowed to focus only on the politically active and the physically aggressive, who came to stand for the whole. This is a kind of generalizing, but one that, unlike later group representations, still used recognizable individuals to act as the communal shorthand. A series of images featuring O'Connell combined physiognomic techniques with caricature exaggeration. Playing on British fears of imperial dissolution and national dysfunction, the image of Irish Frankenstein emerged.

Initially, most caricaturists focused on the political agitators in Ireland itself. With the influx of Irish people and Irish labor into London and other major cities, the scope widened to include immigrants in the portrayals of the Irish menace. Political prints played on the physical threat of the Irish, while the immigrant issues focused on the Irish simian strength that so disturbed Carlyle. These divergent concentrations implicitly recognized the primacy of culture and context with respect to race, emphasizing the difference between the Irish in England and the Irish in Ireland.[46] Ultimately, however, aggression and tirelessness were two sides of the same threatening coin. The image of an Irish monster-man grew to increasing prominence throughout the nineteenth century, a creation who both threatened and reassured English viewers— threatened because he was depicted as dangerous and played on very real anxieties about England's politically unstable neighbors and volatile urban cores, and reassured because as long as he could be cartooned, he could be contained.[47]

Putting Paddy to Paper

Many art historians have noted that like other codes of etiquette, cartooning styles became significantly more restrained, less politically poignant, and less stinging in the Victorian era.[48] In addition to changing British tastes, an important factor in this shift was influence from across the channel in France. Ever sensitive to fashions in France, British artists picked up on the more tempered nature of their Continental counterparts.

As Judith Wechsler has charted in detail, French cartooning developed along different, more restrained lines than British cartooning because of severe censorship laws that were lifted only during the Second Republic (1848–1851).[49] In a particularly famous example, French caricaturist Honoré Daumier depicted the "Citizen-King" Louis Philippe as a pear, an image that proved virtually uncensorable. Merely evoking the shape made the necessary reference or minimum clue to communicate the idea, similar to the "Paddy cap" that came to represent Irishness.[50]

The French technique of using food imagery rather than animal analogies as a characterization technique was in part necessitated by censorship laws and perhaps was in part due to the comparatively lower popularity of physiognomy in France.[51] Animal images, with their similar faces that provided the opportunity for physiognomic representations, held greater utility for an English audience. Nevertheless, at the height of the potato famine, the Irish were identified strongly enough with potatoes to visually become them.[52] In an 1845 cartoon from *Punch*, the potato, a crop destined (and proved) to fail, bears the face of O'Connell, whose repeal movement was, according to the artist, similarly destined to destroy the Irish people (Figure 4.2).

As O'Connell continued to agitate, artists continued to exaggerate. In the autumn of 1835, O'Connell proposed a parliamentary motion in favor of repealing English rule in Ireland. This proposal was soundly defeated, prompting O'Connell to adopt the motto "A real Union or no Union." A few months later, in the print "Real Union with Ireland" in *Figaro in London*, a cheap working-class publication, an apelike O'Connell crossed the Irish Channel over the heads of the Duke of Wellington and the Duke of Newcastle while holding aloft the head of the king's brother, the Duke of Cumberland (Figure 4.3).[53] The Whig government, advancing more slowly over the heads of Irish Anglican bishops, faded into the background of the image. The English figures were all easily differentiated representations of specific individuals. Of various physiognomies, the dukes in question could be distinguished immediately as different people, even if viewers did not know precisely which people they were. The Irish bishops were all of a piece. Distinctions in Irish character, and even in Irish religious affiliation, had become irrelevant. O'Connell became the Irish, and, underscoring the political and economic issues at stake in Irish agitation and immigration, O'Connell was a threatening, oversized monster.

O'Connell was a large and powerful man, and his physical stature was emphasized both in caricature and by those who encountered him in person. Upon meeting O'Connell in 1838, Caroline Fox, a keen reader of faces and a noted diarist, recorded in her journal that "his mouth is beautifully chiselled and his nose *retroussé;* he is an uncommonly strong looking, stout-built man, who looks as if he could easily bear the weight of the whole House upon his shoulders."[54] Fox's more sympathetic rendering of O'Connell's physiognomy may have been related to her understanding of his cause. Of his political opinions she wrote that "he spoke with energy, pathos, and eloquence . . . He gave a grievous account of the Catholic importation—but I absolutely must have a paper."[55]

Despite the proliferation of Irish images in the late 1820s and the 1830s, it was only in 1841, with the founding of *Punch,* that the mocking

Figure 4.2. "The Real Potato Blight of Ireland," *Punch* 9 (1845), insinuated that the destruction wrought upon the Irish by the dramatic failures of the potato crop was being repeated by Daniel O'Connell.

images of Irish Paddy became truly ubiquitous.[56] Until that point, depictions of the Irish were multivalent and emphasized individuals, as well as groups, within the Irish community. Although *Punch*'s depiction of the Irish was not uniformly negative, at least in its early years, it was one of the most powerful agents for creating and cementing images of the monstrous and later the simian Irish in the minds of the viewing public.[57] *Punch* took the subject of the Irish and gave it new life, combining language, art, and science to produce a common entertainment experience that both reflected and produced Victorian ideas. Along with other comic periodicals, *Punch* shared in the development of visual symbols— including the "Paddy cap" —that became the minimum costuming clue needed to conjure Irishness and, in particular, Irishness as imagined by *Punch*.[58]

Figure 4.3. "Real Union with Ireland," *Figaro in London,* 31 October 1835. A subtly simianized Daniel O'Connell is shown crossing the Irish Channel over the heads of British politicians.

The timing of *Punch*'s establishment is particularly significant, coming immediately on the heels of the foundation of O'Connell's Repeal Association in 1840. Now an official organizational slogan, the term "repeal" provided many artists with inspiration and creative material. For example, John Leech's 1843 cartoon "The 'Repeal Farce'; or, Mother Goose and the Golden Eggs" mocked the movement as a shortsighted attempt to gain profit (Figure 4.4).[59] (Mother) Britain, in the form of Mother Goose, was

Figure 4.4. John Leech, "The 'Repeal Farce'; or, Mother Goose and the Golden Eggs," *Punch* 4 (1843). The goals of the repealers were mocked as the greedy and shortsighted notions of a backward people.

pitted against a vacant and clueless-looking Ireland, not yet entirely monstrous. The emphasis was on Paddy's stupidity, which made his thoughtless brutality all the more dangerous. With one hand, Paddy clutched his head, while the other brandished a sword with the word "repeal" written on it, indicating the Irish commitment to violent action.

In this image, Paddy's nose was distinctly of the pug variety. Noses carried particular physiognomic import as the likely first feature that others encountered, as well as one with discrete types that could be easily analyzed. Anatomist and physiologist Alexander Walker contended in his 1834 medical physiognomy text that "this form of nose is sometimes unseemly . . . Persons possessing this in excess are often not merely pert, but impudent, indelicate, or filthy."[60] Walker invited his readers to share his conclusions and noted that the difference between those with superior noses and those, like the northern Irish, with inferior noses, was obvious:

> The truth of this will be evident to all who contrast a nose which is elevated and delicately formed, with one which is flat and coarsely formed—the expanded but beautiful nose of a Rousseau, that pattern of sentiment, with the degraded organ of a northern Irishman, for instance, crushed above and protruding below, the ascription of sentiment to which would be absolutely ridiculous, and which accords only with practical indulgence, or with passion.[61]

Walker provided a specific example of the delicately formed nose that emphasized the rarity and individuality of the traits it represented. For the degraded organ, he offered an entire group, the largely Catholic, mostly farming northern Irish. With respect to such coarseness, individuality was irrelevant.

In addition to a pug nose, Paddy's jaw was prognathous; although he was not yet explicitly simian in this prefamine image, this protrusion set the visual framework for the ape-man he was soon to become. The caricature of 4 November 1843, "The Irish Frankenstein," was the next stage in this development and the first in a long series of Frankenstein-themed images.[62] This was the first instance of the monster being explicitly indicated as the imaged Irish became increasingly threatening, if also increasingly unsophisticated and animalistic.

The potato famine began in 1845 and sparked legislation to deal with the poverty and starvation. Vast emigration greatly depleted the population of Ireland, while those repealers who remained turned to more radical agitation.[63] Many of the Irish were impatient and angry with the British governors, a feeling that lasted long after famine relief was scaled significantly back in 1849.[64] In July 1846, the Young Ireland movement withdrew its support from the Repeal Association in response to O'Connell's willingness to ally himself with the Whigs.[65] This marked a dramatic shift in both the actions and the depictions of the Irish protesters. In the image of 22 August 1846, titled "Young Ireland in Business for Himself," Leech represented the growing fears of Irish agitation (Figure 4.5).[66] The character of Young Ireland had become completely apelike, while the arms

Figure 4.5. John Leech, "Young Ireland in Business for Himself," *Punch* 11 (1846), showed a completely simianized Paddy who was turning to violence to achieve his goals.

dealer, a grotesque and degenerate character, was inhuman.[67] The arms dealer's hat was extremely similar to those shown on O'Connell in other Paddy pictures, linking him to this radical agitation despite his repeated attempts to come to a peaceful agreement.[68] Despite important political and ideological distinctions, Irish activists were collapsed into one animalistic, easily identifiable enemy.[69]

Complementing *Punch*'s visual images of animalization were verbal ones linking the Irish, apes, and zoos. These themes were connected through physiognomic hierarchies that mirrored imperial hierarchies. In 1848, a blurb appeared in *Punch* under the suggestive title "How to Tame Ireland." The article proposed a solution to the problems of Ireland "which will instil the utmost joy, we are sure, into the breasts of all loyal subjects living in Ireland." To suture the divisions among Irish activists, Catholics, and Protestants, "Government has determined on sending to that unhappy country the proprietor of the *Happy Family*—a zoological republic, in which the wildest animals elbow one another in the same cage—to see whether Irishmen cannot be induced, or made, to live peaceably together." The first stages of the project would be experimental, "tried upon a Young Irelander, an Old Irelander, and an Orangeman. He will shut them up in a room, and not allow them to leave it till they have shaken hands together, and have but one idea, one impulse in common—the benefit of their native country." *Punch* was suspicious of the approach, arguing that animals could not so easily be controlled: "We confess we have our doubts . . . The talented tamer of animal passions, however, is sanguine of the result. The best wishes of the intelligent accompany the gentleman on his noble mission of peace."[70]

The Irish had become animals to be "tamed" in the service of empire. Even the peaceful Old Irelanders and the Protestant Orangemen were lumped together as inferior species, and distinctions in class and culture were made irrelevant in the perceived face of race and nationality. Using the language and metaphor of a sideshow exhibit of a "happy family," a place where people were caged and observed for amusement, this article proposed an experiment orchestrated by a "gentleman" experienced in dealing with "the wildest animals." He had had great success with these animals, but *Punch* doubted that he could duplicate this success with an apparently even wilder set of beasts. Despite these doubts, "the intelligent" wished the tamer the best success in dealing with this lower order of being.

During the famine, caricaturists presented the Irish as manipulative and well fed, taking advantage of British funds for their own pecuniary and rebellious purposes. In 1846, "Height of Impudence" linked the Young Ireland movement with famine relief by accusing the Irish of taking funds

from England and allocating them to arms purchases (Figure 4.6).[71]
Paddy had become almost completely apelike; his bending posture was
a sign not only of (false) deference but also of an inclination to walk on
all fours. *Punch* continued in this vein as a result of increasingly harsh
attitudes toward famine relief. According to the portrayal in "The English Labourer's Burden," the animalistic Irish, rather than taking away
jobs, were riding on the backs of the weary old Englishmen who were
shouldering the load for these self-satisfied (rather than starving) rascals
(Figure 4.7).[72]

The increasing simianality of these images, soon to be made explicit,
referred not just to the ape proper but also to the physiognomic principles

Figure 4.6.   John Leech, "Height of Impudence," *Punch* 11 (1846). A simianized Paddy attempts to use famine relief funds to purchase arms.

of apelike features. George Jabet's 1852 satirical physiognomy text *Notes on Noses,* originally published in 1848 as *Nasology* under the name Eden Warwick, combined humor with science to create human hierarchy. Drawing on anthropological authorities, Jabet noted that "Dr. Pritchard asserts and as every ethnologist admits—that protruding jaws indicate a low state of civilization, an animal and degraded mind . . . The flat, depressed Nose, which always accompanies the prognathous jaws, is likewise an indication of a similar mind."[73]

Figure 4.7. "The English Labourer's Burden," *Punch* 16 (1849). The simianized Irish were portrayed as taking advantage of famine relief and placing the burden of their survival on the backs of the English working class.

Here Jabet referred to all so-called lower states of civilization, explicitly linking the Irish and the Africans and calling on the imperial discourse of the wild colonial savage and bringing it to the British Isles. In quoting James Cowles Pritchard, one of the founders of modern anthropology and a prominent monogenist, Jabet argued that even those who believed that all races descended from one source established hierarchies among them.[74] The images of the Irish made them animal-like not just in their behavior but also in their innate level of civilization and development.

During and after the famine, many of the images of the Irish told stories similar to those written by commentators such as Thomas Carlyle, Friedrich Engels, and Henry Mayhew. These narratives dealt with the poverty and displacement represented by the Irish immigrants.[75] The images of the Irish as unscrupulous and self-interested resonated with the depictions of O'Connell and, in so doing, challenged the veracity of his peaceful claims. Following the 1857 Belfast riots and the foundation of the Irish Republican Brotherhood by James Stephens in 1858, the images changed yet again.

Enter the Ape: Mr. G'Orilla

They were not subtle anymore. Two 1861 caricatures, "The Lion of the Season" and "A Great Time for Ireland," showed Paddy not as apelike but as an ape (Figure 4.8).[76] These images played on one another, with the Irishness of the first clear only with reference to the second. As part of a larger vogue for stories about apes entering society, these images challenged claims that savages could be seamlessly civilized.[77] Anti-Irish sentiment had reached such a height that, as a writer for *Punch* commented, the "somewhat superior ability of the Irish Yahoo to utter articulate sounds, may suffice to prove that it is a development, and not, as some imagine, a degeneration of the Gorilla."[78] Following the trend of the "happy family" blurb, the Irishman had become totally objectified, an "it" to be commented on in seemingly scientific rhetoric.

As a narrative fantasy from 1862 demonstrates, the Irish were depicted as the "missing link" to an order of being even lower than the blacks, whom they had come to replace rhetorically as the closest connection to animal life: "A gulf, certainly, does appear to yawn between the Gorilla and the Negro. The woods and wilds of Africa do not exhibit an example of any intermediate animal." Imperial scientific exploration might be a misplacement of energy because "in this, as in many other cases, philosophers go vainly searching abroad for that which they would readily find if they sought for it at home. A creature manifestly between the Gorilla and the Negro is to be met with in some of the lowest districts of London and Liverpool by adventurous explorers." The missing link "comes from Ireland, whence it has contrived to migrate; it belongs in fact to a tribe of Irish savages: the lowest species of the Irish Yahoo. When conversing with its kind it talks a sort of gibberish. It is, moreover, a climbing animal, and may sometimes be seen ascending a ladder laden with a hod of

Figure 4.8. "The Lion of the Season," *Punch* 40 (1861) (left) and "A Great Time for Ireland," *Punch* 41 (1861) (right). These two images showed the complete simianization of Paddy; in both social and political contexts, the Irishman had become a gorilla.

bricks."[79] The role of the Irish as laborers was emphasized and belittled; unlike the Africans, it was precisely because of the whiteness of the Irish that their physical work was a source of such mockery and underlying discomfort for other Britons. The idea that the Irish were in fact on a lower scale than Africans was part of the joke, meant to be taken lightly, and at the same time reveals the seriousness of British fears.

It was not just an increase in anti-Irish feeling that fueled this shift to from ape-man to ape.[80] By 1861, Charles Darwin's *On the Origin of Species* had been in public circulation for two discussion- and debate-filled years. However, it was the publication of Paul du Chaillu's accounts of his expeditions to central Africa (in which he confirmed the existence

of gorillas) that made gorillas such a topic of interest in 1861. As Adrian Desmond has demonstrated in *The Politics of Evolution,* evolutionary anxieties and debates had been raging long before and not exclusively because of Darwin.[81] By making Paddy an explicit ape, cartoonists were providing a visual zoo in which to cage and contain the comings and goings of the Irish. Two major threats, the incursion into London and the resulting degeneration of the English worker, and the violent repeal movement, were rhetorically calmed by making the Irish into cageable creatures.

As the century progressed, all Irish converged into the visual image of an ape, which drew on the physiognomic clues that made this metaphor meaningful. The Irish became an increasing political and economic presence, and their physiognomy degenerated into an animal-like state. The face of the Irish became the face of an ape, with all the implied and unambiguous physiognomic associations. The face of the Jew also became increasingly explicit and explicitly geographic. Through a combination of visual and linguistic cues, the affluence of the Sephardi Jews was subsumed by increasingly uniform Jewish depictions. The difference between Jews of different backgrounds was denied in pursuit of an identifiable Jewish face. The wealthy and assimilated Sephardi Jewish community was visually erased as all Jews gradually were collapsed into the poorest segments of the Ashkenazi Jewish community.

Enter the Jew: If I Were a Rich Man

Many of the traditional physiognomic notions of "the Jewish race" linger today, particularly the Jewish nose.[82] The idea of a Jewish face collapses people from a number of different places into one strangely amalgamated group. There is very little allowance for the fact that Jews come from many different countries and have accordingly differing appearances. In particular, little or no distinction is made between Sephardi and Ashkenazi Jews when discussing or depicting the "Jewish face."[83] From the late eighteenth century through the nineteenth, depictions of Jews featured a largely invented "Jewish dialect," a lisped amalgam of broken English, inaccurate Yiddish, and unintelligible gibberish. First introduced on stage in 1783, this language became the immediate identifier of a Jewish character, independent of that individual's actual fluency or linguistic background.[84] Applied indiscriminately, the so-called Jewish dialect was visually mapped onto all Jews, even those born in Britain or from Iberian and other backgrounds where Yiddish was neither spoken nor understood.

Like the Irish imagery, there were many caricatures of British Jews before the nineteenth century.[85] A particularly vitriolic strain of these was produced following the short-lived 1753 Naturalisation Bill. This bill enabled foreign-born Jews to apply for naturalization without swearing allegiance to the Crown and the church. The advantages garnered by naturalization would have affected only the very wealthy. In the mid-eighteenth century, only the Sephardi Jews could claim significant riches accrued through their long and established history of international trade and finance.[86] By the mid-nineteenth century, Ashkenazim in England outnumbered Sephardim, although the Sephardim remained far richer.[87] Inciting great anger over supposed unfair Jewish influence, the bill was repealed in six months. This period likely saw the most aggressive anti-Jewish and largely anti-Sephardi depictions; deeply vitriolic and hostile, this propaganda marked the height of negative Jewish portrayals in Britain.[88]

Depictions of wealthy and worldly Sephardi from around this time began to contain visual links to the recent poor immigrants. With the increasing stream of penniless eastern European immigrants into England in the early nineteenth century, the dominant Jewish visual image of a wealthy Sephardi banker physiognomically marked as shrewd, sophisticated, cunning, and not altogether unkind shifted to incorporate the new Jewish types seen in the streets.[89] Vaguely unsettling, these prints employed physiognomic techniques to skew and mark Jews as problematic.[90] The clothing and accoutrements of a wealthy, long-settled Sephardi Jew were combined with the physiognomic markers of an Ashkenazi peddler. Ashkenazi symbols such as beards, long coats, shaggy eyebrows, and, particularly, hooked noses were drawn on the Sephardi social markers of culture and sophistication. Part of the work of these images was to map the identifiable Ashkenazim onto the Sephardim, who had a great deal of social and commercial contact with their non-Jewish neighbors.[91] Clothing and facial physiognomy were collapsed to produce a new metonymy of identification that I explore in greater depth in the next chapter.

So culturally different were the Sephardim and the Ashkenazim that by the end of the eighteenth century one German traveler noted that "we are astonished at the difference between the Portuguese and the German Jews in . . . dress, language, manners, cleanliness, politeness," so that "every thing distinguishes them, much to the advantage for the former, who have little to distinguish them from Christians." Following a list of differences between the two groups, the author concluded with the puzzling observation that "the physiognomy is the only thing they have in common."[92]

Caricaturists and viewers were unlikely to have a detailed understanding of the differences between groups of Jews from different geographic backgrounds. Rather, they were using the characteristics of the recent and impoverished immigrants as a way to belittle those immigrants' more prominent coreligionists. There is some evidence that even outside the Jewish community, Sephardiness granted superior social position; in Maria Edgeworth's 1817 novel *Harrington,* for example, the Sephardi character Mr. Montenero was consistently described as the royalty of his race. The composite images of the early and the mid-nineteenth century served to discredit the perception that there was any type of superior Jew.

The eighteenth-century image of the Sephardi banker and stockjobber provided a useful focus for anti-Jewish feeling in Britain at the time. The stock market was a seventeenth-century innovation from the Netherlands, knowledge of which many Jews brought with them when they immigrated to Britain. The combination of British fears about the stock market and the move to paper currency were targeted toward the Jews, who were portrayed as affiliated with the shifts that led to large gains and especially losses in money. A number of anti–stock market pamphlets were published that specifically identified the Jews as the major source of danger in this transition. This trend intensified after the collapse of the South Sea Bubble in 1720.[93]

Members of the Sephardi Jewish community had been in England at least since Oliver Cromwell allowed the Jews to return in 1656, if not before.[94] Many of them, particularly the more successful ones, like Sir Solomon de Medina and the Jacobite Sampson Gideon, were visually all but indistinguishable from other Englishmen.[95] They did not wear beards or dress in a unique fashion; Sephardim truly did walk undetected in the streets of London. In fact, despite prohibitions against Jewish voting, it is likely that many Jews used their ability to blend in to participate in the franchise. The 1788 print *Blue and Buff* was produced during a particularly contentious election won by Charles James Fox (Figure 4.9).[96] The Duchess of Devonshire, one of Fox's ardent supporters and a distant cousin, was shown in the background shaving the unlikely beard of a Sephardi Jew. This image implied that without said marker, there was nothing to prevent this man from hiding his origins and casting a vote.[97]

In conjunction with the apparently complete visual assimilation of Sephardi Jews into English society, there was a concerted effort to conflate the older Iberian and new eastern European Jewish residents into one face. Lavater recognized the strangeness of this effort in quoting a scholar who reflected that "it appears to me remarkable that the Jews should have carried with them the marks of their country and race to all

Figure 4.9. *Blue and Buff*, 1788. This print suggested that Sephardi Jews could "pass," which would make it possible for them to vote in elections. (© The Trustees of the British Museum.)

parts of the world; I mean their short, black, curly hair, and brown complexion." Darkness and tight hair were traits linked with animals and animal-like races such as the Irish and the Africans. Jews were distinct from these groups, however, in that their features were neither geographically defined nor as intellectually limited as other, similarly marked groups. The comment continued by noting that their physiognomic markers were linked to distinct characteristics universal to Jews, regardless of where they came from. "Their quickness of speech, haste and abruptness in all their actions, appear to proceed from the same causes. I imagine Jews have more gall than other men."[98]

A particularly striking example of the Sephardi-Ashkenazi combination is the 1792 print *I've Got de Monish* (Figure 4.10).[99] In this work, the hooked nose, wrinkled skin, narrow eyes, and protruding chin of the Ashkenazi were combined with the wig, cane, and elegant clothes of the Sephardi banker. Many viewers would have immediately identified the subject as Jewish because he had what Lavater identified as "characteristics of the national Jewish countenance, the pointed chin, pouting lips, and well-defined middle line of the mouth."[100]

Here was the collision of financiers of very different status: the respected Sephardi banker and the greedy and groveling moneylender. This conflation led to a confusing physiognomic portrait; whereas the posture and bearing of the subject indicated sophistication and elegance, the narrow eyes and pointed chin were cunning and subversive. Lavater equivocated on the implications of many of these traits; for example, a "pointed chin is generally held to be a sign of acuteness and craft, though I know very worthy persons with such chins."[101] Likewise, pouting lips held two possible valences. On the positive side, "Well-defined, large, and proportionate lips, the middle line of which is equally serpentine . . . though they may denote an inclination to pleasure, are never seen in a bad, mean, common, false, crouching, vicious countenance." By contrast, "Very fleshy lips must ever have to contend with sensuality and indolence."[102]

Although Lavater, unlike later physiognomic writers, did not engage in depth with the Jewish nose, he did distinguish it immediately from the English nose and, indeed, the noses of all other nationalities: "The Jews [have] hawk noses. The noses of Englishmen are seldom pointed, but generally round."[103] Lavater continued to list characteristic noses of particular countries. The Jews were unique in this list for having no land-based nationality, and this allowed for an amalgamated blend of features that made no distinction between different types of Jews. This conundrum of religion or race was physiognomically and politically confusing in an increasingly urbanized world. Categories and classification played an important role in encounters between people in crowded streets.

Later physiognomic writers acknowledged the illogic of these combinations but maintained that there was a constant Jewish face. This one face was actually a composite of the accessories of the long-settled residents with the features of the recent Ashkenazi immigrants, linked together to present an image easily identifiable as a Jew. Phrenological innovator and physiognomy writer Johann Gaspar Spurzheim noted that "the Jews, though they have been dispersed over all the countries, and have lived in all the climates of the globe for many centuries, still preserve a particular and distinguishing physiognomy."[104]

Figure 4.10.   I've Got de Monish, 1792, showed the conflation of Sephardi and Ashkenazi traits. (© The Jewish Museum, London.)

By 1806, these combinations had become explicit. The British viewing public was not necessarily aware of the nuances of Sephardi and Ashkenazi differences but could and did conflate the two communities in order to manage and mock them more easily. George Woodward and Isaac Cruikshank's etching *Long Heads upon Change; or, The Return of Ld. Lauderdale* showed a collection of stockjobbing Jews (Figure 4.11).[105] Jews in this profession were almost exclusively affluent Sephardim, but in this depiction, they were given both the invented dialect and the features of Ashkenazi peddlers. Note the long faces and skinny bodies, as well as the sharp noses, pale skin, and, on the third person from the right, the presence of a prominent black beard. Physiognomically Ashkenazi and professionally Sephardi, this print provided a means of visualizing a distinctly Jewish face within the context of the extant Jewish population. Armed with the tools of physiognomy, these caricatures distorted reality to achieve an important rhetorical gain. The relationship of the physiognomic depiction to the actual features became irrelevant with respect to the larger goals of entertainment and containment.

Despite caricaturists' disregard for the social and historical distinctions between different Jewish communities, the caricatures themselves conveyed important physiognomic information. This was particularly explicit in the shapes of the faces, which were long and tapered. Dr. John Cross's 1817 medical physiognomy text paid particular attention to facial shape and the implications of narrow structure, noting that "the tapering of the head and face from above to below, indicates natural cunning—natural only, for the broad face may be trained into artificial cunning, and the sharp tapering face may be retrained into artificial sincerity; not however without leaving correspondent impressions on the softest parts."[106] This image of Jewish stockjobbers was telling a story of shrewd and sharp men, whose sincerity should be treated as artificial and manipulative.

In the 1803 etching *Moses Chusing His Cook* by Johann Heinrich Ramberg, the distinctions between those who were physiognomically Jewish and those who were not were obviously displayed (Figure 4.12).[107] This piece showed the converted Lord George Gordon in his Newgate prison (where he was kept because of a libel charge) surrounded by a prayer quorum *(minyan)* of ten devout Jews. Typically eastern European in feature, his compatriots had sharp noses, beards, deeply lined faces, and often stunted stature. Only the ignorant pig-bearing cook and Gordon himself were not caricatured in this exaggerated and grotesque fashion; lacking the characteristic physiognomy of the Jewish people, the rare English convert to Judaism was not understood to be other in the same

Figure 4.11. George Woodward and Isaac Cruikshank, *Long Heads upon Change; or, The Return of Ld. Lauderdale*, 1806. In this image, the characteristics of Sephardi and Ashkenazi Jews were entirely conflated. (© The Trustees of the British Museum.)

way. Known for the strictness of his observance, Gordon would not have eaten any nonkosher meat, but the pig is perhaps the best-known and most offensive symbol of *treyfe* (nonkosher) food.[108]

Another important trajectory in early nineteenth-century depictions of Jews may seem counterintuitive to the typologies of stunted, underdeveloped, and skinny book learners. The large and threatening fighter representing English boxing champion and Jewish hero Daniel Mendoza challenged notions of Jewish weakness and sedentary nature caused by love of money.[109] The Mendozas were Spanish Jews who could trace their English roots back to 1656, a distinction that became irrelevant as eastern European Jews outnumbered those of Iberian descent.[110] Images of the Jewish boxer disappeared after the first decade of the nineteenth century.

Figure 4.12.   Johann Heinrich Ramberg, *Moses Chusing His Cook,* 1803. This etching highlights the extent to which caricaturists portrayed Jewish physiognomy as inherent and not acquired; Lord George Gordon maintained his Anglo-Saxon features even after his conversion to Judaism. (© The Trustees of the British Museum.)

The image of the late eighteenth- and early nineteenth-century Jewish boxer was widespread enough to be applied even to non-Jews. The 1795 etching, likely by Isaac Cruikshank, titled *A Worthy Alderman and His Friends Canvasing* showed two candidates for election preparing to come to blows (Figure 4.13).[111] Alderman Combe, himself an amateur boxer, threatened to "box the minister," Wm. Lushington, who responded by saying, "Now Mr. Alderman I vil show you vone Jews Blow." Despite Mendoza's native English-speaking ability and Sephardi roots, the accent being mocked was the imagined Ashkenazi dialect. Nevertheless, the physiognomy of the politicians was purely English, from the rounded noses and mild features to the body types and marked lack of beards.

The many prints produced of Daniel Mendoza and other Jewish pugilists fueled a different aspect of the discourse about British Jews, namely, the connection with a shadowy underground.[112] The Jewish boxer did not contradict and actually reinforced other Jewish images. Here was the convergence of two stock Jewish types, Mendoza and Shylock, later revisited as Dickens's Fagin. Unscrupulous Jewish moneylenders required protection; the Mendozas of the Jewish world were easily put to work in that role. In the 1809 print *Killing No Murder, as Performing at the Grand National Theatre,* hawk-nosed Jews were shown enforcing order after the management of the theatre raised ticket prices following the September 1809 fire (Figure 4.14).[113] Mendoza was explicitly referenced as "Dan that sent the [*sic*] there." His legacy in creating a perception of Jewish physical power lingered in this print but was in actual fact short lived. The image of the poor Ashkenazi came to dominate group Jewish iconography even as individual Jews rose to greater political and social prominence.[114]

From Political Strength to Pictorial Weakness

Even those Jewish men with enough property to qualify did not officially have the vote until 1835.[115] Through 1830, all public and civic offices, Parliament, and justice fields were closed to professing Jews. Likewise, many professions, including the bar, medicine, schoolteaching, and admittance to Oxford and Cambridge required a Christian oath.[116] Between 1830 and 1871, these civil disadvantages were gradually eliminated, which precipitated a significant change in the legal and political standing of British Jews. Pointed prints were published at each stage of the removal of Jewish disabilities, usually isolating a specific individual who, like O'Connell and the Irish, came to represent the whole.[117]

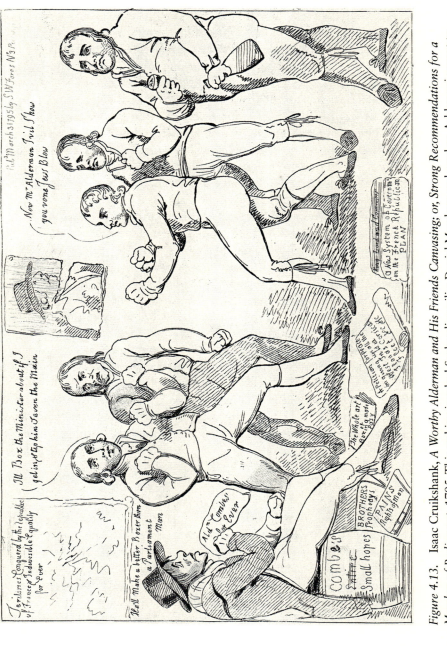

Figure 4.13. Isaac Cruikshank, *A Worthy Alderman and His Friends Canvasing; or, Strong Recommendations for a Member of Parliament,* 1795. This etching invoked Sephardi pugilist Daniel Mendoza and used an Ashkenazi accent to mock him. (© The Trustees of the British Museum.)

Figure 4.14. Killing No Murder, as Performing at the Grand National Theatre, 1809, showed hawk-nosed Jewish pugilists enforcing order following a rise in ticket prices at the theatre. (© The Trustees of the British Museum.)

After wealthy Jews received the vote in 1835, they were still denied the right to sit in Parliament because of the oath to Christ. This issue came to a head in December 1847, when Lionel de Rothschild was first elected to Parliament. Lord John Russell proposed the Jewish Disabilities Bill on 16 December 1847 to allow Rothschild to take his seat, but it was promptly defeated. Similarly, in July 1851, David Salmons was elected to Parliament in a Greenwich by-election, whereupon he took the oath, omitting the problematic concluding Christian words. Salmons actually spoke and voted on the floor before being excluded. It was only in 1858, when Rothschild had been elected five times and Salmons had been elected lord mayor of London, that Rothschild was able to take his seat. Lord Lucan's bill to modify the oaths of the houses was passed on 5 July 1858, but it was not until 1866 that the Parliamentary Oaths Act, allowing ministers to swear the same oath on either the Old Testament or the New Testament, was passed. Shortly thereafter, in 1867, the Second Reform Act was passed, which enfranchised far more British men, including more Jews.

The initial Jewish Emancipation Bill of 1830 was represented in *Knock and Ye Shall Enter,* a print in which an Ashkenazi Jewish old-clothes man and a Sephardi seller, likely from Morocco, waited at the door of the House of Commons (Figure 4.15).[118] The caption, in accented English, read: "Come . . . open the door will ye—I wants to come in—and here's a shentlemans a friend of mines wants to come in too. Don't be afeard. I don't want sheat for nothing. I can pay for it. So help me Got." The Sephardi man was identified as a "gentleman," whereas the Ashkenazi peddler, in a long coat and hat and with a dark beard, heavy eyebrows, protruding jaw, and hooked nose, was most decidedly not. Continuing the association of Jews and money, the peddler offered to pay for his seat. Even when status distinctions were recognized, as in this print, and even for Jewish "gentlemen," the door remained resolutely closed, with a group of obviously English observers clustered in the house and looking on.

An 1834 print, "The Wise Men of the East and the Marquiss of West," published in *McLean's Monthly Sheet of Caricatures,* showed Robert Grant talking to Nathan Mayer Rothschild (Figure 4.16).[119] Grant, the only non-Jew in the picture, was also the most eloquent. Rothschild was not marked as speaking with an accent, but he did bring up a business transaction. The rest all used the by-now easily recognized accented English, which complemented their beards and hooked noses. In particular, the man at the far right, in the long shaggy coat with unfashionably long hair and a full beard, commented on his position outside society. He noted, "Meine Cot, Beards will not be de fashion yet den!"

Figure 4.15. Knock and Ye Shall Enter, 1830. This image showed a poor Ashkenazi peddler and a wealthy Sephardi seller attempting to gain entrance to the House of Commons. (© The Trustees of the British Museum.)

Figure 4.16. "The Wise Men of the East and the Marquiss of West," *McLean's Monthly Sheet of Caricatures* 55 (1834). This print shows the combination of physiognomy, clothing, and hairstyle cues that marked Ashkenazi Jews in caricature. (By permission of the Houghton Library, Harvard University, *44W-1417 F.)

These prints and most subsequent ones drew on an image that had at this point become familiar. The features of the eastern European immigrant were combined with the ubiquitous figure of the old-clothes man to create a single, easily identifiable Jewish type. No longer resorting to combinations of Sephardi and Ashkenazi Jews, physiognomic caricaturists were able to distinguish this once-indistinguishable foreigner for all to recognize. The three major markers, as I have already noted, were the long coat, the beard, and the Jewish nose. Like the Irish cap, the long coat became an immediate sign of Jewishness, such that the physiognomic markers served to remind viewers of the intended associations and reinforce rather than produce them.

Physiognomically, the Jewish nose occupied a strange position in the extensive and detailed nose literature.[120] In *Notes on Noses,* as I wrote in Chapter 1, the author divided all noses into six main classes, in decreasing order of value, starting from the valuable "Roman, or Aquiline Nose" and decreasing through the "Celestial, or turn-up nose," with the "Jewish, or Hawk Nose" occupying the fourth position.[121]

It will not escape the etymologically inclined reader that "aquiline" comes from "eagle," which is similar to the "hawk" description of the fourth type. According to *The Oxford English Dictionary,* the secondary meaning of "aquiline," dated from 1646, is "eagle-like; *esp.* of the nose or features: Curved like an eagle's beak, hooked."[122] As Jabet said, the Roman nose "indicates great decision, considerable Energy, Firmness, Absence of Refinement, and Disregard for the *bienséances* of life," whereas the Jewish nose "indicates considerable Shrewdness in worldly matters; a deep insight into character, and facility of turning that insight to profitable account."[123] The Jewish nose was designed for pecuniary success; the Roman, for leadership and decision making. Despite their similarities, the Jewish nose existed as a distinct category. It became an important fiction on which all physiognomic writers collaborated in order to provide an obvious physiognomic reference point for both Sephardi and Ashkenazi "Jewishness." This was independent of clothing and facial hair, symbols that could be, and indeed were, easily manipulated.[124]

Jabet himself recognized this fiction in his discussion of the Jewish nose. He contended that this feature had extended beyond Jews: "It is, however a fallacy to suppose that the peculiar physiognomy called Jewish is confined to the Jews, or even exclusively characteristic of them. It is in fact a form of profile common to all the inhabitants of Syria . . . This Nose should therefore more properly be called the Syrian Nose."[125] He then commented that this feature was not one to be coveted, because "no very exalted intellectuality is to be looked for from the Syrian Nose."[126]

Others agreed with Jabet. Positive references to being Jewish in nineteenth-century Britain, including the failure to beg that Mayhew and others have noted, were few and far between.[127] In addition to the somewhat ridiculous figures caricatured, there was a darker side to the image of the nineteenth-century Jew. The association between Jews and finance was well known, from the Sephardi banker to the Ashkenazi moneylender. Based on Shakespeare's devilish Shylock from *The Merchant of Venice*, Charles Dickens's famous character in *Oliver Twist*, Fagin, was an amalgamation of many of the traits I have discussed in this chapter. (Dickens later regretted the extent to which Fagin came to represent London Jewry and attempted a corrective with the loyal and benevolent character Mr. Riah in *Our Mutual Friend*. However, Riah was a significantly less central, and indeed less believable, character than was the archetypal Fagin.)[128] Although Fagin was a fence rather than a usurer, he was a manipulative and cunning money-grubber who inhabited the darkest corners of the streets of London.[129] First published serially from 1837 to 1839, the original illustrations by George Cruikshank showed Fagin with the long coat and particularly the hooked nose with which audiences had now become accustomed.[130]

The images of the poor Jewish peddler and this more malevolent version began to overlap, a conflation put to use by comic magazines as even recent eastern European immigrant Jews began to assimilate visually in conjunction with their growing political rights and financial prominence. As the Irish started supplanting the Jews in the streets in the 1850s, in particular taking over the trade of orange selling, the Jews were becoming increasingly upwardly mobile and steadily more invisible.[131] It was precisely when the Jew began to blend in with the crowd that the visual of the Jew became most explicit. Mayhew described the visual assimilation of the London street Jews, implicitly outlining the reasons why the stock type became so important at this time: "Fifty years ago the appearance of the street-Jews, engaged in the purchase of second-hand clothes, was different to what it is at the present time. The Jew then had far more of the distinctive garb and aspect of a foreigner. He not infrequently wore the gabardine, which is never seen now in the streets." Not only Jewish fashion but also non-Jewish tastes had changed, because "at that period, too, the Jew's long beard was far more distinctive than it is in this hirsute generation."[132]

As with the Irish, the presentation of Jewish women was far milder than that of Jewish men. The fact of the indistinguishability of Jewish women was itself a subject of discussion, as can be seen in an 1837 lithograph titled "Is She a Jewess?" published in the *Star* in 1837. Accompanying the print was the answer that "who that has ever looked on the sentimental and languishing face of a beautiful Jewess would not be interested in that query."[133]

Partly, Jewish women were less visible, at least in the role of peddlers that typified their male counterparts. According to Mayhew, "The Jewesses and Jews girls are rarely itinerant street-sellers—not in the proportion of one to twelve, compared with the men and boys; in this respect therefore the street Jews differ widely from the English costermongers and the street Irish, nor are the Hebrew females even stall keepers in the same proportion."[134] Being absent, Jewish women were not the same type of threat to the imperial imagination, and thus their blending into the crowd did not provoke the same type of anxiety and response. Marriages of elite Jewish women to Christian men were not uncommon. Because women were expected to assume the religion of their husbands, Jewish women were less of a threat. Upon entering Christian society, they would cease to be Jewish. Both Irish and Jewish women occupied little of the caricaturists' attention. Rather than being mocked, they were often simply ignored.

The Irish and the Jews were two groups of British citizens who were not immediately or obviously different. These two groups represent two extremes of otherness; the Irish were the most different of those who were similar to the English, and the Jews were the most similar of those who were different. Unlike other foreigners, the immediate visual recognition of Africanness or Indianness was absent for those seeking to separate Irish and Jews from other inhabitants of England. Likewise, the more straightforward anthropological demarcations were simply not sufficient to demonstrate the religious, racial, and class differences of these communities. It was to these ends that physiognomy, and in particular caricature physiognomy, aided in the construction of an Irish and a Jewish face.

As the nineteenth century progressed and the Irish and the Jews gained more political rights, the various visual depictions of them converged into a single, immediately recognizable stock type for each. Collapsing the negative perceptions of various communities into one entertaining visual image, these caricatures belittled their subjects by refusing to acknowledge internal distinctions. In the case of the Irish, this type was an ape that inhabited a visual zoo to justify imperial rule and ease evolutionary fears. With the Jews, the collapsing was itself the point; it removed distinctions between different types of Jews and rendering them all poor and unprofessional. Initially a combination of assimilated Sephardi bankers and Ashkenazi peddlers, the Jewish face became exclusively male and always Ashkenazi.

Physiognomy interacted with rising fears of anonymity by carving out distinct types accessible even in the most superficial interactions. To combat these fears, it was initially individuals who were subjected to physiognomic analyses. As the century progressed, however, physiognomic analyses and depictions moved toward the presentation and creation of group physiognomies. This approach built on the shift in the application of physiognomic techniques that I explored in the previous two chapters. Unlike the initial training of physiognomic perception and its ramifications for individual interactions and relationships, this physiognomic trajectory represents the self-conscious use of physiognomy to shape ideas about large communities and groups of people. Rather than using physiognomy to get information about people, caricature physiognomy applied these principles to give information.

In their depictions, caricaturists were drawing on the relationship between physiognomy and the developing discipline of anthropology.[135] Although anthropological principles focused mainly on nations and peoples abroad, they heavily resonated with the ways in which people living within the British Isles were physiognomically depicted, particularly in caricature. The two approaches complemented each other; physiognomy and visual culture trained British audiences to interpret pictorial cues that were often a part of anthropological presentations, and anthropological ideas deeply influenced notions of inherent differences that physiognomy made obvious. Physiognomic texts all paid attention to national physiognomies, focusing on the work of such racially oriented scholars as Petrus Camper, Johann Friedrich Blumenbach, and Robert Knox.[136]

Part of the reason for the growing popularity of anthropology in the mid-nineteenth century was the increased data available through colonial exploration and expansion. The excitement of empire was associated with the fear of empire, which prompted the attempt to create hierarchies and justify rule through biological imperatives. The depiction of the Irish as apes drew directly on the simianization of the Africans and designated the former even lower than the latter, who captured the sympathy of antislavery activists early in the nineteenth century; in both cases, animal imagery insisted on the inferiority of the ruled and, by implication, the superiority of the rulers.[137] The African discourse, however, noted many gradations of savagery and improvement and granted the possibility and indeed the imperative of civilization by the ruling British colonizers.[138] In the first half of the nineteenth century, the English turned their critical caricature and physiognomic gaze inward and erased such gradations for the internal foreigner. I explore the physiognomic role in anthropological explorations in Chapter 6.

Drawing from classical art theory, as well as rough street drawing, caricature became a highly developed and extremely lucrative art form. Moving from the powerfully sarcastic, biting, and satirical mode of the eighteenth century, by the nineteenth century caricature had become far less aggressive.[139] The use of physiognomy in caricature was not new in the nineteenth or even the eighteenth century; artists had long drawn on these notions to communicate character.[140] It was the increasing circulation of graphic images during the late eighteenth and nineteenth centuries that combined with the growing application of physiognomic ideas and scientific rhetoric. This combination produced a new shared language that gave meaning and power to the messages embedded in the caricature images and to the ways in which they were understood by audiences and artists alike.[141]

By the 1860s, the face of the male Irish and the face of the male Jew, and their accompanying physiognomic implications, were disseminated across various media, particularly comic magazines. These once-invisible and as-similable foreigners became identifiable as both of and apart from other inhabitants of England and Britain. Physiognomy assisted Britons not only to recognize but also to imagine and indeed image the demarcations of religion, race, and empire.

The power of caricature to classify and contain rested on the training of vision and the sharing of a joke. But images did not have to be funny to be physiognomic. In the next chapter, I use a case study to explore the diagnostic role of facial, clothing, and follicular physiognomy in psychiatric photography. The photographs of asylum superintendent Dr. Hugh Welch Diamond served diagnostic, classificatory, and public-relations purposes. Although Diamond's images reflected a kind of reality, they acted as a mediated mirror that expressed the view of the photographer and the observer about the state of mind of the subject.

CHAPTER FIVE

Photographic Physiognomy

Through a Mediated Mirror

N 1861, the English middlebrow family monthly *Cornhill Magazine* published an article discussing the strengths and weaknesses of physiognomy and phrenology.[1] Although the article granted that late eighteenth-century innovator Johann Caspar Lavater "showed more clearly than it had ever been done before that rules there must be, and a system there is, in the language of the human form," it was sharply critical of his failure to demonstrate that very system.[2] Rather, the article contended, Lavater's legacy was "no order, no logic, no finish—nothing but a dense tangled shrubbery of facts, most of them stunted and but half developed."[3]

This lamentable state of disordered affairs was, however, on the cusp of change, according to the *Cornhill*. With the aid of photographic reproducibility, the article argued, physiognomy was about to achieve its long-elusive set of rules, become a true system of classification, and take its place among other sciences:

> It is to be hoped that the discovery of the photograph will prove to be the dawn of a new day for [the physiognomist]. As the science of chemistry was nothing until a perfect balance was invented, and as the science of physiology was really unknown until the microscope was improved, so it may be that the faithful register of the camera, supplying us with the countless numbers of accurate observations, will now render that an actual science which has hitherto been only a possible one.[4]

As the next edition of the magazine read, "It is equally true that with such portraits and engravings of portraits as we have had, it has been utterly impossible to get beyond the nebulous science of a Lavater. We required the photograph."[5]

The *Cornhill* was not alone in heralding photography as the redemptive technology of physiognomic claims. In an 1856 paper to the Royal Society, Victorian asylum doctor and well-known photographer Hugh Welch Diamond emphasized the ways in which photography aided physiognomy.[6] Diamond used his camera not only to chart but also to instigate "the characteristic features of different mental diseases in their commencement, continuance, and cure."[7] With the aid of the camera, Diamond hoped to overcome the challenges Lavater faced in his quest to classify physiognomic types. Lavater bemoaned his lack of trustworthy evidence, relying as he did on artists of varying skill levels: "I shudder when I remember the supposed likenesses which are found between certain portraits and shades, and the living original . . . Each slander, in which there is but a shade of truth, is as usually supposed to be the full and exact truth, as are so many thousand wretched portraits supposed to be real and exact likenesses."[8]

According to the *Cornhill*, with the aid of mechanical objectivity over space and time, the contested terrain of physiognomic efficacy would soon become irrefutably proved and universally accepted.[9] The photograph would provide the necessarily exact archive that was missing from Lavaterian examinations. The photograph, in essence, would maintain the shared experience of physiognomy but remove its subjectivity.

In making these predictions, the *Cornhill* was missing the point. The strength of photographs was precisely that they were not reproductions but productions made by photographers, who could and did emphasize physiognomically meaningful symbols. The likenesses produced by the camera were highly mediated, a condition that Hugh Welch Diamond deliberately used to expand the range of physiognomically meaningful signs. Trained largely on female patients for whom there was a wide range of sartorial and hair nuances, Diamond's camera captured the external markings of madness, which included facial features, expression, carriage, bearing, and grooming. In the case of the mentally ill, the mirroring function of photographs was enhanced by the intermediary of both the camera and the photographer to aid viewers to see what might remain obscured in person.

Diamond turned his camera onto his mostly female patients at the Surrey Country Lunatic Asylum for diagnostic, classificatory, and, most intriguingly, therapeutic purposes. The first practitioner of diagnostic photography, Diamond was an innovator, both in his conceptions of the self and in the ways in which he captured them photographically.[10] He was an innovator in the more traditional sense as well, exploring and explaining a number of new photographic techniques. It is, however, his therapeutic and communicative theories that I seek to excavate here. Through close readings of Diamond's asylum photographs, in conjunction with his own commentaries and those of asylum doctor John Conolly, I explore Diamond's notions of the individual (insane) self and the ways in which he used photography to produce and export his physiognomic ideas.

Conolly used photography for public relations rather than therapy, directing his commentaries to other doctors and the lay public rather than the patients. For him, pictures of asylum residents underscored the importance of proper grooming and humane conditions in the treatment of the mentally ill, especially those patients whom he classified as "fallen women." The fallen women, whose conditions of abnormality were subject to circumstance, could be and were redeemed and cured by a change in those very conditions. For Conolly, pictures documented but did not effect a cure. Written language chronicling the biography of the subjects was a necessary component of Conolly's use of photography, while Diamond's goals of therapy, physiognomic diagnosis, and record keeping could be met largely by images alone. Diamond's three main audiences—other doctors, photographic exhibition viewers, and especially patients—did not need language to explain what he was showing them. As an advocate for the insane, Diamond was part of a growing group of asylum doctors, led by Conolly, who protested systems of restraint. As an advocate of visual imagery as therapy for his patients, it was Diamond who was the leader.

Diamond insisted that looking at photographic representations of themselves provided patients with the accurate self-reflection required to force them to recognize their illness. He chronicled a number of cases in which, through the combination of art and science, "photography unquestionably led to the cure."[11] For Diamond, cure emerged from acknowledgment of insanity, and treatment consisted of matching internal understanding with external representations. Madness developed out of a schism between the way a patient appeared and the way she thought she looked. In this, Diamond pushed physiognomic principles in a dramatically new direction that established a discourse of internality, a concept echoed by later doctors Jean-Martin Charcot and Sigmund Freud.[12]

Photography did not usher in the *Cornhill*'s predicted new era of scientific physiognomy. Nor, contrary to Diamond's own stated goals to the

Royal Society, did photographic physiognomy produce a universal language of diagnosis.[13] What physiognomic photography did do, in the hands and through the eyes of Diamond, was increase the rhetorical power of physiognomy by extending it to clothing, hair, and other metonymical markers of states of mind. Through his exhibitions and his writings, Diamond invited large audiences to execute analyses on his constructed images, standardized across time and space. These invitations were also extended to the subjects of the images. Diamond's medical photographic project invited patients to turn the physiognomic gaze inward on themselves as a therapeutic device. He used his images to both get and give physiognomic information and, in so doing, produced it. Diamond's photographs, then, were mediated mirrors that helped viewers see the subjects through the eyes of the photographer.

Not accidentally, the use of the term *mirror* evokes associations with the psychoanalytic writings of Jacques Lacan. Although I do not engage explicitly with Lacanian theory, I borrow the use of the mirror as a self-fashioning metaphor, whose reflection shows the fantasy of the united self.[14] What interests me is the mirror as a construction of selfhood and individuality, a means to see self as specific and removed from others. This individuality and recognition of self are precisely what Diamond was striving to construct. With his camera, Diamond acknowledged the need for mediation because direct and unmediated reflections sustain fantasies rather than force a confrontation with them.

Many feminist scholars have usefully challenged the mirror metaphor and have argued that when women look in the mirror, they see not the individual self but the gendered collective, members of the social category of female and feminine.[15] Although Diamond's images of female patients certainly engaged with gendered representations, he designed his pictures to insist on the individual self. This approach stands in sharp contrast with the commentary of John Conolly, who was interested in groups—fallen women, the poor, and the asylum patients that hardship conditions produced. Diamond and Conolly used the same set of images to discuss very different kinds of physiognomy, namely, that which identified individuals and that which could be used to characterize groups. What Diamond and Conolly had in common was the use of physiognomic representations to allow many different kinds of audiences to see what they otherwise could or would not. Through the application of physiognomic principles, Diamond's images provided access to sites normally obscured: the hidden depths of the mental asylum and the even more hidden depths of the deranged human mind.

The Eyes of Dr. Hugh Welch Diamond

Diamond, unlike many other physiognomic practitioners, explicitly engaged in the questions of change, in behavior and on the face.[16] Many of his photographs were before-and-after sequences that charted the process of cure through physiognomic improvement. In contrast to other medical physiognomists and physiognomic innovator Johann Caspar Lavater himself, Diamond never conceived of physiognomy as a vast and detailed system of human classification that required additional data to realize its potential.[17] Again unlike Lavaterian physiognomy, Diamond's photographic analyses were tracing behavior rather than personality because Diamond believed that a mind gone wrong could be righted. Insane behavior was marked not only in the face but also in the clothing, hair, and body of the patients. Finally, unlike Lavater, Diamond allowed no space for the instinct of his observers; orchestrating his images to support rather than produce physiognomic analyses, Diamond left little to chance. For Diamond, the camera was a tool that he used to reproduce his own vision and allow others to see what he saw. In so doing, Diamond was training his audience in photographic viewing and physiognomic signs.

Diamond was the superintendent of the Female Department of the Surrey County Lunatic Asylum from 1848 to 1858, at which point he resigned his position under somewhat mysterious and scandalous circumstances.[18] His tenure at the asylum coincided with his growing interest in photography, to which he devoted a great deal of time and energy. Not content with a superficial level of skill, Diamond worked hard to master and even pioneer a number of innovative photographic techniques, which he generously shared with other interested so-called gentlemen amateurs.[19]

Diamond's generosity to the photographic field was recognized by a £300 purse presented in 1855 by a group of amateur photographers, one of whom was the physicist Michael Faraday.[20] Contributions were requested in various publications, including an early volume of the *Asylum Journal of Mental Science,* which commented that "the services rendered by Dr. Diamond to photography . . . have incited a numerous and influential body of photographers and archaeologists to mark their sense of obligation by presenting him with a testimonial."[21]

Widely respected, Diamond was well known for his photographic as well as his medical skills, and particularly for the ways in which he blended the two. His articles about photographic physiognomy appeared in medical, photographic, and cultural journals, including the professional *Asylum Journal*, the specialist *Journal of the Photographic Society*, and the highbrow cultural journal the *Athenaeum*. The broadness of Diamond's appeal was witnessed by the various publications in which he was featured; his *Athenaeum* obituary noted that "Diamond is also to be remembered for the assistance he rendered photographers at moments when they were in urgent need of a scientific tutor endowed with artistic discernment, sufficient knowledge, and manipulatory adroitness." This aid was given generously: "Diamond, without fee or any thought for material reward, acted as scientific instructor to the increasing number of persons who were from different motives interested in the new art."[22]

For Diamond, the pursuit of science and the pursuit of art were intermingled, and both were done in service of the training of the self. The idea that photography could be used for self-improvement, drawing on the resources of both art and science, was a common thread throughout his work with interested amateurs and especially with his patients.

Diamond worked toward repairing an omission lamented by the prestigious medical journal the *Lancet* after "passing through the rooms of the Photographic Society" and finding "so few photographs which had any bearing of what kind soever upon surgery, medicine, and the allied sciences." Given that "photography is so essentially the Art of Truth— and the representative of the Truth in Art—that it would seem to be the essential means of reproducing all forms and structures of which science seeks for the delineation," according to the *Lancet*, "it is much to be regretted that the great resources of the photographic art . . . have not yet been more fully applied to the purposes of our art."[23] In bringing photography to medicine and medicine to photography, Diamond sought to satisfy the requirements of both.

Diamond's reputation as a psychiatric photographer was cemented for both scientific and artistic audiences during his 1852 exhibit at the London Society of Arts. This display, titled "The Types of Insanity," was composed of a series of photographs that he had taken of his asylum patients.[24] With his pictures, Diamond was joining a tradition of medical illustration practiced by such eminent physicians as Sir Charles Bell, whose studies linked expression to anatomy, and Diamond's predecessor at the Surrey County Asylum, Sir Alexander Morison, whose 1838 atlas *The Physiognomy of Mental Diseases* made extensive use of portraits to discuss the facial features and expressions associated with insanity.[25] Likewise, in France, asylum physician J. É. D. Esquirol had more than 200 patients at the Salpêtrière asylum sketched for his *Mental Maladies: A Treatise on Insanity.*[26]

The critical response to Diamond's display was positive. Viewers were particularly impressed by Diamond's skillful harnessing of the power of the photographic medium to capture the pathos of insanity effectively. In its glowing review of the exhibit, the *Athenaeum* noted that "the Doctor has been enabled to produce a group of portraits of insane and idiotic people who could probably not be induced to remain quiet long enough to be taken by the other processes. This is but one of the many ways in which photography may be made subservient to science."[27]

Reflecting on his work, Diamond emphasized the role that photography played in faithfully rendering and preserving a record of insanity because "photography gives permanence to these remarkable cases, which are types of classes, and makes them observable not only now but for ever." Photographs were not only permanent but, unlike other painted portraits of the insane, accurate, offering "a perfect and faithful record, free altogether from the painful caricaturing which so disfigures almost all the published portraits of the Insane as to render them nearly valueless either for purposes of art or science." Although Diamond did not explicitly acknowledge the role of the camera and the photographer in producing physiognomic effects, his use of pictures emphasized the mediation inherent in his "perfect and faithful record."[28]

To Diamond, the "painful caricatures" were medically problematic and physiognomically unhelpful. The representations they produced were not just useless for purposes of record keeping, diagnosis, and therapy but were also harmful because they presented inaccurate images that communicated false information. The mad could not look at these distortions as a way to get a truer sense of self; doctors could not use them to standardize illness categories; laypeople could not view them as a way to calm their fears about the insane. Photographs, as, in Diamond's words, "the copy *drawn to life*," offered a solution to all these objections.[29]

As in the photographic project of late nineteenth-century Salpêtrière asylum doctor Jean-Martin Charcot, Diamond used his camera to bring not just photographic representations but also physiognomic signs into being. Charcot used photographs to chart the various stages of hysteria and, eventually, as a tool to produce them. He too was obsessed with the recording function of the camera and ignored the role of the photographer in excavating the effects that the camera mediated. Overhearing the words of Diamond, Charcot protested his invisibility in the archiving process: "What a marvel this would be if I could, in fact, fabricate illnesses according to my whims or fantasies. But in fact all I am is a photographer. I describe what I see."[30]

Like Charcot's after him, Diamond's images of the exterior contributed to the construction of interiority that he both excavated and produced. In his writings and his pictures, Diamond, unlike his colleague John Conolly, expressed the belief that images speak louder than words. Diamond asked, "What words can adequately describe . . . the peculiar character of the palsy which accompanies sudden terror without hope?" Diamond answered himself, acknowledging that in both pictures and words, he and his camera were doing the talking: "Yet the photographer secures with unerring accuracy the external phenomena of each passion, as the really certain indication of internal derangement, and exhibits to the eye the well known sympathy which exists between the diseased brain and the organs and features of the body."[31] That which "the Photographer catches in a moment," namely, "the permanent cloud, or the passing storm or sunshine of the soul," offered the key to decoding "delirium with raving fury and spitefulness or delirium accompanied with an appearance of gaiety and pleasure." Photography "enables the metaphysician to witness and trace out the connexion between the visible and the invisible in one important branch of his researches into the Philosophy of the human mind."[32]

Although Diamond's images were powerful as therapeutic tools and artistic representations, they alone could not effectively produce a language of the insane self for all viewers. It took the commentary of John Conolly on the photographs to make these images meaningful in a diagnostic and public-relations context. The importance of Conolly's commentary for Diamond's photographs emphasizes Roland Barthes's argument that the photograph is a "message without a code," from which meaning is made by the text that surrounds it.[33] Diamond too added interpretive cues in his setting and staging of the images. However, for Diamond's most proximate audience, the pictures alone were all that was needed.

Diamond's commitment to communicating his vision was effective in reaching his colleagues in the asylum world. His admirers and collaborators in the pursuit of photography were equally able to access his images and ideas, and many of them emulated his work.[34] Diamond has rightly been lauded in historiography as a pioneering diagnostic photographer and a major contributor to the development and dissemination of photographic techniques.[35] One of the most prominent and controversial photographic manipulators was Henry Peach Robinson.[36] Robinson dedicated his 1869 book *Pictorial Effect in Photography* to Diamond "as a tribute of the sincerest and warmest respect and esteem" for "one of the fathers of photography."[37] Diamond was not just a highly influential doctor; he was also one of the major photographic innovators and writers of the nineteenth century. His role as a therapist and his use of the camera and its images as therapeutic technologies have been more overlooked. In a radical move, Diamond suggested using his photographs to treat patients—not as a pleasant pastime akin to games and dances, and not as healthy labor like working in the fields or at crafts, but in order to force patients to see themselves through Diamond's eyes. In this, Diamond was subtly proposing a concept of self and an idea of illness that were highly performative and representational.

This therapeutic approach was possible only because, like some of the caricaturists I explored in the previous chapter, Diamond reoriented the physiognomic discourse to include external symbols outside the face, such as hair, body, and clothing. For him, the face itself was an important diagnostic and record-keeping device, but it was the other markers of insanity, the ones he emphasized in his pictures, that provided him with a point of therapeutic access that would lead to change. These pictures stood witness to the patients' state of being. The opportunity for accurate self-reflection was, Diamond wrote, a particularly valuable aspect of asylum photography: "There is another point of view in which the value of portraits of the Insane is peculiarly marked.—viz. in the effect which they produce upon the patients themselves."[38]

To Diamond, the face, the hair, and the clothing, that is, the *physiognomy*, of his patients had the potential to be transformative of concepts of self. The physiognomic photograph was a reflection of an inner world in the classic physiognomic formulation, but it was one that could be altered. Diamond gave as an example a patient whose "delusions consisted in the supposed possession of great wealth, and of an exalted station as a queen."[39] Showing her photographs of all the other patients who fancied themselves queens "was the first decided step in her gradual improvement," which led to her being "discharged perfectly cured."[40]

Diamond's principles suggested that concepts of the self determined health and illness as reflected not just in appearance but also in understanding of appearance. In order to understand appearance, a mirrored reflection was not enough. In looking at a mirror, patients would see what they expected to see; only through the distance provided by the mediation of photography could the necessary shock and later recognition be achieved. Mediation had power not only to provide distance but also to furnish the necessary signs marking illness. Rather than being purely mimetic, photographs revealed a different kind of truth, dependent on the photographer and his tools. Unlike Karl Marx's

1867 critique of the commodity fetish, in which he argued that reproduced signs of objects replaced the objects themselves, Diamond's copies were value added, excavating what was obscured through the naked eye.[41] Diamond staged his photographs and props to make meaningful those markings that, without an intermediary, remained invisible to the patients.

The success of Diamond's approach was contingent on patients believing in photographs as mimetic and powerful representational objects. They had to believe that they were (finally) seeing themselves as others saw them. What they were really looking at were images of how Diamond saw them; as their doctor, his eyes were to be trusted. The camera, then, became a producer rather than a recorder. The camera both brought into being the physiognomic signs with which Diamond infused his scenes and acted as the mediating object that created the distance necessary to allow patients to see themselves through the camera's—Diamond's—eyes. As John Tagg has argued, the truth-value attached to the photograph bound the body to a particular identity and created a representational archive for surveillance and control.[42] Here, the surveillance was being done both by Diamond and those viewing the photographs, but the possibility of (self-)control was being urged on the patients themselves. The patients were special kinds of photographic subjects; they were meant to be transformed by their own images, thereby (much like museums housing instrument collections) rendering these representations invalid soon after they were produced and viewed.

Diamond was taking the notion of moral management—granting privileges based on appropriate behavior—and pushing it in a new direction.[43] He was establishing normative standards not through actions but through appearance, and he was asking patients to recognize those same norms. In a sort of early art therapy, Diamond was using photographs to reveal the patients' inner states, but rather than the patients, it was he and his camera that were offering the revelation. The therapy was not in the production of art as a leisure activity (as in moral management) nor in an exercise in subconscious personal exposure (as in the art therapy movement pioneered in the 1940s), but in the training of personal judgment and of self-sight.[44] From this followed self-care, which would bring about physiognomic and mental change. Personal judgment was, according to Diamond, absent from patients when they encountered themselves directly in mirrors. It took a photographic copy for patients truly to see themselves, and this attested to a different form of truth than a strictly mechanically objective rendering. The mediation offered by the camera forced a different way of seeing.

Picturing Madness

Diamond's patients, as inhabitants of a large (and growing), underfunded public asylum, were mostly poor, often long-term inhabitants, many of whose families had little or no hope of cure.[45] There is no evidence that Diamond procured permission from his patients or their families to take and display these photos. Diamond's reviewers were initially equally uninterested in interrogating the ethics or appropriateness of the images and their subjects. The first hostile review of the photographs, which argued that it was in bad taste to exhibit them anywhere but a physician's office, appeared only in 1859.[46] Because the patients were poor dependents, it is possible that both Diamond and early reviewers thought that such permission was unnecessary; in his next posting, at a private asylum that he opened in Twickenham in 1858, Diamond took no (extant) photos of his patients, perhaps because their rich families or they themselves objected.

The living conditions of the patients were relevant not only because they provided Diamond with compliant subjects, but also because, according to some Victorian doctors, poverty contributed directly to mental instability. In his writings in general and in his commentary on Diamond's photos in particular, Dr. John Conolly attributed mental and visual physiognomic disorder in (women) patients to social circumstances, such that a corresponding change in those circumstances could effect a cure.[47] Conolly sought to clothe the naked, metaphorically and literally. In so changing their surface, he believed that he would affect their interiors. Again, the state of the body and of that which adorned it reflected the state of the mind, and photographs provided the necessary mirror that inspired patients to adorn their bodies appropriately. To Diamond and Conolly, clothing became as important a physiognomic symbol as the face, and one that was manipulable by the patients themselves.

The first image I examine is likely the best known, both for its content and for its iconography (Figure 5.1). In this photograph, the patient is wrapped in a black shawl or mantle, evoking notions of poverty, deprivation, and salvation. The shawl hints that the patient may be a "fallen woman," a theme underscored by the gap in the shawl over the left breast area. Her eyes are focused away from the viewers and look off to the side in an exhausted, blank stare. The patient's cheekbones are highlighted and suggest undernourishment or a lack of physical health. Far from enjoying the experience, she seems to have no interaction at all with the photographer or any other viewers, present or future. She sees no one, including herself. Most striking is the garland placed around her head by Diamond himself as he was arranging her pose. A powerful symbol of insanity, the garland likens this sitter to Shakespeare's Ophelia, a character often used in Victorian art and literature to represent the asylum madwoman.[48]

Figure 5.1. Hugh Welch Diamond, Plate 32, 1850s. Diamond placed a garland around this subject's head, likening her to Shakespeare's Ophelia, a frequently used Victorian symbol of female madness. (By kind permission of the Royal Society of Medicine.)

Doctors also used the Ophelia image. John Hitchman, in his final address as president of the Association of Medical Officers of Asylums and Hospitals for the Insane, exhorted his colleagues to feel empathy for their patients. Following the approach of Conolly, his mentor, Hitchman called on fellow asylum doctors to "listen to the sweet and gentle voice of yonder woman . . . How touchingly she warbles like poor *Ophelia* . . . What a pitiful spectacle of a sweet mind lying in fragments before us." In a final identifying touch, Hitchman noted that "she has decked herself with a spring garland."[49]

The mantle theme is continued in a number of Diamond's poses, including plate 27, plate 30, plate 42, plate 44, plate 46, and plate 50 (Figure 5.2). In all these pictures, the sitters are wrapped, often huddled, in some type of ragged shawl or blanket. Both infantilizing and impoverishing, these pictures draw on the power of photography to isolate an evocative state of being and freeze it for continuous associations. The patients in these images were stopped in a particular moment in time that was revisited with each viewing of the photographs. What viewers— including the subjects themselves—saw were people who looked as though they had just recently been rescued and had blankets placed on them for warmth or comfort. These mantles dominate the images and draw the eye away from the very faces that Diamond claimed to be highlighting. These blankets also serve to make the sitters appear to be in a state of undress, or at least not fully dressed, hinting at a lack of personal care and hygiene associated with insanity.

In the image on the left, the subject clutches a dead bird in her hand. With her head tilted slightly up, she appears deliberately to be looking away from the victim. It is unclear if she is mourning or celebrating its death, or if she is aware of it at all. Birds were one of many Victorian and particularly Pre-Raphaelite symbols of a woman's virtue; the dead bird here mirrors the woman's state of mind, fallen and destroyed.[50] The darkness of the background causes the woman to blend into it; fading away, she and the bird stand on either side of the life/death divide. Unlike the bird, however, she can still be saved. The photograph on the right shows a woman with messy dark hair covered by a loose shawl. Her hands are also resting in her lap, with the top one clutching at the bottom with a clawlike grip. She looks directly at the camera and at the viewers but does not seem to see anything. Her dress and her shawl are both striped, but with contrasting patterns that make her appearance unsettling and jarring for the viewers.

The themes of poverty and salvation were underscored in the language of Conolly in his commentary on Diamond's photographs, published in the *Medical Times and Gazette* in 1858.[51] Conolly's commentary acted as a narration that provided additional details to those visible in the illustrating pictures. In a classical physiognomic approach, Conolly wrote a great deal about the physical features of these subjects, but he also focused closely on the more easily altered and noticeable external symbols, intertwining the two. Of a patient "labouring under religious melancholy," Conolly read the text of her face and her clothing interchangeably. Working his way down the body, Conolly drew readers' attention to "the high and wide forehead, generally indicative of intelligence and imagination; the slightly bent head, leaning disconsolately on the hand; the absence from that collapsed cheek of every trace of gaiety; the mouth inexpressive of any varied emotion; the deep orbits and the long characteristic eyebrows." These features communicated consistent information

Figure 5.2.   Hugh Welch Diamond, Plates 27 and 30, 1850s. Two examples of Diamond's frequent use of blankets or mantles to invoke pathos for his subjects on the part of his viewers. (By kind permission of the Royal Society of Medicine.)

about the patient's state of mind because "all seem painfully to indicate the present mood and general temperament of the patient." Likewise for the patient's fashion style and grooming: "The black hair is heedlessly pressed back; the dress, though neat, has a conventual plainness; the sacred emblem worn round the neck is not worn for ornament."[52]

Conolly's written commentary was an important part of the codification of medical physiognomic symbols, both physical and sartorial, which drew heavily on his own therapeutic approaches and concerns. Thirteen years before his writings on Diamond's pictures, Conolly published that "dress is women's weakness, and in the treatment of lunacy it should be an instrument of control, and therefore recovery."[53] Unlike Diamond, Conolly did not need patients to see how they were really dressed to inspire them to choose to change their clothes; clothing change, with or without choice, was alone a powerful therapeutic tool. Alongside this theme, the class of the subjects was an important line of analysis for Conolly, reflecting his sense that poverty and deprivation could lead to serious mental imbalance. In his comments, Conolly noted both individual markings and those that indicated membership in a particular social group. He thereby used photographic physiognomy as a means to identify both specific and general characteristics.

In his commentary on the "suicidal melancholic" pictured on plate 3 (Figure 5.3), pictures of a woman who appeared to be begging something of the viewer, Conolly offered an analysis of her social background, noting that like many patients, "it is evidently not the portrait of an educated or refined person, but a woman of the poorer ranks of life,—from which ranks our large crowded county asylums are filled." By using the word "evidently," Conolly supported those physiognomists who argued that life experience was evident in the face and body, because asylum clothing provided few social clues. Explicitly connecting economic and moral failure to mental failure, Conolly warned his audience not to judge those who seemed to have little choice: "And the worst of them, too impatient of this lot . . . deviate from the walks of industry . . . It is easy to moralize on these things, and virtuously to condemn; but God alone can judge such matters justly. If a man would try to do so, he must realise to himself an almost unfurnished home, and hungry children, and rent to pay." Such economic hardship could place an unbearable burden on the mind, one, Conolly pointedly noted, that his comfortable and well-off readers could not understand: "He must fancy the state of his mind under the privation of all indulgences and all amusements, and in the utter absence of all comfortable recreation for mind or body. Who is there, more happily placed, who can estimate or even imagine the physiological results of all this combination of misery and privation?"[54]

Conolly went on to analyze the photograph in detail. In addition to the "inclination of the head to the right, the starting muscles on the left side of the neck, the excessive corrugation of the integuments of the forehead,"

Figure 5.3.   Hugh Welch Diamond, "Suicidal Melancholy," 1850s. The clothing and hair of this subject offered insight into both her disease and her social status. (By kind permission of the Royal Society of Medicine.)

which "all tell the same story of intense and painful emotion," he commented on "the copious and dishevelled hair[, which is] parted with no care, but straggles in sympathy with a tortured brain."[55] He concluded his analysis with an "actual history of the patient," who was "born of a mother on whom wretchedness had already done its work . . . Her sole inheritance was poverty and labour, and a brain disposed to disease."[56] Conolly left readers with a gesture toward inherited degeneration, hinting that the state of the daughter began with the propensities of the mother.[57] Using the image as a text from which to read not only behavioral but historical characteristics of the subject, Conolly merged the photograph with the patient and employed physiognomy as the key to penetrate this representation. In his reading, however, Conolly was citing details that he already knew (and his audience did not) and offering his background knowledge to support his ideas. Unlike Lavaterian physiognomy and the pocket variant that followed, for Conolly, photographic physiognomy proved rather than produced his conclusions.

In this photograph, the patient's head was tilted, but she looked more directly at the camera and the viewers. Her interaction with the camera is striking in its distinction from other images; in addition to eye contact and begging hands, her dress stood out rather than fading in. She had no blanket or shawl, and even the sides of her chair were visible. This image was designed to underscore the humanness of the patient. Where the other photos evoked pathos at the patients' difference and deadness, this one emphasized her liveliness.

This image, more than others, acted as a mirror not just for the subject but also for other audiences. In this woman, viewers saw someone not so different from themselves, someone whose desperation indicated a desire to change. The possibility of cure through the simple expedient of clothing changes and through more complicated therapeutic endeavors seemed a realizable hope. The pathos in this image was not because the woman appeared so different and so deranged, but precisely because she did not.

Two striking before-and-after sequences of sickness and cure demonstrate that to Diamond and Conolly, the physiognomy of insanity and sanity was best represented photographically by changes in fashion sense and self-presentation. The visual result for both doctors may have been the same, although they differed on how these changes were brought about. For Diamond, the photos instigated the cure, while for Conolly, they chronicled it. These pictures in particular highlight the trust that viewers had to have in the photographers and commentators; because the images were arranged by the photographers long before they were released, viewers had no evidence outside the images that a cure actually occurred, and that the images were arranged in an accurate temporal sequence. Here, the mirror acts to reflect time, showing all viewers, including the subjects of the images, the changes that they could not themselves compare without the photographic medium.

Plate 14 showed the progress of a woman through the stages of puerperal insanity and cure (Figure 5.4).[58] Although there were changes in her expression, the most obvious improvement was found in her personal comportment and attire. In the initial stages of the disease, she was dressed in plain clothing with messy and apparently unwashed hair, on which, in a rare direct reference to his photos, Diamond commented in his 1856 paper that she had reached "that stage of Mania which is marked by bristled hair."[59] Here Diamond noted that she progressed along a predictable disease course that made her one of many similar maniacs.

Clothing provided important diagnostic clues to the nature of the patient's disturbance. Influential Victorian asylum doctor Sir John Charles Bucknill, discussed later in this chapter, charted the progression of mental states through states of dress and noted that "the patient's dress not unfrequently presents characteristic traits indicating the direction of insane delusion." However, clothing eccentricities indicated a more developed mania; earlier in the disease, patients preferred no clothing at all, "but these indications belong to a later period of the disease, and it may be taken as a general rule, that in the earlier stages of mental disorder the dress and personal condition of the patient are neglected." On occasion, "There is great intolerance of dress, the patient seeming to suffer irritation from the customary articles of clothing. The propensity to remain wholly or partially nude is frequent."[60]

According to Conolly, the patient in plate 14 continued along Bucknill's course of development because she at times "tore her clothes out of an excess of animal spirits."[61] Her hair was highly disordered, and she showed complete disregard for it. The third picture marked the beginning stages of improvement, although the therapeutic means were not recorded here or elsewhere.[62] Her hair was tidy and brushed, and Conolly commented that she was "neatly dressed."[63] He made this claim—despite an inability to see what she was wearing—because she was covered in the shawl that represented the coming redemption while still firmly situating her as uncured. Conolly's commentary echoed that of Diamond, who noted that "the Hair [sic] falls naturally and the forehead alone retains traces, tho' slight ones, of mental agitation."[64] As in many of the other pictures, hands remain an important point of communication with viewers.

Figure 5.4. Hugh Welch Diamond, "Puerperal Mania in Four Stages," *Medical Times and Gazette,* June 1858. This sequence chronicled a patient's path toward recovery, visually notable in changes in clothing and hairstyles as well as facial expressions. (By kind permission of the Royal Society of Medicine.)

Here the patient's hands are hidden, a fact that represents her lack of control. It is only when she is presented as recovered that her calmly clasped hands are visible.

It was in the final picture, in which she was, according to Diamond, "clothed and in her right mind," and according to Conolly, "represented in bonnet and shawl," that the patient was pronounced cured.[65] She was wearing more clothes, which was an important photographic physiognomic marker of sanity. The most significant addition for Conolly, however, was the presence of a bonnet. Uncovered hair was a source of great anxiety for him, and many of his comments revolved around the patients' state of bareheadedness.

So do the pictures themselves. The next sequence of recovery and cure, on plate 15, showed a woman who had been diagnosed with religious mania (Figure 5.5). While she was in the throes of madness, her hair was messy and uncovered, and her dress was disordered and lacking accessories. When she recovered, this patient was neatly tied, belted, and literally re-covered

Figure 5.5.   Hugh Welch Diamond, "Religious Melancholia and Convalescence," *Medical Times and Gazette,* October 1858. As with the previous figure, the patient's improvement was marked by changes in clothing, hairstyle, and facial expression. (By kind permission of the Royal Society of Medicine.)

with a bonnet on her head. Of another cured patient, Conolly noted that "subsequent photographs are scarcely to be recognised as being likenesses of the same patient," particularly because "the hair is well arranged."[66] This picture does not require Diamond's cause and effect; although it chronicled improvement, it is not clear if the second side is a direct result of the first. The time gap between the two pictures is also erased through photography—between the melancholia of the left side and the convalescence of the right, many visual appearances were left unrecorded.

In showing patients their pictures, Diamond was holding up his mediated mirror not only of the patients' state of mind but also of their station in life. Plate 17 showed two different patients, both of whom were, in the words of Conolly, "illustrative of some of the modifications of features and expression in women who have fallen into the habits of intemperance."[67] Again, the subjects were hatless women in disheveled attire and with disorderly hair. The begging pose in plates 3 and 4 was repeated by one of the patients, an attempt to evoke pathos from the viewers. Of this first subject, Conolly noted that she had been reduced to a state of poverty from "a respectable station," losing everything to the pawnbroker, including "the clothes of her mother and herself."[68] The other patient, with "disordered, uncombed, capriciously cut hair, cut with ancient scissors or chopped with impatient knife," had less possibility of redemption because she had been born into a "low and degraded life, into whose mind, even before madness supervened, no thoughts except gross thought were wont to enter." Even she, however, was to be treated with mercy; her fall to "singing in a public house" was a predictable outcome of her circumstances.[69] In his commentary on these images, Conolly distinguished the subjects as individuals with unique histories and experiences while simultaneously categorizing them as members of groups whose pathologies progressed along standard lines.

Conolly introduced his discussion of the patient in plate 11 with comments about her headgear, calling her "the old lady in the reversed bonnet" (Figure 5.6).[70] He commented that "one feels sure that once this poor woman was of a merry mind . . . and turned her bonnet round for very mirth."[71] Her mental state was visible from "the strong descending lines from the alae nasi to the depressed corners of the mouth," which spoke to her "alternations of depression with excitement, and make the physiognomy indicative of past attacks of mania and melancholia."[72] Her insanity, he explained, was from "the exhaustion incidental to daily labour," the effects of which were lessened in the asylum because of the "regular life led there, the good food, the general regulations of the place, and occasional Medical treatment."[73] For this lucky patient, "the asylum-influences had a happy effect upon her, and in about eleven months she was discharged cured."[74] Nevertheless, traces of her insanity lingered, he admitted, with occasional "fits of violence," although the most common sign of her former state of mind was her benign "eccentricity of dress," of which there is no visual record.[75]

Figure 5.6.   Hugh Welch Diamond, "Chronic Mania," *Medical Times and Gazette,* April 1858. The state of this patient's bonnet and clothing were particularly indicative of her mental condition. (By kind permission of the Royal Society of Medicine.)

With his photographs of women patients, Diamond was participating in the iconography of Victorian symbols of female deviance and abnormality. In a number of prominent Victorian paintings and engravings all made after Diamond's exhibit, there were repeated images of women about to fall into, in the process of falling into, or recovering from a fall into reduced circumstances (Figures 5.7 and 5.8).[76] A num-

Figure 5.7.   Rebecca Solomon, "A Friend in Need," *Illustrated London News,* 23 April 1859. This wood engraving showed a mother and child in desperate straits, marked in part by the mother's long dark mantle. (Reprinted with permission from Mary Evans Picture Library.)

ber of symbols are familiar from Diamond's pictures, including dark shawls, disordered and exposed hair, and postures of begging or prayer. The rhetorical effect of visual symbols was powerful, as Diamond, an accomplished photographer, well knew. By linking photographs of ostensibly curable patients to those women equally in need of positive change, Diamond and, more explicitly, Conolly, were taking a stand not only about the reversal of mental illness but of moral failure as well. If Diamond's patients could recover (and re-cover) with proper aid, so too could these women. As their downfall was chronicled through sartorial shifts, so, like Diamond's patients, their improvement could be externalized, making changes in both mental state and social circumstance visually manifest.

In Diamond's photos, Conolly's commentaries, and the later Victorian paintings and engravings, Lavaterian physiognomic signs were complemented by metonymical symbols that were more easily manipulable and thus subject to change and possible cure. These symbols were emphasized by Diamond in the staging of his photographs and were underscored by

Figure 5.8. "A Social Contrast: Up in the World, Down on Her Luck," *Days' Doings,* 8 July 1871. This wood engraving showed a before-and-after sequence of a woman fallen on hard times. As in Diamond's images, her desperation is marked by a ragged shawl and messy hair.

Conolly in his writings. For both men, this type of physiognomic analysis did tremendous rhetorical work in their attempts to present the mad as curable and containable without restraints. These poses served to tame images of the mad in the public eye by presenting them as neat, ordered, and utterly human and helped.

Diamond, invested in developing the art form of photography, was participating in the establishment of new conventions and visual symbols that became prominent in the Victorian era. These developments rested on the conditions of possibility set by the increasing prominence of physiognomy as a way of seeing in nineteenth-century Britain. Diamond's camera emphasized hair and clothing, adding elements to the reflections of themselves that patients saw. These metonymical symbols built on, rather than replaced, the physiognomy of facial features. In these photographs, clothing became an archive of past experience that contributed to the reading of the body. Diamond offered multiple sources of meaning in his photographs, which he and Conolly trained viewers—patients and others—to see and understand.

The connections between clothing and character that Diamond suggested in his images were in consonance with German idealist notions explored by Thomas Carlyle in his influential and tongue-in-cheek philosophy of clothes, *Sartor Resartus* (The Tailor Retailored).[77] This experimental text, first serialized in the Tory literary journal *Fraser's Magazine* from 1833 to 1834, demonstrated Carlyle's contention that style and its material manifestations are both a representation of social relationships and the "bodying forth" of internalized reality. In this way, clothing was the externalization of an underlying social and spiritual order, a kind of physiognomy of the self and its relationship to others.

Critic and artist Lady Elizabeth Eastlake personalized Carlyle's ideas and tied clothing directly to individuals and their status and character. She argued for the importance of carefully examining clothing as a source of information in the literary-political Tory journal the *Quarterly Review* in 1847. Eastlake noted that "dress becomes a sort of symbolical language—a kind of personal glossary—a species of body phrenology, the study of which it would be madness to neglect."[78] Both an accomplished photographer in her own right and the wife of the first president of the Royal Photographic Society, Eastlake developed acute skills in reading and interpreting photographs and their clothing messages. Like Diamond, Eastlake used the photographic medium to increase the power of sartorial signs for greater physiognomic meaning. However, unlike Diamond, Eastlake used physiognomic photography to eradicate the individual and to capture what was common across characters rather

than what was distinct. Eastlake, with her commentary on urban photography, saw the medium as a way to learn about common characteristics; she erased rather than excavated individuality. Diamond, although
engaged in establishing conventions for a large group—the mad—used
his pictures to represent very specific people. His focus on personal detail was a key aspect of the success of his therapeutic endeavor; offering
only group features would undermine the mirroring function of his
photographs.

   Graeme Tytler has noted that Victorian authors, in contrast to their
predecessors, used clothing descriptions not just to construct literary
portraits but also to communicate physiognomic and character information.[79] For example, in his 1853 masterwork *Bleak House*, Charles Dickens played with the notion of physiognomically significant clothing. In
this story of doubles and exchanges, the elegant Lady Deadlock managed
to disappear into the city masses, becoming what Mrs. Snagsby's servant
described as "a common-looking person, all wet and muddy."[80] This transformation, from beautiful aristocrat to invisible commoner, was achieved
by changing her clothing and thus her social status. In his pursuit of what
he called "the dress," the detective, Mr. Bucket, gave form to the way in
which Lady Deadlock's clothes literally became her, or rather, how she
became nothing more than the indistinguishable dress in which she chose
to hide.

Captured by Camera

Throughout the first half of the nineteenth century, a number of asylum
directors advocated the abolition of physical restraints as a form of treatment. John Conolly introduced nonrestraint in the Hanwell Asylum in
1839 and has often been credited with initially recognizing the therapeutic advantages of physical freedom. However, it was the twenty-three-
year-old house surgeon at Lincoln, Robert Gardiner Hill, who first developed nonrestraint in 1834.[81] Conolly, motivated by both medical and
humanitarian concerns, was the most visible advocate of the approach
and generated widespread support for its application.

   Speaking against the iconic story of the liberation of the insane from
their chains, Michel Foucault has shown the ways in which the nineteenth century saw an internalization of these very restraints.[82] He argued that systems of surveillance and moral treatment were a different, and in many ways equally powerful, form of restraint. Diamond's
physiognomic photography offered a new technology of chaining
that urged patients to judge themselves through Diamond's eyes. The

mediated mirror not only reflected patients but also defined and confined them.

Despite a commitment to abolishing physical confinement, doctors continued to emphasize the importance of instilling a sense of judgment and limitation on patients. Hill, in outlining his treatment approach, commented in a footnote that "it is essential . . . that the patient should be aware that he is observed . . . and aware also that the person who observes him is powerful enough to control him."[83] Thomas Wakely, surgeon, radical member of Parliament, and founder and editor of the influential medical journal the *Lancet,* strongly supported the work of Conolly while noting that Conolly's system was, in fact, forcing a different type of confinement than that of physical chains. In the pages of the *Lancet,* he recognized the inadequacy of the term "nonrestraint," which, he wrote, "is not literally correct, for when the system is most rigidly carried out, the patient is *confined* to the asylum, and in many cases to his room." Instead, Wakely suggested the "humane system," which recognized that modern restraint was a significant improvement over the past because "this confinement is not felt like fetters; it is less degrading, irritating and exasperating, than ligatures on the limbs. The restraint is little more severe than the voluntary confinement of servants to the house, or of workmen to their daily task." Like Conolly, Wakely supported improved conditions as an important aspect of therapy and cure. Wakely noted that in severe cases, particularly the "violent, raving maniac has, however, necessarily to submit to further restraint; the keepers arms are called into action, and have to supply the place of the straight waistcoat, straps and chains."[84]

Diamond's camera and the cameras of other asylum superintendents who followed his approach were equally a form of control and restraint, while simultaneously acting as a therapeutic technology. Always already an observational activity, physiognomy became a more powerful surveillance technique with the recording mechanism of the camera while at the same time, under Diamond's control, it became a way of extending compassion and dignity. Surveillance, in this context, was both a way of exerting control and a way of allowing a group of unseen people to become seen. Photographic physiognomy, like physiognomical labeling and diagnosis more generally applied, was a powerful and multivalent force laden with intention.

Diamond masterminded and designed his pictures for maximum sympathetic and communicative effect, using not just the images but the process by which they were taken to control the way others saw his patients and the way they saw themselves. For Conolly and Diamond, both active advocates of "nonrestraint," photographic physiognomy was a therapeutic breakthrough that allowed a form of mental restraint that released patients from the tyranny of the physical.[85] In consonance with physiognomic dictates, improvement in the condition of the body worked in tandem with improvements in the mind.

Sir Dr. John Charles Bucknill, mentioned earlier with respect to clothing and diagnosis, was one of Diamond and Conolly's most important professional supporters. The first editor of the *Asylum Journal of Mental Science,* founded in 1853 as the publishing organ of the Association of Medical Officers of Asylums and Hospitals for the Insane, Bucknill frequently endorsed the use of physiognomy by doctors in diagnosing mental illnesses, in addition to treating it. In 1858, he coauthored the first and most influential psychiatric textbook of the nineteenth century, titled *A Manual of Psychological Medicine,* the frontispiece of which contained seven lithographic copies of photos taken at the publicly funded Devon County Lunatic Asylum (Figure 5.9).[86] The caption read "Types of Insanity," and the appendix contained a detailed description of each case. Bucknill's coauthor, Dr. Daniel H. Tuke, in addition to being a descendant of the famous York Retreat founder William Tuke, was also the author of a prizewinning essay on the set topic of Improving the Condition of the Insane.[87]

Both Bucknill and Tuke followed the lead of Conolly in nonrestraint campaigns and Diamond in the use of physiognomy as a diagnostic device. Other practitioners emulated Diamond's more creative application of photography and employed it for therapeutic purposes. T. N. Brushfield, superintendent of the Surrey County Lunatic Asylum, and Sir William Charles Hood, medical superintendent of the famous Bethlem (or Bedlam) Asylum, wrote about the role of photographic portraiture in bringing about the cure of mental disorder. In an 1857 letter to the *Journal of the Photographic Society,* Brushfield admitted that he had not studied Diamond's photographs in depth and knew his work only at the level of "an ordinary newspaper article," but from his own experience, he still agreed with him that "patients are very much gratified at seeing their own portraits." He recounted an anecdote in which "a patient, who was formerly one of our most violent cases, begged for a portrait of herself, that she might send to her son, who was in Ireland, to show how much better she was."[88] Here Brushfield acknowledged that seeing really was believing by granting the son the ability to diagnose improvement from the evidence of a photograph. Similarly, the patient herself saw the photograph as a

Figure 5.9. John Charles Bucknill and Daniel Hack Tuke, frontispiece from *A Manual of Psychological Medicine: Containing the History, Nosology, Description, Statistics, Diagnosis, Pathology, and Treatment of Insanity; With an Appendix of Cases* (London: John Churchill, 1858). The most influential psychological textbook of the century, this book contained seven photographs illustrating the physiognomy of different patient types.

witness of her cure rather than an agent in it; Brushfield used photographs like Conolly rather than like Diamond.

The interest of Conolly, Diamond, and all these public asylum superintendents in photography was strongly linked to their commitment to improving the lives of the patients in their asylums. Photography provided a public face for the mad and rendered them as picturesque as the sanitized subjects of mid-Victorian slum photographs. Private asylum superintendents did not have the same public-relations or fund-raising concerns, and this led to schisms between the two groups in the new Association of Medical Officers of Asylums and Hospitals for the Insane. Diamond, in an 1852 letter to photographic innovator William Henry Fox Talbot, explained the hesitancy of private doctors to publish commentary on portraits of mental patients in the soon-to-be-established journal of the association. Diamond apologized that "I fear our proposed journal will not be brought to bear—The idea was that each medical officer should furnish a given quote." Getting quotes from doctors in private asylums proved challenging because "at present we do not act with that unanimity which would be desired. Having admitted the proprietors of private Asylums as members we find our ideas are different & we have different interests to support."[89]

Diamond's pictures and Conolly's commentary drew attention and appreciation from doctors, photographic critics, and viewers interested in photographic exhibitions. In so doing, they sanitized and rendered picturesque the profile of the nonrestrained mad for a wide audience, including those who controlled funding for public asylums. Diamond's pictures came in the wake of the turbulent 1840s, a decade of economic depression and recovery, the Irish potato famine, political turmoil with the overturning of the Corn Laws, and an assassination attempt on Prime Minister Sir Robert Peel in 1842. The assassin, Daniel McNaughton, was found to be suffering from a persecution complex and later lent his name to the laws detailing the definition of criminal insanity that emerged from his case.[90] In the wake of McNaughton's trial and in conjunction with the ongoing 1842 National Lunacy Inquiry came the 1845 Lunacy and County Asylums Act. This act stipulated that pauper lunatics should be sent to asylums, for which increased funding was made available.

Unlike his private asylum colleagues, Conolly was on a mission to publicize his patients and their environment. Well aware of the value of visual evidence, especially when paired with explanatory text, Conolly encouraged the use of illustrations to highlight the conditions in his publicly funded asylum. As the *Illustrated London News* commented in an 1848 caption beneath an illustration of the Twelfth Night Ball at Hanwell

(Figure 5.10), "The accompanying engraving presents a very interesting illustration of the non-restraint system pursued at Hanwell . . . Good humour and mirth prevailed during the entire evening, not a single circumstance occurring to mar the happiness which all appeared to enjoy."[91] The article praised the nonrestraint approach and used this image to underscore its benefits, both to the patients and to those who chose to look at them.

Conolly's support of photographic physiognomy was strongly connected to his interest in improving asylum conditions. His writings revealed a deep concern about poverty and the effects that it had on mental health and its corresponding physiognomic indicators. For example, he asked about one of his patients, "Walking feebly homeward, hungry, and faint, and assailed with offers of food and wine and money, what could poor girls so placed do but yield to temptation?"[92] To Conolly, proper conditions in the asylum were critical to treatment, given that it was often poor conditions that led to the patients' present illnesses.

Figure 5.10.   "Twelfth-Night Entertainments at the Hanwell Lunatic Asylum," *Illustrated London News,* 15 January 1848. Propaganda pieces such as these underscored the value of treating asylum patients without physical restraints. (Reprinted with permission from Mary Evans Picture Library.)

By demonstrating the potential for patient cure as he did in his commentary on Diamond's photos, Conolly effectively used the pictures to illustrate how improved conditions in asylums improved conditions in patients' mental health, and as evidence for that improvement. Photographic physiognomy was a means to represent disease categories that were not only mental but also circumstantial. For Conolly, one of the important roles of photography was to reveal the possibility of cure under the correct conditions of physical comfort. At the same time, the camera could easily document the effect that proper conditions had on the state of the patient. Conolly commented in a nonrestraint treatise in 1856 that "to be well clothed, to have a comfortable bed and sufficient good food every day may, of course, be considered as having peculiarly comforting effects on pauper patients, too long accustomed to scanty fare, and miserable lodging, and wretched clothing." For those potential patients, who "often come to the asylum half starved," the first step in their treatment was nourishment, because "good food is not infrequently of far more consequence to them than medicine of any kind."[93]

Like Diamond's photographs, Conolly's writings and analyses were embedded in concerns outside the strictly diagnostic; alongside his therapeutic hopes for photography, he was interested in underscoring the value of nonrestraint in the eyes of Victorians. To this end, he appealed to those eyes to remove much of the fear and revulsion they felt about asylums, and with that removal, he hoped, would come additional support and funding for these asylums. Diamond's images showed the possibility of cure and the importance of humane treatment in the pursuit thereof. None of these would be possible without public support.

In good conditions and in strictly choreographed settings, patients could be presented in a more attractive fashion; gone, or so claimed Victorian psychiatrists, was the expression of fear that Conolly asserted early nineteenth-century doctor and illustrator Sir Charles Bell noted in the faces of the "outrageous maniac" upon his visit to an asylum. Conolly wrote in response to Bell's writings that "in those times, the galleries and cells of asylums presented vivid expressions of malady to the artists: such as now will be looked for in vain." The artists were capturing the visual manifestations not just of disease but of conditions, because "it was not simple malady indeed which was generally depicted in the faces of the wretched people who then raved or moped in such places: but malady aggravated by mechanical coercion, or by neglect, or by positive cruelty."[94]

Conolly read the physiognomies of Diamond's subjects, like those of the patients of Bell's time, as representing not only their mental states and disease categories but also the ways in which they, as individuals, had been treated in the past. Consonant with those urban physiognomists whom I examined in Chapter 1, who believed of passers-by that their "social condition as their histories, [is] stamped on them as legibly as arms are painted on a carriage panel," Conolly read faces and photographs as biographies of the patients under Diamond's care.[95] Changing external conditions could change internal states of mind, which would have resulting effects on the appearance of the patients. These changes would not be merely aesthetic; the mental health of patients would improve under better conditions, thereby improving their physiognomies.

Early illustrators of the insane were reproducing the inhumane methods of treatment and the nature of the asylum environment in addition to the physiognomy of insanity. As a sketch and accompanying text from Alexander Morison's *Physiognomy of Mental Diseases* showed, "He is represented with the leather sleeves made use of in the Hanwell asylum" (Figure 5.11).[96] Conolly argued that *his* Hanwell provided a much more accurate picture of the true face of the mad. His asylum had nothing to fear from private objections and public outcry; he welcomed the photographer's camera to capture not only the face of insanity but also its surroundings.

By presenting pictures of relatively neat, ordered, and restraint-free patients in their textbook, Bucknill and Tuke calmed fears about the appearance and behavior of the mad, as well as reinforcing the sense that their improved condition was due in part to the more humane treatment that they received. Bucknill and Tuke recounted an anecdote in their textbook about the reactions of one surprised visitor to the calmness of the hospital and the patients: "We have seldom been more amused by the disappointment of a friend, than we were by that of an accomplished gentleman, who has now, for years, made it his business and his delight to read Shakspere [sic] to the English public." This friend came to the asylum seeking inspiration for his roles, but "after patiently examining the numerous inmates of the Devon Asylum, he pronounced his opinion that they were all 'stale, flat, and unprofitable.' Doubtless they were so in his point of view, for he said, 'Where is the poetry of madness? I see none of it—no flashing eye, no foam on the mouth. Why, your people are as sober and respectable as a vestry meeting!' "[97]

Rather than feeling attacked by their guest's complaints, Bucknill and his staff felt honored by the implications. "It was a great artistic disappointment; but, rather flattered than abashed, we admitted that, since the insane had been treated on rational and humane principles, they had ceased to offer the best and most constant examples of exaggerated passion."[98]

The accuracy of the photographic images presented in their textbook was of particular importance to Bucknill and Tuke's agenda of visually acquainting the public with their patients. As they wrote, the expectations

Figure 5.11. Man in Leather Gloves, from Alexander Morison, *The Physiognomy of Mental Diseases* (London: Longman and Co., 1843). This patient was restrained by leather sleeves and a type of straitjacket. (Courtesy of the Pennsylvania Hospital Historic Collections, Philadelphia.)

of this gentleman guest about the appearance of the mad were based on widely held misconceptions drawn from misinformed and overly eager artists and writers. These chroniclers were capturing not just the physiognomies but the environments of madness, which, although they were historically inextricable, Bucknill and Tuke, among others, were prying apart. "If we may trust the descriptions transmitted to us by dramatists, poets, and painters, the facial expression of insanity was much more intense in the olden times, than at the present day; and the idea entertained of a madman, by the public is more frequently taken from such descriptions than from personal observations."[99]

In lieu of these personal observations, the observations of the camera were the next-best thing and in some ways even better. Through photographs, especially when accompanied by explanatory language, viewers could see the true face of the mad. The distance provided by the camera and the mediation inherent in its mirror produced effects that were often obscured or ignored in person. The camera, rather than acting as a silent observer, was in fact as active as the eyes behind it, using its advantages to emphasize external physiognomic markers that would, according to Diamond, produce therapeutic change.

Hugh Welch Diamond's photographs, rather than acting as mechanically objective physiognomic reflections, were in fact highly manipulated and staged. Contrary to the predictions of the *Cornhill* and indeed Diamond himself, photography did not provide incontrovertible evidence for the scientific efficacy of physiognomy. This condition was far from crippling, however; it was precisely because of the mediated nature of the photographs that they were effective as therapeutic and rhetorical tools. Photography provided an important medium by which to call into being physiognomically and therapeutically meaningful signs, which Diamond used to help patients see themselves through his eyes. The mediation inherent in Diamond's photographs made them a far more effective mirror than a looking glass, which only reinforced the mental images already present in the minds of the mad.

In their written analyses, both Diamond and Conolly were reading far more than facial features; they concentrated on clothing and hair to highlight the potential for cure in comfortable conditions. Diamond and especially Conolly showed that given the right environment, deprived women could recover, both morally and mentally. The symbols in the images emphasized the conflation of moral and mental degradation, while the before-and-after sequences highlighted that these fallen women could indeed rise again and become re-covered.

Photography assisted Diamond and Conolly in the project of expanding the power of physiognomy by making use of the advantages of photography over the naked eye. In addition to providing mediated distance for the patients to view themselves, what photography could do, almost effortlessly, was capture and preserve clothing cues, especially as they changed over time. In so doing, Diamond's physiognomic photography contributed to and established conventions in the iconography of female insanity.

Clothing had long been an important social and character symbol; this trend developed dramatically in the nineteenth century as increased social mobility made distinctions all the more significant. Diamond and Conolly documented and expanded this trend by including clothing in the diagnostic framework. In the imperial discourse, especially in travel literature and later advertisements, nakedness or lack of Western clothing had been the mark of savagery; dressing up the natives marked the first stage of civilization. For example, the clothing of Man Friday was an important priority for Robinson Crusoe.[100] So too in England; as William Hogarth's *Rake's Progress* chronicled, one of the first stages of an improvement in social station was an improvement in clothing. In the same way, degradation in dress marked social and mental degradation. Asylum photography formalized the relationship between civilization and sartorial appropriateness, taking Hogarth's trajectory and showing how it could be reversed in the service of cure.

Dutch painter Gérard de Lairesse reflected on the power of clothing to change the way in which a subject was not only perceived but actually was: "I think, also, that the common and usual dress of a person is a great addition to likeness; for no sooner is the dress altered, but the look does the same and shews [sic] itself either more or less pleasing and agreeable; and thereby the person becomes more or less known."[101] Novelist and critic Edmund Duranty's 1856 article "Confession d'un peintre" underscored the importance of clothing in English society in particular: "This society seemed to me to express itself through differences in attire: people who wear smocks and aprons have ideas, feelings, and faces quite unlike those who wear frock coats."[102]

Photography changed the nature of the physiognomic subject from one immediately and instinctually assessed to one observed over time. The framing of the subject lay in the hands of the photographer, Hugh Welch Diamond, and his commentator, John Conolly. Rather than recording extant physiognomic cues, Diamond's camera often produced them and used them for therapeutic and rhetorical ends. Diamond's discussions of photographs focused on their therapeutic, diagnostic, and record-keeping potential. The different uses of his images spoke to different audiences, including exhibition viewers, fellow doctors, and, especially, his patients—the subjects of the photographs. Written language was far less important than the symbols contained in the pictures themselves. Conolly, on the other hand, was more interested in the role of photographs as document archives than as treatment technologies. For Conolly's audiences of medical professionals and the asylum-fearing public, language needed to accompany the photographs to provide the narration for which the images were illustrations.

Drawing on a long tradition of diagnostic physiognomy, Diamond combined the powerful technologies of photographic representation and scientific classification to communicate his personal vision as a universal one. In his skillful melding of art and science, Diamond included clothing and hair as important physiognomic signs and thereby predetermined the ways in which his viewers would read his images. Diamond both recorded and produced his vision through manipulation of the clothing and hair of his patients and subjects. In this way, Diamond's physiognomic photography captured and reproduced the metonymical as well as the physiognomic face of madness.

As a photographer, Diamond used clothing and iconographic symbols to maximum artistic effect. As a doctor, he used them to maximum rhetorical effect. As a therapist, he used them to maximum representational effect. In the end, all these effects amounted to the same thing: Diamond, with Conolly, used the camera to disseminate his eyes widely and to show the helpable and curable face. Diamond invited his various audiences to gawk at his patients and suggested that by looking at them, viewers could, in true physiognomic form, begin to know them. Through this process, Diamond widened the scope of physiognomically meaningful symbols by which to demarcate individual distinction. Conolly used these same images to explore identifying group features.

Diamond and Conolly's work laid the framework for the kind of looking proposed by eugenicist Francis Galton. As I discuss in the next chapter, Galton ushered photographic physiognomy into the anthropological discourse of large-group identification. Galton's photographic spoke to a type of restlessness with Diamond's diagnostic approach. Not content with portraits of individuals that might or might not contribute to a larger profile of type, Galton refocused Diamond's approach by pushing Conolly's interest in group representation. Although Galton's work continued to highlight the metonymical role of clothing and hair introduced by Diamond, it excised the principle that lay at the heart of the Diamond's project, namely, the use of photographic physiognomy for accurate self-identification. Rather, Galton used photographic physiognomy exclusively to identify and classify groups. He thereby turned individual photographic subjects into iterated objects that were but small components of a larger whole.

CHAPTER SIX

Diagnostic Physiognomy

From Phrenology to Fingerprints

P HYSIOGNOMY MADE ORDER out of an increasingly disordered world. An accessible form of classification and diagnosis, physiognomy resonated with the educated and noneducated alike as a way to make sense of others. Many scholars, following the lead of Michel Foucault, have chronicled the nineteenth-century drive to classify and codify everything from museum manuals to dream dictionaries, which in turn rendered people and their ideas legible, visible, and governable. Physiognomy offered the opportunity to organize humanity and diagnose their characters.

As a classification technology, physiognomy had numerous professional applications, in addition to its daily uses in private life. At the beginning of the century, doctors in particular were interested in the diagnostic opportunities offered by physiognomy. Phrenologists, too, saw the advantages of casting their project as *the* scientific physiognomy. The scientizing of physiognomy was itself a nineteenth-century project that recast a set of artistic, divinatory, religious, and etiquette ideas as a diagnostic and classificatory practice. The late eighteenth-century physiognomic revival offered a program of data collection and compilation that, in the hands of doctors, anatomists, and, later, anthropologists, became the basis of a system of diagnosis and judgment.[1] Problems of reproducibility dogged the development of physiognomy, but as of the middle of the century, photography provided physiognomic evidence that could be examined over time and widely disseminated. When physiognomy was combined with photography, it seemed poised to categorize people not only for medical diagnoses but also for biological and anthropological research across the British Empire.

But what or who, specifically, was being represented in the photographic record? Specificity, it turned out, was not the point. Rather than describing specific individuals, photography and photographic physiognomy captured the character of the masses in a new kind of generalized group diagnosis. Around the middle of the nineteenth century, when photography advanced to the point of being physiognomically useful, the discourse about physiognomy itself shifted. In conjunction with developing Victorian notions of nationhood and class, physiognomy became anonymous; it took the individual out of the equation. Although the nation, defined by Michael Lind as "a concrete historical community defined by a common language, common folk ways, and common vernacular culture," was one kind of group, there were specific classificatory subsets, including, as I have discussed, the Irish, the Jews, and the insane.[2] The poor were perhaps the most massed, defined not only without subjectivity and individuality but often, as Anthony S. Wohl has shown, without humanity.[3]

The classificatory power of physiognomy was often harnessed implicitly rather than explicitly. Many did not accept the scientific value of physiognomy, but because of its ubiquity, they could not avoid engaging with its principles and language, if only to reject its claims. Charles Darwin, for example, considered physiognomy very carefully as a potential source of evidence for his writings on expression and emotion. For anthropologists such as Sir Francis Galton, physiognomy was an ideal way to explore what separated one group of people from another.

I will not add much to the extensive literature about eugenics and social Darwinism.[4] Instead, I want to use Galton's work to highlight one of the processes that this book has been tracing, specifically, how Victorians came to think about group character. Through this process, the individual was not entirely erased but was reduced in significance as a meaningful category. Physiognomy, initially a way to determine something about someone specific, became a way to talk in generalities by tying facial features to group features and making communities in England and from across the empire visible and identifiable. As a group diagnostic, physiognomy did important work in importing empire and giving meaning and coherence to a once-nuanced and fragmented amalgamation of individuals. What was lost was precisely that nuance and individuality.

But how did the English get there? When did the individual cease to matter in the search for classification and legibility of human types? Scholars such as E. P. Thompson and Linda Colley have written now-classic works outlining the process by which Georgians and Victorians thought of themselves as part of larger wholes.[5] Peter Mandler has pointed out that the notion of a British "subject" became widespread by the 1880s.[6] Some of the factors that contributed to this process are very straightforward—urbanization and increased circulation of visual images and media generally—but others, as Thompson and Colley chronicled, work in more subtle and pervasive ways, including war, religion, and class stratification. What they did not address in their magisterial works is what, in the face of these coherent groups, happened to the individual. How did people think of their own selves while they were connecting to others as part of a larger whole? What role did technologies of identification play in representations of the specific and the general self?

In this chapter, I argue for a more personal approach to the minimalization of the self starting from the mid-1860s. Like all the processes I have outlined in this book, the transition to grouping occurred across the intellectual and social spectrum. The motivations for various people involved might have differed greatly, but the result was the same—the face, initially a diagnostic of the individual, became a description of the masses. As highlighted by writers like Lady Elizabeth Rigby Eastlake and Galton and his disciples, the notion of self was relevant only insofar as it represented deviation from the norm.

As we have seen, by the middle of the nineteenth century, physiognomy had transitioned from a way of learning and communicating about the specific to a way of understanding and predicting the general. Racial, religious, and social differences were rendered visually identifiable by imagined physiognomies, but these cues often broke down, and this breakdown forced new forms of diagnosis and differentiation. Physiognomy shows that the endpoint of classification and the building of British identity were not just the production of a unified nation and empire but a shift in emphasis away from the individual. In response, as the century reached its close, the individual reemerged in new manifestations inspired by physiognomic understandings. The project of using external features to identify internal traits of specific people had fractured into the radical exteriority of fingerprinting and the radical interiority of psychoanalysis. Physiognomy provided the conditions of possibility for both.

Phrenology: Too Close for Comfort

Physiognomy made legible the invisible human interior. By penetrating this mystery, the nature of human behavior possibly could be solved. One of the great attractions of physiognomy was this legibility and the fact that it drew on the visual senses to make meaning. Sight was widely accessible, and the act of seeing required few, if any, complicated systems and guidelines. James V. Werner has pointed out that the first half of the nine-

teenth century was filled with calls by writers for science to be made accessible to the public. These demands were enabled by the accompanying
claim that every individual could engage with science, and that each,
knowingly or unknowingly, had the tools to do so.[7] Physiognomy satisfied two developing demands of the early nineteenth century: it created
order, and it did so in a way that invited widespread participation.

The accessibility of physiognomy, coupled with its power to organize,
answers one of the major questions that physiognomy presents to the
historical eye, namely, why there was a drive to scientize physiognomy.
Physiognomy had happily functioned for generations in the realms of art,
etiquette, divination, and religion.[8] In the early nineteenth century, there
was a strong effort among practitioners to place physiognomy in the scientific realm. This drive sparked numerous debates about the designation
of physiognomy as either an art or a science.[9] This designation problem,
which seemed to have great urgency at the beginning of the nineteenth
century, was soon overlooked. Without any real resolution of the question, physiognomy flourished in a number of media and entertainment
realms, as well as offering guidelines for interpersonal interaction. I have
been careful not to place the scientific efficacy of physiognomy at issue in
the way in which this book is framed.[10] In fact, I have sought to show
how physiognomy developed and did important work in the nineteenth
century independent of intellectual approbation. Nevertheless, there were
those for whom the status of physiognomy was a pressing problem that
grew as another practice began to encroach.

Phrenology, the practice of correlating the strengths of various mental
faculties with the size of their representative bumps on the skull, emerged,
according to its advocates, from physiognomy.[11] Phrenological writers
argued that phrenology was the elusive key to scientizing physiognomy.[12]
With a clear biological mechanism and a discrete set of categories by
which every person could be judged, phrenology was even more ordered
than the order-inducing physiognomy. Physiognomy, the story goes, was
eclipsed in the academy by phrenology, around which the marks of disci-
plinary status soon accumulated. Unlike physiognomy, there were phrenological journals. Societies were devoted to its teaching and research.[13]
As phrenology grew up, it grew over physiognomy, the traces of which
could be found in various practical applications and media representations that were artifacts of shared culture rather than intellectual rigor.[14]

Texts abounded with names like *Physiognomy and Craniology; or, A
Manual of Phrenology;* although these works apparently dealt with physiognomy, they focused almost entirely on the skull and its faculties.[15] According to these books and the historiography around them, physiognomy

provided the basis for phrenology, a more exact and superior scientific system that was less accessible, more expert, and therefore more valuable.[16] Physician and minister Joachim Zender, for example, claimed that "physiognomy is the necessary concomitant of craniology," while prolific phrenology writer R. B. D. Wells wrote in 1843 that "physiognomy is built on phrenology and physiognomy."[17]

The links to physiognomy posited by the phrenologists were not far fetched; both approaches strove to make the invisible internal human visible through physical and material means.[18] Both linked the complicated nuances of behavior to corporeal markings that could be accessed and evaluated. Most important, both strongly empowered readers to make judgments and draw conclusions about those they read.

Physiognomists fought valiantly to distinguish their practice from the encroaching and more commercially successful and intellectually respected cranial counterpart.[19] Lecturer on anatomy and physiology at the University of Edinburgh and physiognomic writer Alexander Walker devoted many pages of his 1834 monograph to "the refutation of phrenology," which he called "an erroneous doctrine."[20] He contended that "with a little knowledge of the brain, of which Gall and Spurzheim were miserably destitute, it is easy to show the causes of the blunders committed by these craniologists."[21] With frequent reference to physiology and neurology, he then outlined the ways in which craniologists had "egregiously erred."[22] Literary critic and essayist William Hazlitt agreed with Walker on the superiority of physiognomy over phrenology and commented in his essay debunking phrenology that "it appears to me that the truth of physiognomy (if we allow it) overturns the science of craniology."[23] Likewise, pocket physiognomic texts such as the humorous 1848 *Nasology; or, Hints towards a Classification of Noses* staunchly distinguished between physiognomy and phrenology, "utterly repudiat[ing] the doctrine of the phrenologists."[24]

A less sophisticated preference for physiognomy, represented by the system innovated by Johann Caspar Lavater, over the phrenology of Gall, was expressed in an 1828 article in the cheap *Mirror of Literature, Amusement and Instruction,* a sixteen-page, two-penny weekly geared toward the respectable lower-middle classes. The most reasonably priced of its type, this periodical sometimes reached sales of over 80,000 copies an edition.[25] In this article, the physiognomy of a rather unhappy young man was discussed, and the writer concluded that "if that lank-and-leather jawed gentleman . . . do[es] not commit suicide before September,– Lavater must have been as great a goose as Gall."[26] It is notable that the article assumed not only universal knowledge of these thinkers but also that there was consensus about the goosehood of Gall and the legitimacy of Lavater.

At stake for the physiognomists was not just the independence of physiognomy as a set of ideas but also its existence. There were many real distinctions between the two systems, but they also had a great deal in common. The underlying similarities could have drawn physiognomy toward, rather than away from, phrenology. However, it was precisely because physiognomy was so similar to phrenology that it had to insist on its differences. Unlike physiology and anatomy, and, later, biology and anthropology, with which physiognomy was frequently aligned in order to strengthen and add depth to physiognomic principles, phrenology threatened to obscure it entirely.[27]

Mario Biagioli has argued that the process of distinguishing between two intellectually similar ideas can be seen as an evolutionary struggle.[28] In order to carve out independent space for itself, an idea should seem to be as different as possible from those with which it shares an intellectual environment. This differentiation of space is precisely what physiognomists were attempting to achieve with respect to phrenology, and exactly what phrenologists were trying to prevent. In pointedly separating their work from that of phrenologists, physiognomic writers were engaging in what Biagioli called "intellectual sterility," refusing to inbreed with other ideas in order to ensure the survival of their own.[29] Of course, this sterility was selective; physiognomy could safely incorporate strengths of other intellectual ideas that were distinct enough from physiognomic principles to allow for fruitful interbreeding rather than engulfment. Likewise, other fields, including anatomy, physiology, medicine, and biology, could safely draw on the diagnostic advantages physiognomy had to offer to bolster their own endeavors.

Physiognomists need not have tried quite so hard. By the end of the nineteenth century, phrenology faded from the classification conversation.[30] What phrenology lacked, ultimately, was visual legibility. Phrenological sittings required two people to interact closely through touch. Less an act of reading than physiognomy, phrenology demanded expertise, interaction, hapticity, and a not-inconsiderable amount of time on the part of both the subject and the reader. Although phrenology flourished and even eclipsed physiognomy in the eyes of the fluctuating early nineteenth-century scientific establishment, physiognomy lasted far longer. This longevity was partly due to the accessibility of physiognomy and also, largely, the lack of need for consent and interaction. Physiognomy was simply not relational in the same way as phrenology. While phrenology was, in essence, a self-improvement tool to increase the relative size of one's bumps and their associated traits, physiognomy was hardly that reflexive.[31] Rare was the person who executed elaborate physiognomic readings on himself or herself, or on others with their consent or even knowledge.[32]

Above all, the endurance of physiognomy was due to its flexibility. Physiognomy was able to read what people wanted to understand in the context of the urban experience. When early Victorians were interested in individuals, physiognomy acted as a diagnostic for individuals. When they were interested in groups, physiognomy was adapted accordingly.

Doctors and Diagnosis

While phrenology was, at heart, a deeply individualistic descriptor, physiognomy developed into a diagnostic for group characteristics. Phrenology, with its more rigid framework, was not as easily adaptable, both on its own and as a companion for other scientific pursuits. The flexibility of physiognomy made it a powerful tool for a wide range of social pursuits and scientific and intellectual endeavors. Among the first professional communities to realize the diagnostic potential of physiognomy were those ministering to the mad; for them, diagnosis at a distance was often a physical necessity.[33]

In addition to the practical advantages that physiognomy offered to asylum doctors, insane patients presented as ideal candidates for physiognomic analysis. One of the major objections to physiognomy that Lavater and later writers confronted was "the universality, and excess of dissimulation among mankind" that rendered physiognomic results false in the face of self-conscious manipulation.[34] Through at least the end of the nineteenth century, doctors understood the mad to be incapable of physiognomic faking or, indeed, manipulation of any kind.[35] Supporting the notion of the mad as transparent, English "student of physick" Thomas Tryon wrote in 1680 that "when men are so divested of their *Rational Faculties,* then they appear naked, having no *Covering, Vail* [sic], or *Figg-leaves* [sic] before them, to hide themselves in, and therefore they no longer remain under a Mask or Disguise but appear even as they are, which is very rare to be known in any that retain their *Senses* and *Reason;* for those two serve to cover and hide the Conceptions, Thoughts, and Imaginations."[36]

For nineteenth-century asylum doctors, themselves struggling for professional recognition among the medical community, physiognomy was a useful and possibly reproducible diagnostic technology. By insisting on the scientific status of physiognomy, doctors of the mad, including, as we have seen, Hugh Welch Diamond and John Conolly, were able to draw on its potential as a telling method of observation. It was in part due to the wide acceptance of physiognomy as efficacious that it proved a useful tool for asylum and, later, other physicians. In 1806, the eminent physician Sir Charles Bell wrote a well-received text about facial expressions of the mentally ill.[37] Following the success of Bell's work, French physician J. É. D. Esquirol produced sketches of the mad in the Salpêtrière asylum that found a wide audience in England in the *Dictionnaire des sciences médicales,* reprinted in his *Mental Maladies: A Treatise on Insanity.*[38] Doctors used physiognomy to reassert the value of visual diagnostic skills in the wake of rising challenges to tacit knowledge in favor of classification and standardization.[39]

Diamond and Conolly were among the first to merge photography and physiognomy in a diagnostic context. In their work, they were constantly balancing individual identification with group generalizations in their attempts to produce a classification system for mental illness. In so doing, they widened the scope of physiognomically meaningful signs to include sartorial symbols and styles of self-presentation. Their efforts were a microcosm of the larger trajectory of physiognomic thought, which moved from describing specific people to categorizing entire types.

In the wake of Diamond and Conolly's negotiation of the general and the specific, eugenic pioneer Sir Francis Galton forced its rupture. Galton ushered photographic physiognomy into the anthropological discourse of large-group identification. For him, portraits of individuals, like those done by Diamond, produced no meaningful classificatory evidence about the nature of humanity. Such studies, which "select individuals who are judged to be representative of the prevalent type," were "not trustworthy, because the judgment itself is fallacious. It is swayed by exceptional and grotesque features more than by ordinary ones, and the portraits supposed to be typical are more likely to be caricatures."[40] Galton was aided in his classificatory quest by the nature of photography and the ways in which it was understood. While Diamond used photographs to great effect to highlight specificity, Galton exploited photographic exposure to capture the elusive average, the general group type.

Diamond was, of course, not the first to think about photography in conjunction with physiognomy. The changes in physiognomy wrought by the photographic experience were highlighted by two anonymous articles written by artist and critic Lady Elizabeth Eastlake for the prestigious literary criticism magazine the *Quarterly Review.* The first of these articles, an 1851–1852 lengthy and in-depth analysis of the status of physiognomy and the various published monographs on the subject, argued that the great power of physiognomy lay in its unique ability to distinguish individuals from the anonymous urban mass: "How else, in the similarity of age, size, dress, and habits in thousands of individuals, should one man convince another of what he knows so well—namely, that he is himself . . . To lift up a countenance to the world, secure of its identity, is the rightful inheritance of man—and proud of its identity, that of a good man."[41]

However, Eastlake continued, the anonymity of the streets extended to the faces of its inhabitants, rendering most people inappropriate subjects for passing physiognomic analysis because with "regards [to] the exercise of the physiognomical faculty, it is undeniable that the majority of mankind have, at first sight, 'no characters at all.' Two-thirds of those faces which pass us in the street tell us nothing of their mission. The life is not in them, the wires are not at work—they show their features, but nothing more."[42]

In the absence of lengthy encounters, Eastlake argued, physiognomy was useless for most fleeting city glimpses of the common mass of humanity. Photography, in theory, provided the technology to mimic long-term interaction, which was otherwise impossible in the urban experience. As Eastlake chronicled, unfortunately for the physiognomic analysis of individuals, the results of photographic physiognomy served to highlight only the characteristics of groups, whose distinguishing features were dulled and blurred. The eye of the camera, to Eastlake, unearthed only that which was coarse, raw, and general, shared largely by the lower classes. For example, "If the eye be blue, it turns out as colourless as water; if the hair be golden or red, it looks as if it had been dyed, if very glossy it is cut up into lines of light as big as ropes." Some features, those that were widespread among certain groups, lent themselves more to photographic reproduction, because "rougher skin, less glossy hair, Crimean moustaches and beard overshadowing the white under lip, and deeper lines, are all so much in favour of a picturesque result."[43]

Eastlake's photographic physiognomy eradicated the individual, in direct contrast to earlier analyses of specific faces. Like Diamond, Eastlake understood photography to have the power to classify and confer categories of meaning. Because of the shortcomings of photography to highlight individuality, Eastlake of necessity turned to clues other than the face from which to make physiognomic deductions.[44] Photography excelled in the capture of these symbols, but at the cost of artistry and aesthetic value.

In her writing, Eastlake exhorted readers to "examine a little more closely those advances which photography owes to science—we mean in an artistic sense." To do so, "We turn to the portraits, our *premiers amours* now taken under every appliance of facility both for sitter and operator." These photographic portraits excelled at highlighting specificity because "far greater detail and precision accordingly appear. Every button is seen—piles of stratified flounces in most accurate drawing are there,—what was at first only suggestion is now all careful making out,—but the likeness to Rembrandt and Reynolds is gone!" Eastlake explained that in direct contrast to the sartorial focus, the face remained incomplete, which led to this sad loss of artistic merit: "There is no mystery in this. The first principle in art is that the most important part of a picture should be best done. Here, on the contrary, while the dress has been rendered worthy of a fashion-book, the face has remained, if not so unfinished as before, yet more unfinished in proportion to the rest."[45]

Eastlake challenged the artistic aspirations of photography, an endeavor in which both she and her husband, the first president of the Royal Photographic Society, were deeply engaged. In this article, she echoed her earlier sentiments about the difficulty of reading character in many faces, a problem compounded by the limitations of photography. Rather than facilitating the necessary time for the face to reveal its secrets, the medium of photography highlighted rough features, marring and eliminating refined beauty in favor of glaring character. Eastlake argued that photography emphasized only gross and extreme character and revealed the characteristic features of the poor or coarse. It was the less desirable deviants—the mad and the (poor) bad—who could be easily analyzed as members of the group with which they shared characteristic, and sometimes inhuman, features.[46]

The struggle between individual and group physiognomic identification was eloquently expressed in Charlotte Brontë's 1853 novel *Villette*. Lucy Snowe, the decidedly unglamorous heroine, was obsessed with physiognomic and phrenological analyses of those she encountered, despite her own commitment to remaining unnoticed.[47] This plot backfired, of course, because Lucy was visible through her very plainness among the young beauties and fashionable teachers. It was her deviance and lack of adherence to type that marked her as remarkable and, ultimately, uniquely lovable. Her lover, M. Paul, penetrated the costume of her clothing, saying, "Other people in this house see you pass, and think that a colourless shadow has gone by. As for me, I scrutinized your face once, and it sufficed."[48]

M. Paul, rather than reading the clothing symbols that marked her membership in the community of the dull, relied on his instinct to read the signs inherent in her face. Just as the photograph could selectively portray group characteristics, so too could Lucy's peers see only those external symbols that she deliberately chose. It was up to M. Paul to use physiognomy to penetrate the individuality written on Lucy's face to discern her true nature. It was precisely this individuality that Eastlake's photographs were unable to portray. Diamond, however, skillfully combined both clothing and facial cues to harmonize them into one predetermined message.

Lucy, well aware of the physiognomic power of clothing for most observers, was careful about her plain style and fashion choices. She was equally cognizant of the ways in which clothing acted as more than costume, coming to represent the person and even becoming the person. She refused to don a man's clothes during her performance in a school play; although she said of the costume pieces that "I don't object to some of them," she resolutely maintained, "I won't have them all." Rather, she solved the demand for "something . . . to announce you as of the nobler sex" through the resolute of her daily, rather than her stage, costume: "Retaining my women's garb without the slightest retrenchment, I merely assumed in addition, a little vest, a collar, and a cravat, and a paletot of small dimensions."[49] It was precisely because Lucy's femininity and "women's garb" were so repressed and understated that she most feared to lose them. With her already shallow grasp on her sexuality, Lucy could not risk it being overtaken by the costume that would become her.

Physiognomic metonymy extended from the faces of the poor to their very smell. Poverty and those who inhabited it were a stinking, indecipherable mass. As Alain Corbin has shown, the presentation of poverty as perceptually problematic was essential to the categorization of the poor as inferior.[50] Physiognomic thinking created the conditions of possibility for the olfactorization of the poor, which, in turn, eliminated their existence as visual beings. According to Chris Otter, smell alone denoted poverty and rendered physiognomic identification irrelevant.[51] Although I agree with Otter that smell overtook sight in the case of poverty, in my formulation, smell was itself a kind of collective Victorian physiognomy that functioned only because individual traces merged in a powerful group effect.

Photographs of individual faces may in fact have been difficult to recognize. Journalist and social commentator Henry Mayhew recounted an anecdote about his visit to a photographer's studio. The photographer boasted about his ability to pawn off leftover pictures on the wrong customers, a trick, he claimed, that was aided by people's inability to identify themselves: "The fact is, people don't know their own faces . . . Directly they see a pair of eyes and a nose, they fancy they are their own."[52]

Kate Flint attributed this lack of recognition to the novelty of the notion that the self could be fixed and objectified.[53] Although the static form of photographs was certainly part of the challenge in making sense of faces, an equal challenge was presented by the isolated nature of the images. Without context, the self was obscured, particularly in the second half of the nineteenth century. Equally, many Victorians did not think of themselves in isolation and self-identified only as part of a larger whole. This made individual portraits confusing and, as in this exaggerated claim, illegible.

The power of photography to unearth and expose the extremes of the human condition en masse was articulated in an 1867 article in the *Living Age,* an American magazine consisting largely of reprints of English and American newspaper and journal articles. The critic argued that "a good photograph often possesses a subtlety of resemblance which brings out characteristics of race or mental capacity scarcely seen in the original, but which undoubtedly exist."[54] Photography not only had the power to capture features not immediately discernible but also called into being their visual manifestation. To this critic, photography was a creative process that brought to the surface a hidden physiognomic truth. In this way, the work of the photographer converged with that of the painters, actors, and caricaturists that I have examined, all of whom were engaged in the physiognomic possibility of creation by mapping types onto the face.

Rather than representing the culmination of nineteenth-century physiognomic discourse, photography was part of its continual growth and development. As the needs of its users changed, physiognomy and the language that accompanied it adapted. In his photographs of the physiognomy of mental illness, Diamond highlighted both individual and group traits in the service of his humanitarian, diagnostic, and therapeutic goals. Later practitioners, most notably Sir Francis Galton, abandoned Diamond's careful negotiation and used photographic physiognomy only to unearth group traits, to which end Galton innovated new technologies. With this shift toward general identification, physiognomy converged with the anthropological and ethnographic discourse. As Joanna C. Scherer has argued, the photograph was and remains one of the primary documents from which anthropological data were gathered at the end of the nineteenth century.[55] In its copious use of observation to identify somatic and sartorial commonalities among groups, this discourse rested on the central physiognomic precept that looking at people, or even at their photographic representations, was a way to know them.[56] Physiognomy invited observers to gawk. Anthropology required it.

As the nineteenth century progressed, numerous other professional communities borrowed from physiognomic language and ideas to further their own classificatory and diagnostic projects. These included biologists and anthropologists, such as Sir Francis Galton and, perhaps unwillingly, Charles Darwin. Darwin's *Descent of Man* (1871) was, as Jonathan Smith has shown, an extended argument with Sir Charles Bell's natural theological approach to expression.[57] Darwin engaged more explicitly with physiognomy and expression in *The Expression of the Emotions in Man and Animals* (1872). Although Darwin dismissed physiognomic analysis, Smith has argued that Darwin's work was situated in the visual tradition established by physiognomy, and that he often borrowed from physiognomic conventions.[58] It was, however, Darwin's cousin Francis Galton who found an enduring home for physiognomy for the twentieth century and beyond.

Charles Darwin and the So-Called Science

Although Charles Darwin is usually situated historiographically as a naturalist or general science intellectual, his later work tended strongly toward the anthropological or, more specifically, the anthropology of biology. In both *The Descent of Man* and *The Expression of the Emotions in Man and Animals,* Darwin engaged with the social, racial, and even religious consequences of his claims and created classification schemes across cultures and societies and, more subtly, across species. In these endeavors, Darwin drew heavily on photographic evidence and incorporated the visual conventions of physiognomy even as he repudiated their efficacy.

With the exception of a brief anecdote about Darwin's nose in Chapter 1 and a discussion about evolution in Chapter 4, I have come amazingly far in a book about Victorian science without engaging seriously with the person who dominates the Victorian history of science. For some, this omission has, I am sure, been truly glaring. Others may appreciate the attempt to situate Darwin in his appropriate Victorian place—important, but not always central, not all the time.[59] But the time has come.

It is not a stretch to bring Darwin into the physiognomy story. Darwin really did write and think about physiognomy, if only to reject it. As Jonathan Smith has chronicled in detail, Darwin approached physiognomy with an open mind, first reading Lavater in 1838 and taking copious notes found in his records on expression. Darwin pondered the possibility that physiognomy might provide some evidence for inheritance and asked, "Is there—anything in these absurd ideas.—do they indicate mind & body retrograding to ancestral type of consciousness."[60] In his correspondence with both Sir Charles Lyell and Asa Gray, Darwin returned repeatedly to the question of the design of facial features and revealed some lingering curiosity about the state of his much-analyzed nose.[61] In an 1861 letter to Lyell, Darwin asked if he would "honestly tell me (& I should really be much obliged) whether you believe that the shape of my nose was 'ordained & guided by an intelligent cause?' "[62] Darwin recounted this tongue-in-check question to Gray in subsequent letters, demonstrating his doubt about both divine design and physiognomy.[63] While writing *The Expression of the Emotions,* Darwin returned to these questions and ultimately maintained his original skeptical assessment of physiognomy. He commented in the introduction to his first edition that "he who thinks that remarks of this [physiognomic] kind throw any light on the meaning or origin of the different expressions, takes a very different view of the subject to what I do."[64]

Darwin's rejection of "the so-called science of physiognomy" was not for lack of trying to understand it.[65] In addition to his careful reading of Lavater and those who came before him, specifically Giambattista della Porta and Charles Le Brun, in the compilation of Jacques Louis Moreau, Darwin maintained a long-term collaboration with asylum doctor Sir James Crichton-Browne.[66] Darwin's reliance on the expertise of Crichton-Browne was a reflection of the belief chronicled earlier in the chapter that the uncontrolled faces of the insane were uniquely suited to physiognomic analyses.[67] Despite this collaboration, Darwin used only one of Browne's photographs in *The Expression of the Emotions,* to illustrate "erection of the hair in man and animals."[68] Crichton-Browne's physiognomic photography of his patients did not prove useful to Darwin's theories, which failed to locate any kind of taxonomy of species of madness.[69] Throughout his collaboration with Crichton-Browne, Darwin examined physiognomy critically and thoughtfully, and his rejection of these principles was considered and researched.[70] It was also, as Rosemary Jann pointed out, incomplete.[71]

Although Darwin distanced himself from physiognomy, in part to avoid the taint of illegitimacy that accompanied it, he knowingly or unknowingly mimicked much of the language familiar to readers of physiognomic texts. Like many physicians, physiologists, anatomists, and even phrenologists and astrologers, Darwin recognized the advantages of subtly aligning himself with a set of ideas that were easily accepted and understood. The merest hint of physiognomy was not enough to condemn Darwin as unscientific but certainly helped in the absorption of his ideas of human-animal comparisons. Such comparisons, like many of Darwin's writings, threatened the supremacy of human beings in the hierarchy of life. When read through physiognomy, a practice long accustomed to cross-species comparisons, Darwin's writings could reinforce a teleological conception of development in which humans were predictably superior to the animals they resembled.[72] Although this was only a very minor part of the application of physiognomy, for some of Darwin's readers, it was a soothing one.

Some reviewers, of course, got it wrong, casting Darwin as a physiognomist for better or for worse. Both the *Journal of the Anthropological Institute* and the *Athenaeum* tied Darwin to Lavater and in some cases gave Lavater the intellectual advantage.[73] Although Darwin may have tried to put distance between his project of human-animal classification and that of the physiognomists, the links, both visual and literary, were powerful.

Despite these connections, however, Darwin's writings were unconcerned with the nature and identification of the individual. Although his evolutionary ideas created hierarchy and classificatory order in a way for which physiognomists were always striving, Darwin's detailed historical mapping complicated the understanding of humanity at that moment. Like Diamond, Darwin had to confront the slippage between making order on a small scale and setting up macro systems, and applying those systems to any given individual. In *The Expression of the Emotions*, Darwin provided a new kind of legibility for the face that connected it to other faces and other kinds of faces in other places and at other times. On the basis of his extensive questionnaires and research efforts, Darwin concluded that "the same state of mind is expressed throughout the world with remarkable uniformity."[74] When Darwin was confronted with a given expression, he could connect it to internal emotions cross-culturally and even across species. He could explain what a person was feeling at the time the emotion was captured photographically. What he could not do was tie that emotion to a particular person's experiences or explain why it was expressed at that moment. From Darwin's perspective, there was no problem: he did not want to make those connections. But in so (not) doing, he was applying physiognomic language and slowly taking the person out of the picture.

Darwin's use of photography as his medium of choice was part of the nineteenth-century process of generalization of individuals to types.[75] As we have seen, photography highlighted the mass average rather than the individual unique, especially as the century progressed. Ironically, given the personal offense many people took at his work, Darwin was not particularly interested in specific individuals. In this, he was joined by, and indeed the inspiration for, his younger cousin Francis Galton.

Framing Francis Galton

The connection between photography and physiognomy varied depending on the photographer and the viewer. It also depended on the kind of photography being done. Diamond, for example, managed to harness quite well the power of the photographer to aid his physiognomic and artistic goals. Despite the poor quality of the lithographic reproductions of Diamond's work, Conolly effectively explicated and expanded on Diamond's work for a large medical audience.[76] Diamond and Conolly used photography to continue a project of medical physiognomic classification dating back at least to the beginning of the nineteenth century. Lady Elizabeth Eastlake inhabited a different space, in which classification— and therefore physiognomic classification—told the story of types of people rather than individuals. Sir Francis Galton shared Eastlake's inclination to consider communities as classificatory fodder. In all aspects of his statistical analysis, Galton was deeply uninterested in specifics. He cared about exceptions only insofar as they could educate him about the nature of the average.

Like his cousin Charles Darwin, Galton had early exposure to practices of human classification based on external physical manifestations.[77] During a bout of the depression that plagued him throughout his life, the twenty-seven-year-old Galton consulted a phrenologist in April 1849.[78] His choice of an advisor may have been motivated by an experience he had as a child at King Edward's School. Upon being examined by a phrenologist affiliated with the University of Cambridge, Galton and his parents were told that this "boy has the largest organ of causality I ever saw in any head but one, and that is the bust of Dr. Erasmus Darwin."[79] Supposedly unaware that Galton was Erasmus Darwin's grandson, this phrenologist came across as prophetic in his predictions. Dejected by his lack of academic success, Galton was likely eager for this kind of positive encouragement.

The results of that reading seemingly inspired Galton to embark on an African exploration in 1850. Comforted by the report claiming that his failure to meet academic expectations was caused not by lack of effort or will but rather by lack of natural endowment, Galton gave himself permission to maximize the other traits that he had in abundance, including curiosity and creativity. Raymond Fancher has argued that it was these early experiences that strengthened Galton's commitment to the idea of innate abilities, which in turn led to his attempts to systemize hereditary intelligence and emphasize the importance of inheritance.[80] Even before he applied the principles of physiognomy to his statistical work, young Galton imbibed the physiognomic language of his day, referring to his face as his "phiz" in a letter home from university on 3 November 1840.[81]

Following his disappointing years at Cambridge, Galton embarked on a series of explorations and drew from his experiences abroad and at home to publish extensively on travel, hereditarianism, statistics, and genius. In 1878, Galton proposed his own photographic-physiognomic synthesis in the very particular form of composite photography. In radical opposition to Diamond's approach, Galton sought to capture the essential identifying features of a classificatory type by exposing many instantiations of that type on the same photographic plate. Not content with choosing generic individuals as representative samples, Galton shifted Diamond's project both in theoretical approach and in mechanism and deployed a highly specific and highly technical photographic mode.[82] He pushed the statistical implications of Eastlake's claims that photography unearthed a common coarseness of feature among those of the same group. In so doing, Galton discarded the identification of individuals and completed the gradual shift that physiognomy had been undergoing from midcentury.

In Galton's composites, each subject was photographed for an equal fraction of time, which ensured that only common features would appear in the image. Those features that were idiosyncratic and unshared would be underexposed and thus unseen. Galton claimed to be capturing the ultimate physiognomic average and, correspondingly, the degree to which each individual did not adhere to the general case. Of this project, Galton wrote that "composite pictures are . . . real generalizations, because they include the whole of the material under consideration. The blur of their outlines, which is never great in truly generic composites, except in unimportant details, measures the tendency of individuals to deviate from the central type."[83]

Galton published a series of his composite studies of Jewish boys in the *Photographic News* in April 1885.[84] Statistician and Galton disciple Karl Pearson wrote admiringly about these studies that "we all know the Jewish boy, and Galton's portraiture brings him before us in a way that only a great work of art could equal—scarcely excel, for the artist would idealise from *one* model."[85] Galton actually used multiple models to produce one nameless image that encapsulated all those young men into the one definitive Jewish boy. Namelessness was a research principle for Galton, who did not want to attach any unequalizing depth or personality to a given subject. Upon examining pictures provided by Director-General of Prisons Sir Edmund Du Cane in 1877, Galton requested that the pictures be presented in three groups according to crime, and that all names be removed.[86] By removing names, Galton in many ways removed the humanity and subjectivity from those he studied. Mirroring the process of objectification that I outlined in Chapter 1, Galton's physiognomic analyses exerted power over the powerless by removing the identities of his research material.

As Alan Sekula has pointed out, Galton disregarded those features that provided the evidence for deviation from type.[87] Galton shared with Eastlake the belief that it was the coarse features, those easily captured on film, that defined character. Composite photography abandoned the attempt to mediate between the demands of specificity and generality by finding the former uninteresting. Galton granted no significance at all to the physiognomic signs of individuality, dismissing them as "unimportant details."

Galton's various intellectual efforts—statistical analysis, composite photography, anthropological exploration, biological hereditarianism, and fingerprinting—were all engaged in the project of classifying and identifying human types. To do so, he drew on the principles and legacies of physiognomy that mapped character onto external physical traits and allowed access to identity. Galton thus offered new forms of differentiation for those who failed to make visual distinctions among and within groups. He claimed that "whatever difficulty may be felt in the identification of Hindoos, is experienced in at least an equal degree in that of the Chinese residents in our Colonies and Settlements, who to European eyes are still more alike than Hindoos, and in whose names there is still less variety."[88] Along with the ability to create difference, physiognomy provided a logic for inherited characteristics—the face one was born with determined one's future.

Although Galton was highly innovative in many ways, he was following in the footsteps of the efforts of others in the project of human classification. These included Petrus Camper and Johann Friedrich Blumenbach, who laid the foundation of (racial) anthropology and eugenics movements, and whose works were frequently referenced by nineteenth-century physiognomists.[89] Later anthropologists, including London Anthropological Society founder James Hunt, drew heavily on physiognomic writings in framing their projects.[90] Hunt and his followers were largely concerned with the study and classification of peoples encountered through imperialization.[91] Drawing on the physiognomic principle that observation of others facilitated knowledge of them, they categorized these communities and tribes by common facial structures, styles of dress and decoration, and cultural customs about eating, shelter, celebrations, and life-cycle events. Anthropologists further blurred the distinction between physical and decorative visible features by using both types of symbols to construct meaningful pictures (and photographs) of their subjects. Photography provided anthropologists with classificatory evidence that was both portable and timeless; as Roland Barthes has famously noted and I hinted in the previous chapter, photographs deny history and remove time, making every viewing experience immediate and dependent on the observer's context.[92]

Elizabeth Edwards has shown that anthropologists and other scientists ascribed authority to photographic evidence through personal recommendations and networks of information exchange rather than a straightforward acceptance of mechanical objectivity.[93] Personal recommendations came from respected observers who vouched for the data contained in the photographs, in a new twist on Steven Shapin and Simon Schaffer's "virtual witnessing."[94] In this way, anthropological principles emerged from cultural representations by making meaning out of imperial photographs and their settings.

Many scholars, including, notably, Benedict Anderson and Elleke Boehmer, have argued that textuality was central to empire and colonialism.[95] Although Anderson's notion of empire and its colonial transmission was overly unitary, his analysis of the role of media in the construction of community demonstrated the importance of cultural representation in framing relationships.[96] Literary communication networks constructed and maintained the imaginary and the actuality of the empire and, in John B. Thompson's formulation, encouraged media agents to look beyond nationalistic borders.[97] I would like to propose an equally important "visuality of empire." It was through pictures of people and places, as much as through reports, diaries, letters, and memoirs, that Britons at home constructed their notions of empire and their place in it.[98]

Britons encountered imperial images in a variety of settings, most dramatically at the 1851 Great Exhibition in London, which, through the auspices of Thomas Cook's travelers and their souvenirs, brought the world to the Crystal Palace.[99] The extended physiognomic conversation of the first half of the nineteenth century enabled viewers to make meaning from colonial photographs and paintings, which reinforced the messages they received from best-selling explorers' and missionaries' tales.[100] Britons looked from a comfortable distance that allowed them to judge without even having to encounter. The empowerment and objectification of the physiognomic relationship that I explored in Chapter 1, in which rich men analyzed poor women and criminals, was extended to large groups of people—the poor, the problematic, and, especially, the foreign and exotic. Much like passers-by in the streets of London, inhabitants of colonized lands needed to be made legible. As Barbara Korte has chronicled, traveling was a visual experience, and traveling records emphasized the act of seeing that which was different.[101] Although pictures of these far-flung places and their inhabitants seemed to highlight human and geographic differences, application of physiognomic principles helped people make sense of these images and, at times, unearth similarities.

In his approach to composite photography, Galton was adding a new twist to prevailing anthropological methods. Throughout the second half of the nineteenth century, explorers and other researchers of family and kinship followed the principles of generalization set out by French engineer and economist Pierre Guillaume Frédéric Le Play and, later, French philosopher Maurice Halbwachs.[102] Although these two thinkers were different in many ways, they shared a commitment to representative informants and tasked researchers with making deliberate choices among their subjects to select those most typical and most trustworthy. Select individuals stood for the social whole, and their experiences and claims could be generalized to the group. Galton inverted this process; rather than generalizing from an individual to a group, he produced a group composite that was compressed into an individual representation. The principle remained the same, however—an average sample could come to stand for the whole. Deviations and nontypical results were to be ignored.

George Levine has explored Galton's statistical analyses in great depth and has focused in particular on Galton's struggle to balance the needs of the individual with the good of the group.[103] Levine has convincingly shown that Galton's statistical analysis allowed him to place individual aberrations in a larger context that considered these anomalies as part of a predictable whole. In this context, the individual as individual bore almost no significance and had meaning only as part of a calculated and meaningful system. Much like the emerging scientific method of the nineteenth century, in which a given fact was relevant only in connection with numerous other facts, the individual mattered only with respect to other equally fragmentary individual parts.[104]

Turning the Inside Out

Galton's ideas about inherent criminality prompted him to propose an aggressive eugenics campaign, in which selective breeding would preserve only the best features of the British people. In its various forms, Galton's notions lingered through the twentieth century, finding their most explicit expression in the Nazi propaganda and extermination programs of the 1930s and 1940s.[105] Although there are obvious overlaps between physiognomy and eugenics, especially the notion of static personality as correlated with measurable features, I am more interested in focusing on something else close to Galton's heart. Fingerprinting, in which Galton played a major role introducing to British police work, marked a point of departure for physiognomy that carried the relationship between the exterior and the interior in a number of very different directions.

For Galton, the primary use of somatic identification was to prosecute the guilty rather than to exonerate the innocent. In an inversion of Eastlake's arguments (discussed in Chapter 1) that physiognomy protected unfairly targeted strangers, Galton argued that "in civilized lands and in peaceable times, the chief use of a sure means of identification is to benefit society by deflecting rogues, rather than to establish the identity of men who are honest. Is this criminal an old offender? Is this new recruit a deserter? Is this professed pensioner personating a man who is dead? Is this upstart claimant to property the true heir, who was believed to have died in foreign lands?"[106]

I am not claiming that Galton was influenced by physiognomy and phrenology alone, but the physiognomic mind-set of the nineteenth century did contribute to Galton's approach to the classification of human types. In Galton's hands, photography and statistics combined to change the emphasis of identification from individuals to groups, or, specifically, to individuals as representatives of groups. Galton was interested in the normative average, such that without the general case, the specific became meaningless. Physiognomy, always malleable and subject to its context, was, through Galton (among others), turned completely on its head.

Fingerprinting, in Galton's hands, did similar work in shifting emphasis from individual character to representative statistical averages. Although Galton neither invented the practice nor introduced it to Britain, he received credit for both these deeds. Fingerprinting had been in use in the British Empire from at least 1858, when Sir William Herschel had local businessman Rajyadhar Konai press an imprint of his hand on the back of a contract. Herschel, the chief magistrate of the Hooghly district of Jungipoor, India, was searching for ways to hold locals to their commitments by reinforcing their signatures. He made it a practice to have all contracts witnessed in this way, later moving from the handprint to that of one finger. As his collection of prints grew, Herschel began to appreciate the identification applications of these additional signatures and started to use them for that purpose.

In Japan, similar developments were afoot from 1870. Dr. Henry Faulds, British surgeon-general of Tsukij Hospital in Tokyo, began noticing finger and hand marks in ancient Japanese pottery. Faulds developed his own system of identification and classification based on these examples, which he forwarded to Charles Darwin in 1880. Darwin, elderly and in poor health, passed the information to Galton, his younger, healthier cousin. Galton eventually pursued these data in 1888 by placing a request for further information on fingerprinting in *Nature*.[107] Herschel responded by passing on his entire collection to Galton, along with his own experimental findings on the longevity and uniqueness of an individual's fingerprints. Galton developed a classification system that, according to Faulds, was directly copied from his own.[108]

From this point follows a long history of the introduction of fingerprinting to police work. Fingerprinting eventually supplanted Alphonse Bertillon's system of anthropometric record keeping.[109] Through fingerprinting, Galton realized his goal of identification without individuality. Fingerprinting enabled large-scale and efficient classification of individuals while at the same time removing all question of character from this external sign. Although fingerprinting was physiognomic in the sense that a surface feature—the whorls of a finger—allowed knowledge of who someone was, it was radically unphysiognomic in that the internal features—nuances of character and behavior—were irrelevant. Although it was designed to identify precisely one person, the character of that identified individual was irrelevant to the process. The self was sidelined as the internal and external were flattened into two-dimensional fingerprint representations. The body, in Alan Sekula's terms, was an archive of experience and internality, but that internality, at least in the initial stages of fingerprint identification, was ignored.[110]

Although the fingerprint and the composite photograph were seemingly very different technologies, they both removed questions of character from representation and identification. As a practice, fingerprinting produced no meaningful information about types. Galton did not find any group or racial whorl patterns from which to create or support the categories he established with his composite photography. Fingerprinting offered no means of classification, no larger system, no hereditary commonalities, and no general claims. Ironically, the culmination of Galton's work was a project that contributed nothing to his notion of biologically determined group types. Galton wrote that his "great expectations [about fingerprints'] use in indicating Race and Temperament . . . have been falsified . . . I thought that any hereditary peculiarities would almost of necessity vary in different races, and that so fundamental and enduring a feature as the finger markings must in some way be correlated with temperament." To Galton's disappointment, "It may emphatically be said that there is no *peculiar* pattern which characterizes persons of any of the above races. There is no particular pattern that is special to any one of them, which when met with enables us to assert, or even to suspect, the nationality of the person on whom it appeared." Any observed distinctions, Galton conceded, were labor intensive with very little payoff: "The only differences so far observed, are statistical, and cannot be determined except through patience and caution, and by discussion of large groups."[111] Fingerprinting was a trace clue that provided only a correlative piece of information linking a print to a person but communicated nothing about behavior, character, or type. Although fingerprinting was an incredibly powerful technology of identification, on its own, it was ultimately meaningless.

Flattening Physiognomy

Unlike the layering of the internal and the external embodied by physiognomy, the late nineteenth century saw a dramatic fracturing of the signs of self. In Carlo Ginzburg's formulation, minute details and faint clues came to replace obvious signals in the understanding of identity.[112] Fingerprinting flattened the internal almost out of existence, while other practices turned physiognomic marking radically inward. Rather than using the external to explain and understand the internal, these identification technologies started inside and worked their way out. Starting in the 1860s and continuing through the beginning of the twentieth century, artists experimented with new ways of representing the essence of an image. Marked by impressionism, the silhouette movement, and the emergence of techniques such as hypnosis and psychoanalysis, the relationship between the internal and its external manifestations ceased to be indexical. As a means of accessing the internal through its seen manifestations, these forms of understanding drew on physiognomic principles even as they changed them.

By the end of the nineteenth century, physiognomy seemed to fade from the public eye. It did not disappear, despite a lowered prevalence of published literature and cultural applications in the second half of the nineteenth century.[113] Rather, the photographic-physiognomic synthesis of the middle of the century found a number of new intellectual homes. Physiognomy went in two very different types of directions, both of which followed from the demands of the new ways of visualizing introduced throughout the nineteenth century. The most obvious of these places was the use of classificatory physiognomy to make claims about actual or constructed groups in anthropology and eugenics. The second of these reflects the development of inner space, the construction of interiority, and the use of abstraction to reflect it. The modern manifestations of physiognomy were expressions of radical exteriority and radical interiority, but the two were not always linked, except as forms of diagnosis and classification of the self.

The photographic-physiognomic synthesis was directly involved in the discourse on interior space. French doctor Jean-Martin Charcot, director of the Salpêtrière asylum, explicitly took up Diamond's project of photographic physiognomy as a recording mechanism of mental disturbance.[114] But where Diamond was a painter, Charcot was a conductor, manipulating his patients to produce hysterical events that he captured photographically.[115] Although he too relied on photographic visuality, his most important pictures were performances over which he tried to exert complete control.[116] He and his subjects called madness into being from the inside out. To Charcot, the interior world of his patients was one of possibility that offered the opportunity for hysterical creation and manipulation. The moments of patient independent space created by the Salpêtrière visual regime charted another space to be explored, that of the internal world. By provoking hysterical states through his manipulation, Charcot was implicitly conceding that the possibility of these and other states was constantly in existence. The internal world, whose therapeutic manipulation was introduced by Diamond, became one not to eradicate but to honor.

Like Diamond, Charcot believed in the therapeutic and research power of visual recording. Also like Diamond, Charcot maintained that the photograph was an objective medium.[117] Unlike Diamond, however, Charcot granted the photograph no artistic and creative power. Where Diamond effectively negotiated the interplay between art and science so vital to his work and his various audiences, Charcot ignored it. His denial of the creativity and power inherent in the photographic act led audiences to reject his images as manipulated rather than welcoming the rhetorical power that these manipulations produced. Diamond acknowledged and even welcomed the place of artistic sensibility in his work and displayed his images to an artistically interested public, as well as to fellow asylum doctors. Charcot, on the other hand, did no such thing, and this ultimately led to his professional downfall.[118]

The emergence of psychoanalysis, pioneered by Charcot's disciple Sigmund Freud and Joseph Breuer at the turn of the twentieth century, provided a new, long-lasting home for the interiority displaced by Galton and Victorian typologies. Psychoanalysis turned physiognomy inside out by using the interior to make meaning of the exterior rather than the other way around. In his analysis of Anna O., Breuer's patient and collaborator, Freud illustrated the ways in which physical symptoms were linked to biographical experiences.[119] For example, Anna O.'s inability to drink liquids was eventually traced back to an incident she had witnessed in which a dog drank from a commonly used glass. When the incident was excavated, the symptom was alleviated.[120] Many physiognomists deliberated about, underplayed, or even ignored the impact of life experience, but Freud and those who followed him prioritized it above all else. That is not to say that Freud was not interested in biology; as Frank Sulloway has chronicled, Freud's ideas emerged from an intense and long-term engagement with biological and evolutionary theories.[121] To Freud, human biology required biography, which was the key constituent of behavior and character and, necessarily, of their physical expression. In direct opposition to the traditional physiognomic position that face determines character, to Freud, one's face—and body—were created by everything that happened after birth.

The subject of physiognomy and psychoanalysis could take up books, and here I merely wish to be provocative in gesturing toward this relationship. Psychoanalysis shows one of the many ways in which physiognomic thought continued past its historically recognized heyday, and one of the many hidden trails that trace back to physiognomy. Rather than refer solely to eugenics and social Darwinism, which inevitably appear in any study of modern physiognomic manifestations, I wish to widen the scope of our understanding of physiognomy. All practices that mandate a relationship between the exterior and the interior, and between identity and physicality, are connected to physiognomy. Some had more chilling implications than others.

In the conclusion to this book, I touch briefly on contemporary manifestations of physiognomic practice, ranging from biological-anthropological hand- and finger-size studies to examinations of babies and facial expressions. The technology and methodology have changed, but the principles are, in many ways, the same.

Physiognomy was flexible. Unlike its more scientifically accepted counterpart, phrenology, the classificatory power of physiognomy lay in its accessibility and mutability. As social and cultural ideas about selfhood and identity changed, so too did the application of physiognomy. In this chapter, I have explored how the application of physiognomy transitioned from understanding individuals to describing groups, and the role that photography played in representing and understanding commonalities within types of people. Following the innovative work of Hugh Welch Diamond, key players in this process were Lady Elizabeth Rigby Eastlake, Charles Darwin, and especially Sir Francis Galton. By the end of the century, physiognomy had become an important component of anthropology and imperial exploration.

Although physiognomy never achieved widespread intellectual acceptance, the flexibility and practicality of its practice ensured its lingering use among many professional communities. In the first half of the nineteenth century, physiognomy served as a useful diagnostic tool for doctors and emphasized the importance of visual observation in the practice of medicine. Asylum doctors, in particular, took advantage of the power of physiognomy to produce character information at a distance. When physiognomy was combined with photography, the range of physiognomic readings extended, allowing observers to make diagnoses over time, even in the absence of their subjects. Many thinkers engaged with diagnosis and discussion of human types borrowed from physiognomic language to make their work appealing and interesting to their readers. Charles Darwin frequently resorted to physiognomic conventions in his language and visual analysis even as he rejected the practice itself.

As Lady Elizabeth Rigby Eastlake explained, physiognomic photography captured different clues than the evidence of the naked eye, highlighting communal features and obscuring the individual. Her focus on groups was consonant with mid-Victorian attitudes about class and nationhood as individuals began to think of themselves as components of a larger whole. The photographic-physiognomic synthesis proved particularly useful for Francis Galton, who employed composite photography to create his physiognomic subjects. In so doing, he discarded what was unique about individuals in favor of a visual average. He employed similar techniques in his statistical work, striving to find universal features for a given group and rendering exceptionality irrelevant.

In addition to his work on statistics and eugenics, Galton experimented with other means of identification and description that related to earlier diagnostic and classificatory practices. Galton offered a way to create difference beyond the sometimes inadequate mechanism of visual and facial messages. His work on fingerprinting, although seemingly tied only to specific individuals, was in fact part of his larger endeavor to eradicate character from classification. Fingerprinting removed all internality from the identification process, fracturing physiognomy while at the same time engaging with its underlying principles. Ironically, fingerprints failed to provide meaningful racial or group information but succeeded in linking individuals inextricably to their own bodily marks. With the work of Jean-Martin Charcot, internality began a period of its own intense development for which physiognomy provided the conditions of possibility. By the end of the nineteenth century, internality became a subject of study in its own right in a variety of fields, including the fine arts and especially psychoanalysis.

By the turn of the twentieth century, physiognomic ideas were subtly integrated into a variety of practices, including anthropology, eugenics, psychoanalysis, and, up to the present, targeted neurological and psychological studies. As I explore in the conclusion to this book, lay and practical physiognomy has begun to make a comeback in workshops teaching people how to judge others and interpret the message of their faces. Although, like Darwin, workshop organizers avoid the taint of the physiognomic title, they too are offering physiognomic observers permission to judge.

Conclusion

Seeing Ourselves

THERE ARE ENDLESS PUNS that I have been tempted to use in writing this book. I have mostly resisted, not wanting to detract from the serious nature of this topic. Physiognomy had high stakes. It still does. True or false, right or wrong, physiognomy remains a powerful technology of communication and decision making, a marker of selfhood, and a way of building identity.

The flexibility of physiognomy granted it the endurance that has allowed it to linger in different settings and contexts and even under different names. From its Lavaterian formulation on, physiognomy promised nothing less than the ability to know others just by observing them and learning just by looking. Today, that possibility remains a tantalizing, if elusive, part of the search for what it means to be human, and how people relate to one another.[1] As in the pursuits of the polite and the professional physiognomists, researchers today continue to look for the key by which the system of physiognomic standardization can be unlocked. Also, as with the physiognomists of the nineteenth century, some of today's research is based on the premise that people are always already applying physiognomy; the challenge is to understand the ways in which the judgmental instinct works.[2] The issues around physiognomy remain compelling for both practical and abstract theoretical applications. If physiognomy can be understood, perhaps so can people.

But for me, like my historical actors, the physiognomic mechanism is beside the point. It is by studying physiognomic practice that I learned about its practitioners, people from all walks of life and experiences who converged on the exercise of visual judgment. They all shared a desire to learn about one another and the belief that, girded with the Lavaterian language, they could. Touching on many different parts of lived experience, physiognomy allowed me to penetrate the hidden depths, the invisible internal that lay behind the face of nineteenth-century existence. What I found was a complicated and deeply intertwined society, in which divisions between the educated elite and the working class were less significant than participation in the communication of ideas. Theoretical distinctions between art and science were less important than their practical applications. The boundaries between the observer and the observed, between artist and audience, were less meaningful than their shared nonverbal language. Without the advantage of physiognomic insight, these more important relationships would have remained invisible. Sometimes looking at the surface just is not enough.

A dynamic and ever-expanding set of ideas and type of language, physiognomy, contrary to widespread prejudice, was neither marginal nor esoteric. It was not merely an amusing footnote in the history of brain-localization theory, or literary studies, or artistic techniques. Rather, the rise in physiognomic practice and the extent to which it cut across class lines, educational barriers, and cultural entertainments open up new perspectives on ways in which people managed the changing and often frightening experience of nineteenth-century urban life. Physiognomy was so deeply embedded in Victorian daily life that its context is its content; it is impossible to separate the two. The story of physiognomy is the story of lived experience, of seeing and observing, of learning, and of making decisions and making them quickly. By following physiognomy around, I walked in the path of its communication, describing the ways in which knowledge was produced and amassed value, and the important and often-overlooked role that culture and entertainment played in the construction of ideas. The rise in physiognomic thinking heralded a change in the ways in which Victorians encountered one another; by charting the development of physiognomy, I have charted a change in the nature of human interaction.

The range of physiognomic activity offers historians of Britain tantalizing suggestions about the ways in which Victorians identified and dealt with the questions of urbanization, artistic representation, the emergence of professional categories, the increasing democratization of information, and, underlying all these challenges, the problems inherent in an erosion of trust. In the cities of the nineteenth century, people of all classes, occupations, religions, and backgrounds did not know how to make sense of one another. Physiognomy offered a solution to this very pressing problem of identification and communication. In so doing, it became a language all its own.

The point of physiognomy as a practice—and also of my own historical investigation of its emergence as a cultural phenomenon in Britain—was never only physiognomy itself but rather what it revealed. By studying the practice, I learned about its practitioners and the world in which they lived. Originally intended for an elite audience for whom physiognomy was a way to mediate social prestige, Lavater's vision laid out a system dependent on individual instinct that was itself unclassed. It was also apparently unquantifiable. Although physiognomic skills could be developed and learned, the presence of physiognomic aptitude could not be predicated on or limited by age, occupation, or status. Because of its empowering potential and easily accessibility, as well as its practical and useful applications in the urban environment, physiognomy quickly became a widespread way for all classes of society to make and discuss judgments about others on the basis of brief visual encounters.

Within the framework offered by physiognomy, the visual manifestations of character, often confused with class, increasingly became the critical focus of trustworthiness. Nevertheless, the actual physiognomic correlations between features and personal attributes often remained unexpressed as Victorians quickly came to conclusions based on what they saw. Once made, the conclusions themselves mattered, not how they were derived. Invoking the authority of physiognomy was often enough to justify the instinctive appraisals of others and to create a space in which these appraisals could be shared.

Because physiognomy was always resistant to systemizing (something that was a source of frustration to some physiognomic adherents), its cultural persistence as a practice lay partly in its flexibility, that is, in the ability of its practitioners to suggest rules for its application while always insisting that these rules yield to individual innovation and experience. Physiognomic applications were infused with space for personal judgment and even creativity, rare features in an increasingly mechanical age. In this sense, the historical study of physiognomy illuminates not only the nature of an important practice of nineteenth-century daily life—itself no small feat—but also questions about access to and participation in knowledge production.

As a historian, by resisting the initial temptation to apply anachronistic hierarchies between entertainment and education and between specialized and lay knowledge as sites of knowledge production, I have been able to understand the ways in which the history of physiognomy can be seen as an ultimately unsuccessful attempt to erect such a hierarchy in one domain of practice. The continuing difficulties in turning physiognomy into a "system" explain why, throughout this book, I have drawn on material ranging from elite published monographs and journal articles to private diaries, literature, essays, promptbooks, and various works of art. All these media contributed to the construction and communication of physiognomic knowledge and continued to do so even when physiognomists struggled most valiantly to ground their practice in science. Their struggles in turn give the historian an opportunity to study ways in which early and mid-Victorian scholars and scientists made sense of the problems of reproducibility and classification, the nature of observation, and the status of visual judgment as an art or a science.

What physiognomy shows, in all its forms and practices, is that people are extraordinarily adept at finding ways to read distinction and value into what they see. As physiognomy developed from a mechanism to mediate social prestige to a way to make sense of urban encounters, its flexibility was tested. The ideas were resilient and flourished in creative applications to impose meaning on represented characters in literature, the theatre, and portraiture. The power of physiognomy was employed in the service of imperial and political purposes to construct faces of outsiders even as they began to assimilate visually and politically. Throughout, in the hands of doctors and laypeople alike, physiognomy remained a diagnostic technology with a constant tension between its application to the classification of groups and the identification and judgment of individuals. The introduction of photography to physiognomic practice heightened this tension by producing creative negotiations between the specific and the general in the recording and analysis of photographic subjects.

The story of physiognomy is not a conventional story at all. This book is not a clean narrative with a beginning, a middle, and an obvious end. There is not really an end here at all, mostly because physiognomy did not go anywhere. The search for a way to access the invisible internal through external correlates continues and has even intensified in recent years. This desire for access shares its motivations with many religious and scientific quests relating to humanity and its classifications and interactions. In this respect, physiognomy is perhaps not very different from genetic research and biblical literalism, two areas that offer clues to unlock the puzzling box of the person. Both genetic research and biblical behavioral codes are framed by the pursuit of perfection. If humanity can be explained, it can be improved.

Physiognomy, on the other hand, did not require assumptions of self-improvement. Although some applications involved modification of self and others, most physiognomies were modeled on information acquisition and management, in sharp contrast to phrenology. Even the more rigidly diagnostic manifestations were—with the notable exception of Hugh Welch Diamond—centered on labeling problems rather than fixing them. Nevertheless, the search for perfection was a subtle undertone of many physiognomic pursuits. Inspired by the worshipful framework of Johann Caspar Lavater, some saw physiognomy as a true quest, not necessarily for the divine but for the ideal self. This tendency increased throughout the nineteenth century as humanity became ever more rigidly structured along a classification hierarchy, and physiognomy remained a consistent backdrop to this trend.

What I find compelling about the relationship between physiognomy and improvement is that it returns us almost to the beginning of this unusual kind of story. I refer here not to Lavater but to the reflexive physiognomic practices discussed in Chapter 1. The use of physiognomy for the self rather than others is, I think, the message that has the most enduring undertones. This idea of physiognomy as self-revelatory will guide my work in this conclusion. I will draw together the major themes of this book, but I will do so with an eye toward the present and the future, raising questions about current physiognomic activities and their guiding motivations.

Of course, despite their powerful adherence to doctrines of self-improvement, Victorians were no more naïve about perfection than we are today, which is to say that some pursued it vigorously, others rejected it entirely, a few dreamed of it, and many laughed at it.[3] The absurdity of a perfect body correlating with a perfect mind and soul and the impossibility of achieving that state were reflected in the 1836 lithograph titled *The Body Politic on the March of Intellect* (Figure C.1), published by Thomas MacLean. In the picture, each part of the body has an imperfect face, representing the fragmentation of the human body in all its malformed and misshapen glory. Each face, or body part, has its own visual and verbal pun bemoaning its own inadequacies. The main caption, stemming from the head at the actual head, reads: "Better be hanged than thus be headed." Aside from the clever double entendre, the meaning of this quip is clear: better to be dead than to live life as a physiognomic failure. This image, like many I have examined, is an exaggeration, an invitation for viewers to calm their anxieties by sharing the joke. No one, the picture argues, has a perfect face, and no one really ought to die for this deficiency. At the same time, the idea that a damned face led to a damned life was a real one. Damnation was also not limited to the face; here we see the fragmentation of physiognomy, because people were often

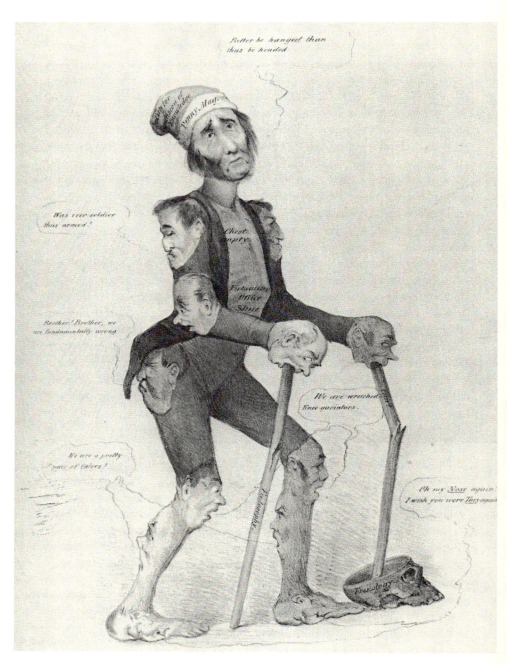

Figure C.1.   The Body Politic on the March of Intellect, 1836, challenged the idea of a perfect body and a perfect physiognomy. (Courtesy of the U.S. National Library of Medicine.)

divided into their component parts to subtract from the power of their whole.

Perfection may have been impossible, but there were certainly those who were better and those who were worse. Physiognomy did its part to help in the sorting, but as a tool, it was framed by the vision of its deployer. Physiognomy could see what the physiognomist saw, depending on the subjectivity of the viewer. Although, as I have repeatedly emphasized, that subjectivity was shared in many ways, it originated from a unitary source—the individual observer. Physiognomic judgment lay always in the eye of the beholder.

Did it matter at what, exactly, the beholder was looking? Did physiognomy work differently when one was looking at a painting as opposed to reading a novel as opposed to viewing a photograph or a play or a wax model? This book has introduced a number of representational forms, including literature, acting, painting, caricature, and photography, through which it subtly explores exactly that question. Both the individual looker and the medium through which the subject was being viewed did matter. Part of the physiognomic progression was about training, not only about the practice and its principles but also about ways of viewing. Physiognomy was part of the process of making sense of media and in turn developing the practice further.

Of course, even in person, people were often self-fashioned representations of themselves. Despite the best aims of physiognomy, people are not transparent. But in self-fashioning choices lie many clues that artists and others engaged in mimesis were eager to understand and exploit. We have looked at how actors, artists, and novelists deployed physiognomic messages in order to self-consciously convey character information. Visuality was an important mediator in this process, but not the only one. Physiognomy and its associated metonymy were also present in the written word.

For Hugh Welch Diamond's photographic subjects, like female protagonists such as *Bleak House*'s Lady Deadlock and *Villette*'s Lucy Snow, sometimes clothing did not become the patients even though it defined them. Diamond deployed photography as therapist, artist, and advocate, coaxing a wide range of viewers to see as and what he wished. His tools were his patients and his asylum, but his tools were also clothing, props, his camera, and his own eyes. Through the vision of his eyes, viewers— patients, doctors, and exhibition visitors—saw, and viewers felt that they knew. Through this process, Diamond widened the scope of physiognomically meaningful symbols by which to demarcate both group adherence and individual distinction.

I ended the last chapter with a reference to interiority and psychoanalysis, but now I take a step back to photography and think about the legacy that its embedded physiognomy has left as we continue to confront media today. Staged pictures of people were a common photographic theme; the physiognomy of these subjects was an equally important focus for both photographers and viewers. As photography continued to develop, however, there was a growing sense among social commentators that mass productions prevented rather than facilitated visualization of the original image as a whole. The most famous such analysis was Karl Marx's 1867 description of the commodity fetish, wherein he argued that signs of objects would begin to replace the objects themselves and in this way obscure their origins as the product of human labor.[4] As Marx struggled to make sense of the new mass media and the politics of aesthetics, his questions centered on the search for value and the ways in which it was produced in commodities. Like physiognomic images, the meaning of commodities lay in their relationship to the original, which, Marx argued, was obscured through the processes of capitalism and their production of value. The commodity, the object, was itself a performance of this value; in this way, its relationship to the original was far from a direct copy. So too with physiognomic analyses; highly complicated, the relationship between the original person and the images from which others were conducting these analyses was deeply embedded in the media and mediators of the images and performances of physiognomic copies.

Marx's discussion provided the foundation for the Frankfurt school's analysis of the faults of modern cultural reproduction, expressed in closely affiliated thinker Walter Benjamin's 1935 essay "The Work of Art in the Age of Mechanical Reproduction."[5] Marx, Benjamin, and even later scholars of audience reception were in dialogue with Victorian and pre-Victorian theorists about the questions of realism and the picturesque. These thinkers were confronting the challenges of mass media and searching for ways to understand and express value, questions that haunt us today in the Internet world. Like today's computer or the film and radio of Benjamin's time, physiognomy and its media changed the way in which people perceived the world around them.

The many physiognomies of nineteenth-century England would not have been possible without the many media of nineteenth-century England. Media helped make physiognomy possible, but what, in that geographic and temporal context, made it necessary? The easiest answer is the most hackneyed, deployed to explain any and all phenomena occurring and around Victorian London: mass urbanization. Because it is hackneyed does not make it untrue but simply uninteresting or less interesting, which is why I have spilled little ink on the numbers and trends of city growth. More interesting is the nature of the city and of the interactions of its inhabitants. Physiognomy helps us follow urbanites around and begin to understand how they moved with and around others in their space, and what they saw and why they saw it when they moved.

Sight, I have argued throughout this book, is subjective. What people saw when they looked at others in various representations was highly individual, but it was at the same time shaped by a long process of communal training and communication. Sight, and in particular physiognomic sight, was a shared subjectivity that depended on the individual but could be understood by the group. The technology of physiognomy did not require special training or rely on abstract forces and unknown authors. Physiognomic results demanded trust only in oneself and one's judgment. Although physiognomic sight could be improved and honed, it could be employed by anyone, and it was.

As physiognomy was employed and deployed, it changed. Physiognomy became a mechanism to describe and define the traits not only of a given person but also of entire groups. It became a technology not only of information acquisition but also of deliberate information dissemination. Physiognomy helped frame the multiple media of mimesis by offering new and enduring minimum cues to conjure character. Audiences and viewers played a very active role in the ways in which physiognomy developed and thus in the ways in which media presented people and ideas about the nature of humanity.

What physiognomy revealed about others, however, is not where this story lands. Rather, what lingers is what physiognomy tells us about ourselves. In Chapter 5, I argued that Hugh Welch Diamond's photographic physiognomy was a mediated mirror that excavated the accurate inner self for people to see and understand. Through the medium of photography, physiognomy became revelatory in a way in which it otherwise was not. But not everyone needed that particular medium to use physiognomy to learn about the self, *oneself* as opposed to the self of others. Physiognomy is most useful, both for the historian and for the self-seeker, as a way to learn about physiognomists. What one sees in others ultimately tells a great deal about oneself.

Emily Brontë, among others, well understood where to focus her physiognomic lens to maximum effect in her 1847 masterpiece *Wuthering Heights*. In one of the great moments of literary manipulation, the housekeeper and surrogate mother Nelly Dean describes the decidedly handsome but generally villainous Heathcliff in glowing physiognomic terms: "A good heart will help you to a bonny face, my lad . . . if you were a regular black; and a bad one will turn the bonniest into something worse than ugly."[6] Strongly ironic in light of Heathcliff's character development, this assessment tells readers more about Nelly than about Heathcliff. Her conventional and pious approach to life is clearly illustrated by her commitment to traditional religious Lavaterian physiognomic principles.[7] Nelly gets it wrong, but that is not the point. Brontë was not, through Nelly, mounting an attack on the efficacy of physiognomy. Rather, she was telling us about the character of Nelly herself.

So what does physiognomy tell us about the Victorians? We learn that they were searching for community and looking for ways to connect to others. We find out that they wanted to trust in their own instincts and skills rather than in a diffuse and elite authority. We discover, unsurprisingly, that they created hierarchy and separated the good from the bad, the mad, and the sad. We note their reflexive use of these despised elements to frame their own self-presentations better. We chronicle their growing insistence on thinking of themselves and others as contributors to a whole rather than individual parts. We comment on their demand for realism in representation while at the same time acknowledging the fantasy of these mimetic acts. We catch their creative side as they invented and imagined distinctions and then called them into being through their visual representations. We know that their vision was mediated through literature, theatre, caricature, and photography. We see the dawning of their obsession with interiority and othering. Then, and only then, do we stop to consider, not the future of the Victorians, but their practice of physiognomy.

We know some of the story, or at least we have produced a narrative that connects eugenics, social Darwinism, physiognomy, and other practices of human classification. In the wake of the tragedies of World War II and its precursors across the world, physiognomy was whispered about in corners and shamefacedly acknowledged.[8] But now it is back, both in obvious ways and in new and subtle costumes. What, and why?

The *what* is easy. A quick Google search or a scan of the local library reveals endless titles on face reading and its associated arts from across the world.[9] These texts promise readers an edge in relationships, in business, and in life skills. Some even offer software that does the work in the comfort of one's own computer.[10] If physiognomy went paperback in the nineteenth century, it has now gone digital.

Such books are unsurprising. Enough time has passed and enough wounds have healed for these approaches to be rehabilitated in wide forums. In our ever more globalized world, the ability to make specificity, to create order, and to assert dominance over a universal urban landscape, with an overload of information similar to the one that the Victorians encountered and had to manage, is elusive. As we have seen, physiognomic practices and ways of seeing offer an accessible way to make sense of cities and of sight. They offer hierarchy, order, and control. They offer groups and ways of placing ourselves within or outside those groups.

The intelligentsia has offered its benediction on rethinking physiognomy in a modern context. Recent articles in the *Economist* and the *New Yorker* (the sacred texts of the U.K. and U.S. chattering classes) have offered reports on physiognomic experiments being conducted to track success in business, in teaching, and in the arts of detection.[11] According to one study chronicled in the *Economist* in January 2008, financial success can be visually identified from photographs. A group of undergraduates were asked to look at the photographs of executives from the top and bottom twenty-five *Fortune* 1,000 list and rate them. Without knowing into which group each photograph fell, the students consistently ranked the top twenty-five highly for competence, dominance, and maturity, with opposite results for the bottom twenty-five. The article ended with a tongue-in-cheek suggestion that market analysts ought to take the faces of chief executive officers into account in preparing their reports. The suggestion was a lighthearted joke, but, to the readers of this book and those who are chronicled in its pages, the idea is not so outrageous. It has been done before.

A more recent article in the *Economist* titled "Physiognomy: Facing the Truth" reported on a study of face shape as an index of aggression as measured by the penalty minutes of hockey players.[12] The study suggested that the differences in face shape were connected to levels of exposure to testosterone in individuals. In response to the article, one online post urged the authors of the study to generalize their claims more broadly, commenting that "Carré and McCormick's results point at the possibility that entire ethnic groups are more aggressive than others due to differences in testosterone exposures during puberty."[13] This letter argued that physiognomic indicators could be used to describe not just individuals but large groups. That too has been done before.

A longer *New Yorker* article profiled Paul Ekman, a psychologist who has developed training courses to teach people how to read facial expressions that are very subtle and often fleeting. Although Ekman's work is not strictly physiognomic, it is predicated on research that shows that expressions are universal, and that the skills needed to read these expressions are universally accessible. A gifted few possess these skills naturally and often excel in fields such as police enforcement, therapy, and the law. (A recent procedural television series on Fox, *Lie to Me,* is premised on a team of crime investigators who solve cases using Ekman's techniques.) Others can be taught, and teach them Ekman and his team do. Ekman's techniques focus on honing vision and looking for signs based on discrete muscle movements. The face reading that we all do many times a day, Ekman has claimed, can be honed. Most of us are not that good at it on our own, but through his lessons we can become so. Such results are tantalizing; who would not want these skills?

These studies are only the tip of the iceberg, the ones that seem interesting, accessible, elite, and yet unthreatening enough to be widely reported. I would love to analyze these current endeavors and reflect on their motivations and causes through my historical perspective, but that is another project for another, or many other, books. There are literally thousands of studies and scores of laboratories doing this work, and I cannot even begin to list them. These get less press, including the recent hand studies in biological-anthropological research that link various characteristics and behavior to the ratio of the subject's fingers.[14] This too, like physiognomy, is an attempt at data collection that links character to its external physical manifestation but, unlike physiognomy, requires complicated apparatus and elite specialists. Other studies include mapping facial preferences in babies, which in turn suggests ideas about how nurturing and care can be reflected in the face.[15]

What about racial profiling? Long an informal practice among police forces, racial profiling has become institutionalized at airports and in other settings in the wake of 9/11. This too is a topic worthy of its own book, and I will not even attempt to summarize the debates and various issues associated with this practice. I only point out its similarities to other, older assumptions about the visual manifestations of group affiliation and its implicated behavioral patterns. Is airport racial profiling the actualization of the fantasized racial traits I chronicled in Chapter 4? Is it the recognition of metonymical cues of facial hair and clothing styles that I tracked throughout this book? Is it a set of conclusions drawn from statistical data, the realization of Lavater's original call for classification? Is it simply, yet again, a way to make one frightened group feel in control by exerting control over others?

I do not know. What I do know is that our own physiognomy practices today have the potential to tell us a great deal about ourselves if we let them. Rather than continually turning our often-faulty analytic eyes outward, perhaps it is time to hold the metaphoric physiognomic mirror to our own faces in order to answer these questions and figure out how to proceed. Physiognomy promises to reveal the hidden secrets locked behind the faces of those we see. Perhaps it succeeds, and perhaps not. I do not really know, and the truth is that I do not really care. What I do know, what I have learned and hope that readers have understood, is that physiognomy can tell us what we think and who we are. It certainly has told us a great deal about the Victorians: their fears, they way they wished to portray themselves, and how they thought about power, identity, and sociality.

Throughout the course of this book, we looked at shifts in human interaction in city streets. We went to the theatre to peek at audiences and actors and how they thought about themselves and their representations. We strolled through art shows and studios to think about viewers and what they demanded in portraits, as well as how artists thought about their subjects. We looked at caricatures as a way to think about cultural concerns, fears of immigration and assimilation, and fantasies of group hierarchy and control. We peered at both sides of the camera lens to see photographs physiognomically and discover a great deal about the photographer, his subjects, and their audiences. Finally, we turned to physiognomy as a broad diagnostic tool to excavate imperial attitudes as Victorians thought about themselves as part of the larger whole. We held physiognomy up as a mirror to the Victorians, and we learned what they saw in themselves as much as in others. We used physiognomy to gather information about the past and, in so doing, excavated the characters of the Victorians themselves, peeking as they were looking, glimpsing their insides as they evaluated the outsides of others.

Diamond, it seems, was right.

Notes

Introduction

1. The long nineteenth century was defined by historian Eric Hobsbawm as starting in 1789 and running through the start of World War I in 1914.
2. James A. Secord, "Halifax Keynote Address: Knowledge in Transit," *Isis* 95, no. 4 (2004): 661.
3. In this approach, I follow the lead of Peter Galison and Lorraine Daston, who destabilized objectivity in their landmark article "The Image of Objectivity," *Representations* 40 (1992): 81–128.
4. Chris Otter, *The Victorian Eye: A Political History of Light and Vision in Britain, 1800–1910* (Chicago: University of Chicago Press, 2008), 84.
5. Ibid.
6. Alison Winter, *Mesmerized: Powers of Mind in Victorian Britain* (Chicago: University of Chicago Press, 1998), 8.
7. Jonathan Crary, *Techniques of the Observer: On Vision and Modernity in the Nineteenth Century* (Cambridge: Cambridge University Press, 1990).
8. Alan Sekula, "The Body and the Archive," *October* 39 (1986): 3–64; Julie Codell, "Expression over Beauty: Facial Expression, Body Language, and Circumstantiality in the Painting of the Pre-Raphaelite Brotherhood," *Victorian Studies* 29 (1986): 255–290.
9. Charles Kingsley, *Charles Kingsley: His Letters and Memories of His Life, Edited by His Wife* (New York: C. Scribner's Sons, 1894), 291.
10. Otter, *Victorian Eye*, 86, has argued that control of visual codes was an important part of the maintenance of Victorian gender roles and social positions.
11. Tom Crook, "Power, Privacy and Pleasure: Liberalism and the Modern Cubicle," *Cultural Studies* 21 (2007): 549.
12. Simon Gunn, *The Public Culture of the Victorian Middle Class: Ritual and Authority and the English Industrial City, 1840–1914* (New York: St. Martin's Press, 2000), 61.

13. Jonathan Conlin, "Vauxhaull Revisited: The Afterlife of a London Pleasure Garden, 1770–1859," *Journal of British Studies* 45 (2006): 718–743; see 719.

14. For example, writers such as Honoré de Balzac, Stendhal, and Wilhelm Karl Raabe, among others, frequently used physiognomic conventions in their novels.

15. For the publication of English-language physiognomy texts, see John Graham, "Lavater's *Physiognomy:* A Checklist," *Papers of the Bibliographical Society of America* 55 (1961): 297–308. I am not going to list the physiognomically oriented manuals published in the nineteenth century; all texts relevant to this book are discussed in the body of the work. France was most similar to England with respect to sustained interest and participation in practical physiognomy. There were a number of French pocket physiognomy guidebooks; Paris was next to London in its scale and pace of immigration. For more on physiognomy in France, see Judith Wechsler, *A Human Comedy: Physiognomy and Caricature in 19th Century Paris* (Chicago: University of Chicago Press, 1982). The prominence of physiognomy in Europe rose at the end of the century with various criminal identification mechanisms, particularly in France and Italy.

16. For texts dealing with the history of physiognomy, see Jennifer Montagu, *The Expression of the Passions: The Origin and Influence of Charles Le Brun's "Conférence sur l'expression générale et particularière"* (New Haven, Conn.: Yale University Press, 1994); Melissa Percival, *The Appearance of Character: Physiognomy and Facial Expression in Eighteenth-Century France* (London: W. S. Maney and Son, 1999); Melissa Percival and Graeme Tytler, eds., *Physiognomy in Profile: Lavater's Impact on European Culture* (Newark: University of Delaware Press, 2005); Graeme Tytler, *Physiognomy in the European Novel: Faces and Fortunes* (Princeton, N.J.: Princeton University Press, 1982); Lucy Hartley, *Physiognomy and the Meaning of Expression in Nineteenth-Century Culture* (Cambridge: Cambridge University Press, 2001); Roy Porter, "Making Faces: Physiognomy and Fashion in Eighteenth-Century England," *Études Anglaises* 38 (1985): 385–396; and John Graham, "The Development of the Use of Physiognomy in the Novel" (Ph.D. diss., Johns Hopkins University, 1960). See also Ellis Shookman, *The Faces of Physiognomy: Interdisciplinary Approaches to Johann Caspar Lavater* (Columbia, S.C.: Camden House, 1993); Michael Shortland, "The Power of a Thousand Eyes: Johann Caspar Lavater's Science of Physiognomical Perception," *Criticism* 28 (1986): 379–408; and Christopher Rivers, *Face Value: Physiognomical Thought and the Legible Body in Marvaux, Lavater, Balzac, Gautier, and Zola* (Madison: University of Wisconsin Press, 1994).

17. Sharrona Pearl, "As Plain as the Nose on Your Face: Physiognomy in Nineteenth-Century England" (Ph.D. diss., Harvard University, 2005).

18. See Johann Caspar Lavater's first German-language publication, *Physiognomische Fragmente zur Beförderung der Menschenkenntniss und Menschenliebe* (Leipzig: Weidmanns Erben und Reich, 1775–1778).

19. Lavater's work was first translated into English by Thomas Holcroft in 1789. Holcroft's translation became the most widely used, even in subsequent editions. Johann Caspar Lavater, *Essays on Physiognomy: For the Promotion of the Knowledge and the Love of Mankind,* ed. and trans. Thomas Holcroft (London: G. G. J. and J. Robinson, 1789). This version was still expensive and available only to the elite; the first widely affordable English-language version of Lavater's writings was published in the *Conjuror's Magazine* in 1792. One could track the development of physiognomy through the changes in the actual books in which it was presented.

20. See particularly Johann Caspar Lavater, "Reasons Why the Science of Physiognomy Is So Often Ridiculed and Treated with Contempt," in *Essays on Physiognomy,* trans. Thomas Holcroft (London: Ward, Lock and Co., 1800), 19–23.

21. Azilé d'Arcy, *Prejudice; or, Physiognomy: A Novel in Three Volumes* (London: A. K. Newman and Co., 1817), 7.

22. Sir James Paget, "Physiognomy of the Human Form," *Quarterly Review* 99 (1856): 453.

23. "Speaking to the Eye," *Illustrated London News* (1851): 452. Established in 1842 by printer and newsagent Herbert Ingram, the *ILN* was the first weekly to accompany the news with illustrations. At sixpence an issue, the *ILN* was affordable by the working classes on a weekly basis. The paper was a strong advocate of the poor and used its pages to further the cause of social reform.

24. Ibid.

25. Lynda Nead, *Victorian Babylon: People, Streets and Images in Nineteenth-Century London* (New Haven, Conn.: Yale University Press, 2000), 57.

26. Lavater, *Essays on Physiognomy,* 1800 ed., 40.

27. As Jonathan Crary and Michael Leja have shown, new visual technologies such as the stereoscope and the panorama challenged the trust people had in what they saw with their own eyes. Through the training of perception, however, they became more sophisticated and learned to become discriminating and skeptical viewers, asking and even demanding to be knowingly tricked. See Crary, *Techniques of the Observer;* and Michael Leja, *Looking Askance: Skepticism and American Art from Eakins to Duchamp* (Berkeley: University of California Press, 2004).

28. For more on virtual witnessing, see Steven Shapin and Simon Schaffer, *Leviathan and the Air-Pump: Hobbes, Boyle, and the Experimental Life Including a Translation of Thomas Hobbes, Dialogus physicus de natura aeris by Simon Schaffer* (Princeton, N.J.: Princeton University Press, 1985). See especially chapter 2.

29. This type of trust and the ways in which the status of the individual affected the nature of his or her claims are established in Steven Shapin, *A Social History of Truth: Civility and Science in Seventeenth-Century England* (Chicago: University of Chicago Press, 1994). For a history of commodity culture in England, see Neil McKendrick, *The Birth of a Consumer Society: The Commercialization of Eighteenth-Century England* (Bloomington: Indiana University Press, 1982).

30. Marjorie Morgan, *Manners, Morals, and Class in England, 1774–1858* (New York: St. Martin's Press, 1994), 3.

31. Although the first modern celebrity was eighteenth-century actor David Garrick, advertising did not become an organized profession until the nineteenth century. With the rise of the cult of celebrity at midcentury, a new figure of endorsement and trust emerged, particularly with the advent of celebrity photography. Celebrity endorsements, freely given or otherwise, were attached to products from figures as disparate as Queen Victoria, Charles Darwin, and singer Jenny Lind. For a discussion of the emergence of celebrity in the Victorian era, see Nicholas Dames, "Brushes with Fame: Thackeray and the Work of Celebrity," *Nineteenth-Century Literature* 56 (2001): 23–51. Victorian photographer Julia Margaret Cameron was quick to capitalize on the potential of celebrity support; upon coaxing endorsements for her pictures from her famous sitters, she used their claims to promote sales of these images through Paul and Dominic Colnaghi's London gallery; see Janet Browne, "I Could Have Retched All Night: Charles Darwin and His Body," in *Science Incarnate: Historical Embodiments of Natural Knowledge*, ed. Christopher Lawrence and Steven Shapin (Chicago: University of Chicago Press, 1998): 240–287.

32. Theodore Porter, *Trust in Numbers: The Pursuit of Objectivity in Science and Public Life* (Princeton, N.J.: Princeton University Press, 1995).

33. Paget, "Physiognomy of the Human Form," 463.

34. Ibid., 454.

35. Secord, "Halifax Keynote Address," 670. Secord specifically points to works by Johann Amos Comenius, Camille Flammarion, and Stephen Hawking as examples of "popular science" that should not fall under a common designation.

36. The "trickle-down" theory of the popularization of science has been replaced by more sophisticated approaches; the shortcomings of the diffusion model were demonstrated in Roger Cooter and Stephen Pumfrey, "Separate Spheres and Public Places: Reflections on the History of Science Popularization and Science in Popular Culture," *History of Science* 32 (1994): 237–267.

37. A cat could always look at a king; before widespread physiognomic knowledge, however, the cat's conclusions were given no credence.

38. Nomenclature debates were a large part of the two-day conference titled "Popular Science: 19th-Century Sites and Experiences," York University, Toronto, Ontario, 2–3 August 2004. (The conference proceedings are available in Aileen Fyfe and Bernard Lightman, *Science in the Marketplace: Nineteenth-Century Sites and Experiences* [Chicago: University of Chicago Press, 2007].) Many of the best approaches to this subject are collected in Bernard V. Lightman, *Victorian Science in Context* (Chicago: University of Chicago Press, 1997).

39. Anthropologists Daniel G. Bates and Fred Plog drew on the work of Franz Boas to define culture as "the system of shared beliefs, values, customs, behaviors, and artifacts that the members of society use to cope with their

world and with one another, and that are transmitted from generation to generation through learning." Daniel G. Bates and Fred Plog, *Cultural Anthropology*, 3rd ed. (New York: McGraw-Hill, 1990), 7. I am interested in a different type of culture, namely, cultural events and entertainment such as the theatre, art shows, and printed publications. I do not use the designations "high culture" and "low culture" because I contend that for the purposes of physiognomic communication, the distinction between the two is meaningless.

40. Demonstrating the existence of science in the pub and other working-class spaces and taking these sites seriously as places of knowledge exchange and communication were themselves innovations, found in Anne Secord, "Science in the Pub: Artisan Botanists in Early Nineteenth-Century Lancashire," *History of Science* 32 (1994): 269–315.

41. Tytler, *Physiognomy in the European Novel*; and Mary Cowling, *The Artist as Anthropologist: The Representation of Type and Character in Victorian Art* (Cambridge: Cambridge University Press, 1989). Hartley's *Physiognomy and the Meaning of Expression*, cited in note 16, is a history-of-ideas monograph on physiognomy and expression that focuses on a small number of scholarly Victorian works on these topics. Wechsler, *A Human Comedy*.

42. See for example the essays in Lightman, *Victorian Science*. The distinction between professional and popular is itself a modern (post-1800) term, and thus the nomenclature debate that I outline is itself necessarily modern. Although the early modern era also featured expert and lay knowledge, there was no category of science as such, and thus no distinction between scientists and nonscientists. There was far more overlap in kinds of knowledge and their practitioners, although historians of the early modern period also struggle with the importantly messy boundary between lay and expert production and practice of ideas.

43. See, for example, Larry R. Stewart, *The Rise of Public Science: Rhetoric, Technology, and Natural Philosophy in Newtonian Britain, 1660–1750* (New York: Cambridge University Press, 1992).

44. Anne Secord, *Artisan Naturalists: Science as Popular Culture in Nineteenth-Century England* (Chicago: University of Chicago Press, forthcoming).

45. Winter, *Mesmerized*.

46. Roger Cooter, *The Cultural Meaning of Popular Science: Phrenology and the Organization of Consent in Nineteenth-Century Britain* (Cambridge: Cambridge University Press, 1984); Roger Darnton, *Mesmerism and the End of the Enlightenment in France* (Cambridge, Mass.: Harvard University Press, 1968).

47. James A. Secord, *Victorian Sensation: The Extraordinary Publication, Reception, and Secret Authorship of "Vestiges of the Natural History of Creation"* (Chicago: University of Chicago Press, 2000).

48. Otter, *Victorian Eye*.

49. Jennifer Green-Lewis, *Framing the Victorians: Photography and the Culture of Realism* (Ithaca, N.Y.: Cornell University Press, 1996); and Jennifer

Tucker, *Nature Exposed: Photography as Eyewitness in Victorian Science* (Baltimore: Johns Hopkins University Press, 2005).

1. Pocket Physiognomy

1. Steven Marcus, "Reading the Illegible," in *The Victorian City: Images and Realities,* ed. H. J. Dyos and Michael Wolff (London: Routledge and Kegan Paul, 1973), 257–276.

2. Jonathan Crary has charted the development of the category of observer and the ways in which the vision of the observer could be manipulated; *Techniques of the Observer: On Vision and Modernity in the Nineteenth Century* (Cambridge: Cambridge University Press, 1990). While Crary presented the subjectivity of vision as a source of concern for nineteenth-century theorists of sight, I am interested in the ways in which the subjective modality itself was an empowering agent, allowing Victorians to contribute to their experiences. As both Chris Otter and Chitra Ramalingam have shown, instrument makers and visual theorists understood many of the visual technologies that Crary explored in a variety of ways, not all of which were subjective. Likewise, subjectivity was not always itself a source of concern. See Chris Otter, *The Victorian Eye: A Political History of Light and Vision in Britain, 1800–1910* (Chicago: University of Chicago Press, 2008); and Chitra Ramalingam, "Electric Instantaneity: Spark Illumination and Photography in London, 1833–1851" (paper presented at the Annual Meeting of the History of Science Society, Crystal City, Va., November 2007).

3. Bernard Comment, *The Painted Panorama,* trans. Anne-Marie Glasheen (New York: Harry N. Abrams, 2000).

4. Kay Anderson has called this confusion a "crisis of humanity," whose increase she charted throughout the nineteenth century in *Race and the Crisis of Humanism* (London and New York: Routledge, 2007).

5. Johann Caspar Lavater, *Essays on Physiognomy,* trans. Thomas Holcroft (London: Ward, Lock and Co., 1800), 99. Artist-physiognomist and engraver to the queen Thomas Woolnoth disagreed with Lavater on the nature of beauty, citing "a great authority" who "tells us, however, that if a person born blind were suddenly to receive his sight, and the first objects he beheld were two females, the one of the greatest Beauty and the other as greatly in want of it, he would be at a loss to know whether he should give preference to Beauty or Deformity. This is just supposing that a taste for Beauty is not natural but acquired, and that such a growing attachment to Beauty would follow in the course of years as to give Cupid his greatest reputation among old men and women." Thomas Woolnoth, *Facts and Faces: Being an Enquiry into the Connection between Linear and Mental Portraiture; With a Dissertation on Personal and Relative Beauty* (London: Author, 1854), 188–189.

6. Marcus, "Reading the Illegible."

7. Engels focused on Manchester rather than on London because he was interested primarily in the industrial North.

8. Henry Mayhew, *London Labour and the London Poor,* 4 vols. (New York: Dover Publications, 1968).

9. Mayhew's work emerged out of his investigative journalism on the conditions in which the London poor lived. He was an active reformer and used his writing to promote his campaigns.

10. Mayhew, *London Labour,* 2:2.

11. Ibid., 2:2–3.

12. Henry Mayhew and John Binny, *The Criminal Prisons of London and Scenes of Prison Life* (London: Griffin Bohn, 1862); Henry Mayhew, *London Characters and the Humorous Side of London Life* (London: S. Rivers and Co., 1871).

13. Mayhew, *London Characters,* 1.

14. For more on Mayhew's motivations and personal history, see Anne Humpherys, *Henry Mayhew* (Boston: Twayne Publishers, 1984).

15. Mayhew, *London Characters,* 2.

16. *Household Words* was established by Charles Dickens and ran from 1850 to 1859. Aimed at the middle class and affordable at twopence weekly, the journal provided social commentary, entertainment, and informational articles.

17. Eliza Lynn Linton, "Passing Faces," *Household Words* 2 (1855): 264.

18. Ibid., 261. This attitude toward London was shared by Henry Mayhew, who wrote that "in the World of London, indeed, we find almost every geographic species of the human family. If Arabia has its nomadic tribes, the British Metropolis has *its* vagrant hordes as well. If the Carib Islands have their savages, the English Capital has types almost as brutal and uncivilized as they. If India has its Thugs, London has its garrotte men." Mayhew and Binny, *Criminal Prisons,* 5.

19. Linton, "Passing Faces," 261.

20. Ibid., 263.

21. Ibid., 262.

22. Ibid.

23. Ibid.,263.

24. Ibid.

25. Sir James Paget, "Physiognomy of the Human Form," *Quarterly Review* 99 (1856): 452.

26. Ibid., 453.

27. Percy J. Edwards, *History of London Street Improvements, 1855–1897* (London: Truscott and Son, printed for the London County Council, 1898), 10.

28. James Silk Buckingham, *National Evils and Practical Remedies, with the Plan of a Model Town* (Clifton, N.J.: A. M. Kelley, 1973), 193.

29. Patrick Joyce, *The Rule of Freedom: Liberalism and the Modern City* (New York: Verso, 2003), 109. The first public street lighting was introduced in Pall Mall on 28 January 1807, although street lighting did not become common in London until 1816 and was not universal in Britain until 1859. Gas lighting spread to the stage proper in 1816, further blurring the line between

street and stage, a process that intensified with the mid-Victorian turn to realism. For the most comprehensive history of Victorian British lighting practices to date, see Otter, *Victorian Eye*.

30. Carolyn Marvin, *When Old Technologies Were New: Thinking about Electric Communications in the Late Nineteenth Century* (New York: Oxford University Press, 1988).

31. Richard Sennett, *The Fall of Public Man* (New York: W. W. Norton and Company, 1992), 27.

32. Although there are crime statistics in England and Wales as of the early nineteenth century, collection methods were made uniform and extensive only as of 1857. Before this time, it is possible to identify general trends, but the introduction of street lights was only one of many factors in shifting crime patterns. For more on the history of crime in England, see Clive Emsley, *Hard Men: The English and Violence since 1750* (New York: Hambledon and London, 2005).

33. These panics were linked to occasional sensational and widely publicized crimes. Ibid., 19.

34. For more on Benjamin and detective fiction, see James V. Werner, *American Flaneur: The Cosmic Physiognomy of Edgar Allan Poe* (New York: Routledge, 2004), 16.

35. Woolnoth, *Facts and Faces,* 22.

36. Lady Elizabeth Rigby Eastlake, "Physiognomy," *Quarterly Review* 90 (1851–1852): 62–63.

37. Woolnoth, *Facts and Faces,* 22.

38. Ibid., 6.

39. Paget, "Physiognomy of the Human Form," 480.

40. Ibid.

41. Marjorie Morgan has pointed out that rapidly changing etiquette and fashion codes provided a way for members of the aristocracy to extend their social superiority in the context of a growing middle class; they invented and changed these rules at such a pace that only those with access to the trendsetters could keep up. Marjorie Morgan, *Manners, Morals, and Class in England, 1774–1858* (New York: St. Martin's Press, 1994), 28.

42. Sennett, *Fall of Public Man,* 26.

43. Ibid., 38, 183.

44. "Lavater," *Encyclopaedia Britannica* (1853–1860): 251.

45. Maggie Angeloglou, *A History of Make-up* (London: Studio Vista, 1970), 96. Victorian middle- and upper-class makeup practices were shrouded in mystery because of the perceived immorality of self-decoration.

46. Simon Gunn, *The Public Culture of the Victorian Middle Class: Ritual and Authority and the English Industrial City, 1840–1914* (New York: St. Martin's Press, 2000), 69.

47. Industry made clothes cheap to produce, and empire made the fabrics cheap to acquire. The excesses of the eighteenth century, particularly with respect to physiognomy, are discussed in Roy Porter, "Making Faces: Physiognomy and Fashion in Eighteenth-Century England," *Études Anglaises* 38 (1985): 385–396.

48. G. W. M. Reynolds, "Etiquette for the Millions," *London Journal* 12 (1845): 184. Emphasis in original. For more on the readership of the *London Journal,* see Michael Hancher, "From Street Ballad to Penny Magazine: March of the Intellect in the Butchering Line," in *Nineteenth-Century Media and the Construction of Identities,* ed. Laurel Brake, Bill Bell, and David Finkelstein (Hampshire: Palgrave, 2000), 98–103.

49. Sennett, *Fall of Public Man,* 167.

50. Christopher Lane, *Hatred and Civility: The Antisocial Life in Victorian England* (New York: Columbia University Press, 2004).

51. "Progress in Waxworks," *Punch* 28, no. 710 (1855): 67. Courvoisier was François Courvoisier, executed on 6 July 1840 for the murder of Lord William Russell. Daniel Good, executed on 28 May 1842, was convicted of the murder of Jane Good, with whom he was living. Good escaped capture and evaded the police for over a month; his actions prompted the establishment of the Detective Branch to develop the efficiency of the police forces. Crime detection improved significantly in the nineteenth century with the gradual establishment of police forces, starting with the Metropolitan Police Act of 1829. This force had jurisdiction only over metropolitan London; although crime rates dropped in London, those of surrounding towns began to rise. The Municipal Corporations Act of 1835 required incorporated towns to establish police forces, but it was not until 1856 that Parliament mandated that all provinces do so. Methods of detection increased in sophistication throughout the second half of the nineteenth century with the application of statistics for identification, particularly with the anthropometric system of Alphonse Bertillon. The end of the century saw the introduction of fingerprinting as a means of identification. It was introduced in Britain by Francis Galton, who had followed its use in India.

52. Ibid. Rush was James Bloomfield Rush, hanged on 21 April 1849 for the murders of father and son Isaac Jermy and Isaac Jermy Jermy.

53. "Comparative Physiognomy," *Punch* 40, no. 1017 (1861). William Godfrey Youngman was executed on 4 September 1860 for the murder of his mother, his two brothers, and his young lady, Mary Wells Streeter.

54. Johann Caspar Lavater and Giambattista della Porta, *The Pocket Lavater; or, The Science of Physiognomy, to Which Is Added an Inquiry into the Analogy Existing between Brute and Human Physiognomy, from the Italian of Porta,* 3rd ed. (New Haven, Conn.: Baldwin and Treadway, 1829), 72.

55. Eastlake, "Physiognomy," 63.

56. Charles Dickens, "The Demeanor of Murderers," *Household Words* 13 (1856): 505.

57. The *Mirror* was an apolitical working-class two-penny journal that ran from 1822 to 1847. Its initial success prompted a host of imitators for which it provided the model.

58. "Spartan Laws," *Mirror of Literature, Amusement and Instruction* 7 (1826): 53.

59. Vanessa R. Schwartz, *Spectacular Realities: Early Mass Culture in Fin-de-Siècle Paris* (Berkeley: University of California Press, 1998).

60. Eastlake, "Physiognomy," 66.
61. Ibid., 62.
62. Paget, "Physiognomy of the Human Form," 486.
63. Ibid., 489.
64. Linton, "Passing Faces," 263.
65. Eastlake, "Physiognomy," 90. Eastlake was gesturing to the question of change over time, with which physiognomists largely did not deal. Lavater conceded the possibility of self-improvement, which entailed overcoming bad impulses rather than actually changing the features of the face.
66. Ibid., 65.
67. Morgan, *Manners, Morals, and Class*, 26.
68. Ibid., 27–28. The loftiest addresses were squares, followed by places and then rows. Lower on the hierarchy were streets, courts, and alleys.
69. "The Historical Portrait Gallery at the Sydenham Palace," *Athenaeum* 1389 (1854): 718.
70. For more on Munby's relationship to working-class women in general and Hannah Culwick in particular, see Barry Reay, *Watching Hannah: Sexuality, Horror and Bodily De-formation in Victorian England* (London: Reaktion Books, 2002).
71. Arthur Joseph Munby, *Munby, Man of Two Worlds: The Life and Diaries of Arthur J. Munby, 1828–1910,* ed. Derek Hudson (Boston: Gambit, 1972), 15.
72. Ibid.
73. Ibid., 55.
74. The tour actually took five years to complete.
75. Charles Darwin, *The Autobiography of Charles Darwin,* ed. Francis Darwin (New York: Prometheus Books, 2000), 27.
76. William Hazlitt, *The Collected Works of William Hazlitt,* vol. 3 (New York: McClure, Phillips and Co., 1902), 307. Hazlitt, a radical republican, continued in the essay to emphasize all the ways in which the position of kings damaged their characters and rendered them unsuitable leaders.
77. Isaac D'Israeli, *Curiosities of Literature* (New York: D. Appleton and Company, 1932), 230.
78. Pierre Le Bas, "Phases of Physiognomy," *Dublin University Magazine* 68 (1866): 475.
79. Ibid.
80. The introduction to this book noted that the "metropolis, has, within a few years, become, as it were, the immense stage on which all the varieties of human aspect and action have been exhibited . . . The Physiognomist has there an ample scope for the study and enlargement of his Science." Johann Caspar Lavater, *The Pocket Lavater; or, The Science of Physiognomy* (Hartford: Andrus and Judd, 1801), v–vi.
81. The first half of the nineteenth century saw the publication of numerous physiognomic monographs, each of which purported to build and improve on Lavater's writings and those of his adherents. These books argued that the failure of physiognomy lay not in its principles, but in the ways in which

they had been explained in prior works. Following the original publication under the name Eden Warwick, the nasology book went through an additional seven editions under the name of George Jabet and the title *Notes on Noses*.

82. George Jabet, *Nasology: or, Hints towards a Classification of Noses* (London: R. Bentley, 1848), 2.

83. Ibid., 3.

84. Ibid., 6, 11–12. Emphasis in original.

85. Ibid., 136–137.

86. Ibid., 10.

87. Ibid., 7.

88. Ibid., 14.

89. Ibid.

90. Ibid.

91. Ibid., 15–16. Emphasis in original.

92. "Noses: A Chapter out of Lavater," *Temple Bar* 94 (1862): 523.

93. "Telling the Character to a Hair," *Punch* 16, no. 410 (1849): 205.

94. "Historical Portrait Gallery," 717.

95. "Physiognomy," *Anthropological Review* 6 (1868): 146.

96. Eastlake, "Physiognomy," 76.

97. Ibid.

98. Munby, *Munby, Man of Two Worlds*, 18–19.

99. Ibid., 19.

100. Sander Gilman, *Creating Beauty to Cure the Soul: Race and Psychology in the Shaping of Aesthetic Surgery* (Durham, N.C.: Duke University Press, 1999).

101. Reay, *Watching Hannah*.

102. Maria Edgeworth, *The Life and Letters of Maria Edgeworth*, ed. Augustus J. C. Hare, vol. 1 (Boston, Houghton Mifflin and Co., 1895), 18. Emphasis in original.

103. "Noses: A Chapter out of Lavater," 524.

104. Reay, *Watching Hannah*, 39.

105. Jabet, *Nasology*, 176.

106. Ibid., 176–177. Dickens's most frequent collaborator, Hablot K. Browne, was nicknamed "Phiz," which, in addition to harmonizing with Dickens's "Boz," spoke to Browne's success in creating and communicating physiognomic meaning.

107. Ibid., 177.

108. The population of London rose steadily from the mid-eighteenth to the mid-nineteenth century, increasing between 16 and 20 percent each decade in the first half of the nineteenth century. By 1750, a full tenth of England's population lived in London, the economic and cultural center of Britain. In 1800, the population was around 900,000, which grew to well over 3,000,000 by 1871. The population of London in 1831 was 1,654,994; in 1841 it rose 18 percent to 1,948,417; 1851 saw a 21 percent rise to 2,362,236; by 1861 it climbed another 19 percent to 3,254,266; 1871 saw a population of

3,883,902. The boundaries of London for the purpose of census taking were firmly established only in 1851; statistics from before that date are approximate. For more on Victorian urbanization, see H. J. Dyos and Michael Wolff, eds., *The Victorian City: Images and Realities* (London: Routledge and Kegan Paul, 1973).

109. Lynda Nead, *Victorian Babylon: People, Streets and Images in Nineteenth-Century London* (New Haven, Conn.: Yale University Press, 2000), 120–121.

110. In addition to the pressures of urbanization, the Great Exhibition of 1851 brought an entire nation together to see the same sights in the same places. The contents of the exhibition were highly educational and innovative; equally so was the opportunity for people across classes and throughout the country to experience wonder together. Forcing technological sophistication on all who attended, the exhibition was part of, and contributed significantly to, the increasing commodification and commercialization of the working, middle, and upper classes alike.

111. Paget, "Physiognomy of the Human Form," 452.

112. Ibid.

113. Ibid., 452–453.

2. Performing Physiognomy

1. Elizabeth Ewan and Stuart Ewan, *Typecasting: On the Arts and Sciences of Human Inequality; A History of Dominant Ideas* (New York: Seven Stories Press, 2006), 7–8.

2. Jonathan Rose, *The Intellectual Life of the British Working Classes* (New Haven, Conn.: Yale University Press, 2001), 99.

3. As I discuss later in this chapter, I use contemporary sociological theories, particularly Stuart Hall's encoding/decoding model, to analyze historical theatre responses.

4. Theatre theorists such as Pier Jacopo Martelli and Johann Christoph Gottsched proposed historically appropriate costuming in the mid-1740s. Their suggestions initially met with mixed success. Allardyce Nicoll, *A History of Early Nineteenth Century Drama, 1800–1850* (Cambridge: Cambridge University Press, 1930), 191. British painters, architects, and managers began to experiment with realistic scenery in the late eighteenth century, and their efforts led to beautiful backdrops that were often more impressive than the costumes and sets.

5. I want to be careful here not to impose a unilateral view of audience; in Raymond Williams's formulation, "There are no masses, only ways of seeing people as masses." Raymond Williams, *The Long Revolution* (New York: Penguin, 1965), 300. The Frankfurt school consisted of a number of thinkers who worked at the Institut für Sozialforschung in Frankfurt, Germany, in the late 1920s and early 1930s. These theorists included Max Horkheimer, T. W. Adorno, Herbert Marcuse, Leo Lowenthal, Norbert Elias, and Erich Fromm. From their work, which included innovative analyses of mass communication and social reproduction, emerged modern

critical theory and cultural studies that built on and eventually challenged their models of passive audience reception. My analysis of the interaction between audiences and actors pushes against the Frankfurt school's contentions about audience passivity in the consumption of capitalist culture. See Max Horkheimer and Theodor W. Adorno, *Dialectic of Enlightenment* (New York: Continuum, 1993), especially "The Culture Industry: Enlightenment as Mass Deception," 120–167.

6. Audience response theory is a rich and contested field; early approaches, like those of the Frankfurt school, framed audiences of mass culture as passive and unthinking entities. Later work began to investigate the role that audiences played in negotiating the material they viewed and consumed. For a broad overview of various interventions and developments, see Will Brooker and Deborah Jermyn, *The Audience Studies Reader* (New York: Routledge, 2003).

7. Stuart Hall, *Culture, Media, Language: Working Papers in Cultural Studies, 1972–79* (Birmingham: Centre for Contemporary Cultural Studies, University of Birmingham, 1980), 128–138. Subsequent scholarship took an empirical approach to Hall's model, notably in work by David Morley and Dorothy Hobson. David Morley, *The "Nationwide" Audience: Structure and Decoding* (London: British Film Institute, 1980); Dorothy Hobson, *Soap Opera* (Malden, Mass.: Blackwell, 2003).

8. Umberto Eco, *The Role of the Reader: Explorations in the Semiotics of Texts* (Bloomington: Indiana University Press, 1979).

9. Music halls, puppet shows, pantomimes, and entertainment spaces geared explicitly to the working classes functioned in different, if overlapping, ways. My analysis is limited to those involved in the respectable stage and the materials they consulted and with which they engaged.

10. My analysis focuses on the application of physiognomic ideas rather than on their deliberate transgression.

11. As numerous scholars have chronicled, racial ideas and imperial impulses were often rehearsed and promoted through theatre. See, for example, Hazel Waters, *Racism on the Victorian Stage: Representation of Slavery and the Black Character* (Cambridge: Cambridge University Press, 2007). Daphne Brooks has shown that the theatre was also a site of protest that offered performers a space in which to challenge modes of oppression and repression. Daphne Brooks, *Bodies in Dissent: Spectacular Performances of Race and Freedom, 1850–1910* (Durham, N.C.: Duke University Press, 2006). See Chapters 4 and 6 for discussions of Victorian racial science and notions of human hierarchy.

12. Theatres also were physically changing; in addition to improvements in lighting and scenery technology, the additional interior illumination sparked a series of renovations and redecorations.

13. The gradual removal of the relatively affordable seats near the stage offered by the pit was the subject of some controversy connected to larger debates about the elitism of the theatre. For a defense of the pit, see Clement Scott's 1875 article in *The Era Almanack,* reprinted as Clement Scott, "A Plea for

the Pit," in *Victorian Theatre: The Theatre in Its Time,* ed. Russell Jackson (Franklin, N.Y.: New Amsterdam, 1989), 50–54.

14. As noted in Richard Sennett, *The Fall of Public Man* (New York: W. W. Norton and Company, 1992), 176.

15. See, for example, the teachings of Aaron Hill, a very early advocate of theatrical realism whose acting guide was the primary reference for eighteenth-century aspiring players. Aaron Hill, *The Art of Acting. Part I: Deriving Rules from a New Principle, for Touching the Passions in a Natural Manner. An Essay of General Use, to Those, Who Hear, or Speak in Public . . . But Adapted, in Particular, to the Stage: With a View to Quicken the Delight of Audiences, and Form a Judgment of the Actors, in Their Good, or Bad, Performances* (London: Printed for J. Osborn, 1746).

16. For debates about Victorian realism, see Michael R. Booth, *Theatre in the Victorian Age* (Cambridge: Cambridge University Press, 1991), 95–98.

17. Ibid., 95; Catherine Hall, "Keynote Address: Macaulay's Nation," presented at the meeting of the North American Victorian Studies Association, New Haven, Conn., 2008; Alison Winter, *Mesmerized: Powers of Mind in Victorian Britain* (Chicago: University of Chicago Press, 1998), 324–328.

18. Russell Jackson, ed., *Victorian Theatre: The Theatre in Its Time* (Franklin, N.Y.: New Amsterdam, 1989), 200.

19. Various scholars have explored the links between literary and other forms of realism, but there have been few studies of all the realisms and their relationships to one another. One of the most comprehensive explorations of Victorian realism is Alison Byerly, *Realism, Representation, and the Arts in Nineteenth-Century Literature* (Cambridge: Cambridge University Press, 1997). Although Byerly uses literature to structure her study, she incorporates a wide range of media and types of evidence. See also Caroline Levine, *The Serious Pleasures of Suspense: Victorian Realism and Narrative Doubt* (Charlottesville: University of Virginia Press, 2003).

20. Levine, *Serious Pleasures of Suspense,* 10.

21. Ibid., 11. Levine drew largely from Ruskin's writings in *Modern Painters,* a series written from 1843 to 1860, in which Ruskin set forth an agenda taken up by the Pre-Raphaelites, whom I discuss in the next chapter.

22. For changes in acting styles, see Alan S. Downer, "Players and the Painted Stage: Nineteenth-Century Acting," *Publications of the Modern Language Association* 61 (1946): 522–576. Another intriguing form of theatrical realism was found in the staging of "shipwreck plays," which used actual ships and detailed seascapes as part of the staging and props.

23. Richard W. Schoch, *Shakespeare's Victorian Stage: Performing History in the Theatre of Charles Kean* (Cambridge: Cambridge University Press, 1998), 34.

24. Ibid., 30.

25. Ibid., 57–61.

26. *The Theatrical Journal and Stranger's Guide* 33 (1872): 212. Many Victorian critics used the terms *realism* and *naturalism* interchangeably; I do not here refer to "scientific naturalism" in its technical sense, as explored in the schol-

arship of Frank Turner, among others. Frank M. Turner, *Between Science and Religion: The Reaction to Scientific Naturalism in Late Victorian England* (New Haven, Conn.: Yale University Press, 1974).

27. Henry Irving, *The Art of Acting* (Chicago: Dramatic Publishing Company, 1887), 18.

28. Gillen D'Arcy Wood, *The Shock of the Real: Romanticism and Visual Culture, 1760–1860* (New York: Palgrave, 2001). Romanticism, Wood argued, emerged as a response to mass marketing and the widening appeal of formerly elite entertainment spaces and visual experiences.

29. Horkheimer and Adorno, *Dialectic of Enlightenment.*

30. See Chapter 1 for a longer discussion of these concerns and the ways in which physiognomy, with its emphasis on instinct, helped suture this crisis.

31. Allardyce Nicoll, *A History of English Drama, 1660–1900,* 2nd ed., vol. 4, *Early Nineteenth-Century Drama, 1800–1850* (Cambridge: Cambridge University Press, 1966), 187–190.

32. Georgian theatrical audiences provided entertainment equal to that of the actors; those seated in the pit up front would often rise in the middle of the show to shout out remarks and would frequently throw fruit and other items onto the stage.

33. As quoted in Wolfgang Schivelbusch, *Disenchanted Night: The Industrialisation of Light in the Nineteenth Century* (New York: Berg, 1988), 195.

34. The relationship between lighting and stage physiognomy is a rich topic that is more fully explored in Sharrona Pearl, "Building Beauty: Physiognomy on the Gas-Lit Stage," *Endeavour* 30 (2006): 84–89.

35. Joseph Strutt and J. R. Planché, *A Complete View of the Dress and Habits of the People of England: From the Establishment of the Saxons in Britain to the Present Time . . . : To Which Is Prefixed an Introduction, Containing a General Description of the Ancient Habits in Use among Mankind, from the Earliest Period of Time to the Conclusion of the Seventh Century* (London: H. G. Bohn, 1842), v.

36. The improvement in the social status of actors mirrored the improvements in theatre respectability more broadly.

37. Johann Jacob Engel and Henry Siddons, *Practical Illustrations of Rhetorical Gesture and Action,* 2nd ed. (London: Sherwood, Neely and Jones, 1822), 53.

38. Ibid., 25.

39. Ibid., 70.

40. Ibid., 71.

41. Ibid.

42. Dion Boucicault *The Art of Acting* (New York: Dramatic Museum of Columbia University, 1926), 49.

43. An Old Stager, *A Complete Guide to the Stage, and Manual for Amateurs and Actors* (London: Henry Beal, 1851), 11–13.

44. Ibid., 15. Emphasis in original.

45. Sander Gilman, *Making the Body Beautiful: A Cultural History of Aesthetic Surgery* (Princeton, N.J.: Princeton University Press, 1999), 61–63.

46. Gilbert à Beckett was a close friend and collaborator of Henry Mayhew.

47. Gilbert Abbott à Beckett, *Man-Fred: A Burlesque Ballet Opera, in One Act* (London: John Cumberland, 1834). Passed in 1834, the Chimney Sweep Act forbade anyone under twenty-one from climbing chimneys. Young, undernourished children, many of whom were sold to master chimney sweeps from orphanages, made ideal instruments for cleaning chimneys. These children often died from choking or getting stuck in the chimney; if they survived, they often suffered health problems in later life.

48. Ibid., frontispiece.

49. Ibid., act I, scene 3, page 13.

50. An Old Stager, *Complete Guide,* 7.

51. Irving, *Art of Acting,* 14. Emphasis added.

52. Ibid., 15.

53. Engel and Siddons, *Practical Illustrations,* 362–363.

54. Max Beerbohm, *The Works of Max Beerbohm* (New York: Dodd, Mead, 1922), 117.

55. The process of switching from gas lighting to electric was hardly smooth; numerous fires and tragedies resulted.

56. Caroline Fox , *The Journals of Caroline Fox, 1835–71: A Selection*, ed. Wendy Trewin (London: Elek, 1972), 183.

57. An Old Stager, *Complete Guide,* 15.

58. Ibid., 11. Emphasis in original.

59. Ibid., 16.

60. T. W. Erle, *Letters from a Theatrical Scene-Painter: Being Sketches of the Minor Theatres of London as They Were Twenty Years Ago* (London: M. Ward, 1880), 30–31.

61. Pearl, "Building Beauty."

62. Erle, *Letters,* 25.

63. Henry Morley, *The Journal of a London Playgoer,* 2nd ed. (Leicester: Leicester University Press, 1974), 28–29.

64. Puppet shows were extremely common in the nineteenth century, particularly those employing the now-classic "Punch and Judy" characters.

65. Morley, *Journal of a London Playgoer,* 69.

66. "Carmarthen Theatrical," *Times* (London), 2 January 1824, 3.

67. "Covent-Garden Theatre," *Times* (London), 19 October 1826, 2. The Mr. Liston in question was Victorian comic actor John Liston.

68. The prototype for the patter baritone was Fred Sullivan, Arthur Sullivan's brother, who inspired the types of roles that patter baritones filled. Michael Ainger, *Gilbert and Sullivan: A Dual Biography* (Oxford: Oxford University Press, 2002).

69. Engel and Siddons, *Practical Illustrations,* 29. Emphasis in original.

70. Ibid., 53–54. Emphasis in original.

71. *The Actor; or, Guide to the Stage* (London: John Lowndes, J. Chappell and Son, 1821), 26–27.

72. Irving, *Art of Acting,* 7.

73. Ibid., 9.

74. John Baldwin Buckstone, *The Dream at Sea: A Drama in Three Acts,* 4th ed. (London: W. Strange, 1835).

75. This claim is based on my examination of literally hundreds of promptbooks from the Harvard Theater Archive.

76. Sennett, *Fall of Public Man.*

77. Charles William Smith, *The Art of Acting* (London: Thomas Hailes Lacy, 186?), 6. Emphasis in original.

78. According to Lavater, birth played a more powerful role than breeding in determining character. He wrote at length about "inexplicable, singularly true, pure predestination" and argued that "each bone hath its original form, its individual capacity of form." But, he continued, physiognomy did continually alter, particularly for the worse: "I have known handsome, and good young men, who, in a few years, by debauchery and excess, have been totally altered." Improvements were also possible because "persons may, at length, combat their vices with their whole force, and sometimes, obtain no small victory." From *Essays on Physiognomy,* trans. Thomas Holcroft (London: Ward, Lock and Co., 1800), 103. The Victorian attitude toward the role of education in self-improvement left more room for change than did Lavater; phrenology in particular was seen as a vehicle for personal growth. This theme is examined in Roger Cooter, *The Cultural Meaning of Popular Science: Phrenology and the Organization of Consent in Nineteenth-Century Britain* (Cambridge: Cambridge University Press, 1984).

79. Smith's attitude stands in sharp contrast to Victorian codes of conformity that I discussed in the previous chapter, wherein the right clothing was often enough to enable one to pass.

80. Stock racial and religious stage types long predated the nineteenth century, but a number of props and features of various types coalesced at this time; of particular note for the purposes of this study are the stage Jew and the stage Irish. The history of the stage Jew is chronicled in depth in M. J. Landa, *The Jew in Drama* (New York: KTAV Pub. House, 1969). For a discussion of the stage Irish, see Annelise Truninger, *Paddy and the Paycock: A Study of the Stage Irishman from Shakespeare to O'Casey* (Bern: Francke, 1976).

81. Smith, *Art of Acting,* 6. Emphasis in original.

82. Irving, *Art of Acting,* 22.

83. Julie F. Codell, "Expression over Beauty: Facial Expression, Body Language, and Circumstantiality in the Painting of the Pre-Raphaelite Brotherhood," *Victorian Studies* 29 (1986): 255–290.

84. Earl Leslie Griggs, ed., *Collected Letters of Samuel Taylor Coleridge,* 6 vols. (Oxford: Clarendon Press, 1956–1972), 3:501. Emphasis in original.

85. Lucy Hartley, *Physiognomy and the Meaning of Expression in Nineteenth-Century Culture* (Cambridge: Cambridge University Press, 2001), 101. Michael R. Booth has also argued for continuities between the realistic theatre and Victorian painting trends. Booth, *Theatre in the Victorian Age,* 95.

86. Wood, *Shock of the Real,* 17–66.

87. William Hogarth, quoted in ibid., 48.

3. Portrait Physiognomy

1. Bernard Smith has shown that Charles Darwin lamented his lack of drawing ability as a weakness that affected him during the *Beagle* voyage. Other Victorian naturalists, including Sir William Jackson Hooker and John Lindley, explicitly developed their skills as draughtsmen to further their botanical observations and descriptions. Bernard Smith, *European Vision and the South Pacific* (New Haven, Conn.: Yale University Press, 1985), 276–277.

2. Anne Secord, "Botany on a Plate: Pleasure and the Power of Pictures in Promoting Early Nineteenth-Century Scientific Knowledge," *Isis* 93 (2002): 28–57. Naturalist and botanical patron Sir Joseph Banks recognized the importance of including skilled artists on collecting expeditions in order to accurately record the specimens in their original states and environments. Drawing on the writings of Richard Walter, Banks pioneered the inclusion of artist-observers on voyages of naturalistic discovery. Smith, *European Vision*, 6–7.

3. Charlotte Klonk, *Sciences and the Perception of Nature: British Landscape Art in the Late Eighteenth and Early Nineteenth Centuries* (New Haven, Conn.: Yale University Press, 1996), 152.

4. Chris Otter, *The Victorian Eye: A Political History of Light and Vision in Britain, 1800–1910* (Chicago: University of Chicago press, 2008), 43–70.

5. David Brewster, "The Sight and How to See," *North British Review* 26 (1856): 176.

6. John Ruskin, *Modern Painters* (Kent: G. Allen, 1883). Ruskin frequently emphasized the importance of studying the rules of nature as a means to understand the laws of art. See, for example, E. T. Cook and Alexander Wedderburn, eds., *The Works of John Ruskin,* 39 vols. (New York: Longmans, Green, and Co., 1903–1912), 22:157.

7. As quoted in Kate Flint, *The Victorians and the Visual Imagination* (Cambridge: Cambridge University Press, 2000), 174. For more on these debates, see ibid., 183–184.

8. Ford Madox Brown, *The Exhibition of Work and Other Paintings* (London: McCorquodale and Co., 1865).

9. Jennifer Montagu, *The Expression of the Passions: The Origin and Influence of Charles Le Brun's "Conférence sur l'expression générale et particularière"* (New Haven, Conn.: Yale University Press, 1994), 107.

10. Giambattista della Porta, *La fisonomia dell'hvomo, et La celeste* (Venetia: Presso S. Combi, & G. La Noù, 1652). Charles Le Brun's lectures are reprinted and translated in full in Montagu, *Expression of the Passions.*

11. Lavater's exact reactions are recorded (in translation) in Joan K. Stemmler, "The Physiognomical Portraits of Johann Caspar Lavater," *Art Bulletin* 75 (1995): 151–168. In this article, Stemmler traced the various portraits of Lavater and his relationship to them. Her close reading of these images alongside Lavater's writings provides a fascinating and useful foray into Lavater's self-image and his attitude toward painting and imagery. I think that Stemmler misunderstands the meaning of the term "caricature" for Lavater

and his contemporaries; regardless, this article is a unique approach to Lavater and physiognomy.

12. Ibid., 160.
13. Johann Caspar Lavater, *Essays on Physiognomy; for the Promotion of the Knowledge and the Love of Mankind,* trans. Thomas Holcroft (London: Ward, Lock and Co., 1800), 170–176. See also 141 and 393.
14. Ibid., 175.
15. The provenance of this etching and engraving is in some doubt; various curators have argued that it is a copy after Gillray.
16. The *Anti-Jacobin Review* was the press arm of the Anti-Jacobin Society, an English group formed to oppose radical political ideas that grew out of the French Revolution. The review, founded by Tory politician and former prime minister George Canning, ran for one parliamentary season, from November 1797 to July 1798. Gillray was a frequent contributor.
17. Secord, "Botany on a Plate," 36.
18. The practice of using inanimate objects to make up a face and body was likely pioneered in the sixteenth century by the Italian artist Francesco Urbini, whose image of a man with a head of phalluses is now displayed in the Ashmolean Museum in Oxford. The genre was practiced extensively by Italian mannerist painter Giuseppe Arcimboldo, whose many paintings provided the model for French artist Nicolas de Larmessin II, whose series of engravings *Costumes Grotesques* (1695) was likely the first example of the rendering of occupations through their relevant equipment. "Physiognomy: You Are the Sum of Your Parts," http://www.georgeglazer.com/collecting/eccentric.html (accessed 15 March 2007).
19. The other Spratt images include "The Circulating Library," "Fish," and "The Mineralogist." The first two of these nonprofessional composites are of women, while the third, a professional category, constructs a man.
20. See especially my discussion of Eden Warwick and his use of *Oliver Twist* in Chapter 1.
21. Isaac D'Israeli, *Curiosities of Literature* (New York: D. Appleton and Company, 1932), 79.
22. Ibid., 50.
23. Jonathan Brown, "Enemies of Flattery: Velázquez' Portraits of Philip IV," *Journal of Interdisciplinary History* 17 (1986): 137–154.
24. Nadia Tscherny, "Likeness in Early Romantic Portraiture," *Art Journal* 46 (1987): 151–168.
25. Montagu, *Expression of the Passions.*
26. Nineteenth-century artists reached a far wider audience with their work than previous artists as painting exhibitions were opened to the viewing public. The spectatorship of these viewers was mediated by the dictates of Lavater and later physiognomic writers; in short, they and the knowledge they brought to their viewings needed to be considered in an unprecedented fashion.
27. Lady Elizabeth Rigby Eastlake, "Physiognomy," *Quarterly Review* 90 (1851–1852): 69

28. William Hazlitt, *The Collected Works of William Hazlitt,* 21 vols., vol. 8 edited by A. R. Waller and Arnold Glover, with an introduction by W. E. Henley (New York: McClure, Phillips & Co., 1903), 133.

29. D'Israeli, *Curiosities of Literature,* 48.

30. "The First Principle of Physiognomy," *Cornhill Magazine* 5 (1861): 569.

31. [Carington Bowles], *The Draughtsman's Assistant; or, Drawing Made Easy* (London: Robert Sayer and Co., 1801), 5.

32. James Merigot, *The Amateur's Portfolio: Being a Selection of Lessons Calculated to Make the Art of Drawing Easy,* 2 vols., vol. 1 (London: S. Robinson, 1821), 2.

33. *Progressive Lessons Intended to Elucidate the Art of Portrait Painting* (London: Thomas Clay, 1824), 23–24.

34. N. Whittock, *The Miniature Painter's Manual* (London: Sherwood, Gilbert, and Piper, 1844), 21.

35. Ibid., 24.

36. Whittock published at least five drawing manuals on other topics.

37. Whittock, *Miniature Painter's Manual,* 66–67.

38. Ibid., 67.

39. *The Manual of Oil-Painting for Young Artists and Amateurs* (London: David Bogue, 1847), 94.

40. Ibid., 95–96.

41. Thomas Woolnoth, *Facts and Faces: Being an Enquiry into the Connection between Linear and Mental Portraiture; With a Dissertation on Personal and Relative Beauty* (London: Author, 1854), 249. First published 1852.

42. Ibid., 3.

43. Ibid., 260–261.

44. Ann Bermingham, *Learning to Draw: Studies in the Cultural History of a Polite and Useful Art* (New Haven, Conn.: Yale University Press, 2000), xii. The transition in the English economy from a "client-based" to a "market-based" system and its effects on painters are also discussed in Richard Wendorf, *Sir Joshua Reynolds: The Painter in Society* (Cambridge, Mass.: Harvard University Press, 1996), 88. Analyses of patronage networks offer useful insights into the support and production of various and disparate types of knowledge, from artistic to scientific. One of the pioneering works in this area is Mario Biagioli, *Galileo, Courtier: The Practice of Science in the Culture of Absolutism* (Chicago: University of Chicago Press, 1993).

45. Bermingham, *Learning to Draw,* xii–xiii.

46. The changes in art patronage and its effects on institutional art production are discussed in Helene E. Roberts, "Exhibition and Review: The Periodical Press and the Victorian Art Exhibition System," in *The Victorian Periodical Press: Samplings and Soundings,* ed. Joanne Shattock and Michael Wolff (Leicester: Leicester University Press, 1982), 88.

47. *Fortnightly Review* 51 (1855): 708, quoted in Roberts, "Exhibition and Review," 88.

48. Leonore Davidoff and Catherine Hall, *Family Fortunes: Men and Women of the English Middle Class, 1780–1850* (New York: Routledge, 2002), 289–

291. Painting manuals are a useful source of information about women's activities, as are the art-supply records that Bermingham examined. Another useful resource is Victorian women's scrapbooks; these detailed and intricate pieces of work contain a great deal of information about Victorian life and culture, as well as providing clues to what these women found compelling and important. Most scrapbooks are the result of countless hours of hard work and concentration and speak as much to women's need to fill their hours as to their skills. The largest collection of Victorian scrapbooks can be found in the Harry Robertson Page Collection at the Manchester Metropolitan University Library.

49. Bermingham, *Learning to Draw.*

50. Ibid., 129.

51. Ibid., 133.

52. Ibid., 132. The London-based Royal Academy of Arts was founded in 1768; applicants who showed appropriate character and talent were admitted free for instruction and membership. The Academy's yearly exhibition opened on the first Monday of May and closed on the first Monday of August. Each artist could display only eight works, none of which was allowed to have been exhibited previously. Membership in the Academy was highly competitive; the number of associates was fixed at twenty, while the number of full members never exceeded forty. An aspiring associate had to wait for a full member to die before being promoted. Because there were far more than sixty artists working in England in the nineteenth century, a number of rival organizations were formed, the most successful of which was the British Institution, founded in 1825. However, none of these groups ever achieved more than second-rate status compared with the Academy, despite the complaints of critics, artists, and even Parliament about the quality of Academy work. For more on the history of the academy, see Holger Hoock, *The King's Artists: The Royal Academy of Arts and the Politics of British Culture, 1760–1840* (New York: Oxford University Press, 2003).

53. Roberts, "Exhibition and Review," 88–89.

54. Ibid., 104.

55. "On Some Pictures in the Royal Academy Exhibition of 1855," *Fraser's Magazine* 51 (1855): 707.

56. Ibid.

57. Roberts, "Exhibition and Review," 86.

58. Ibid.

59. Flint, *Victorians and the Visual Imagination*, 174, 183–184; Klonk, *Sciences and the Perception of Nature*. See especially Klonk's discussions of phenomenalism on this point.

60. Bermingham, *Learning to Draw*, 132.

61. "Fine Arts: Royal Academy," *Athenaeum*, 20 May 1854, 627.

62. Mary Cowling, *The Artist as Anthropologist: The Representation of Type and Character in Victorian Art* (Cambridge: Cambridge University Press, 1989), 91.

63. "The R.A.," *Athenaeum*, 16 May 1868, 701.

64. "Thomas Woolnoth, *Study of the Human Face*" (review), *Art Journal,* July 1868, 228.

65. Sir James Paget, "Physiognomy of the Human Form," *Quarterly Review* 99 (1856): 455–456.

66. Eastlake, "Physiognomy," 69.

67. Ibid.

68. Kenneth Bendiner, *An Introduction to Victorian Painting* (New Haven, Conn.: Yale University Press, 1985), 1.

69. Christopher Wood, *Victorian Painting* (London: Weidenfeld and Nicolson, 1999), 48–52.

70. Ibid., 63.

71. For a discussion of critical response to *Derby Day,* particularly with respect to its use of physiognomic principles, see Cowling, *Artist as Anthropologist,* 232–316.

72. Firth's physiognomic ideas and their expression in his work are chronicled in Cowling, *Artist as Anthropologist,* especially 182–183.

73. Wood, *Victorian Painting,* 91–92.

74. Cowling, *Artist as Anthropologist,* 106. See Cowling for excerpts from the physiognomic writings of these artists. As Julie Codell noted, even with their focus on aesthetics, members of the PRB were prepared to sacrifice beauty for the expression of character. Julie F. Codell, "Expression over Beauty: Facial Expression, Body Language, and Circumstantiality in the Painting of the Pre-Raphaelite Brotherhood," *Victorian Studies* 29, no. 2 (Winter 1986): 255–256.

75. Brown, *Exhibition of Work,* 255.

76. Henry O'Neil, *Lectures on Painting Delivered at the Royal Academy* (London: Bradbury, Evans and Co., 1866), 34.

77. "Fine Arts: Royal Academy," *Athenaeum,* 8 May 1858, 596.

78. O'Neil, *Lectures on Painting,* 37, 36.

79. Originally quoted in Helmut Gernsheim and Alison Gernsheim, *The History of Photography from the Camera Obscura to the Beginning of the Modern Era,* rev. and enl. ed. (London: Thames and Hudson, 1969), 118.

80. See, for example, M. J. Landa, *The Jew in Drama* (New York: KTAV Pub. House, 1969).

81. Johann Jacob Engel and Henry Siddons, *Practical Illustrations of Rhetorical Gesture and Action,* 2nd ed. (London: Sherwood, Neely and Jones, 1822), 137.

4. Caricature Physiognomy

1. See, for example, Marcus Tullius Cicero *De inventione,* trans. and ed. Maria Greco (Galatina: M. Congedo, 1998). For discussion of these conventions, see the foundational text on Irish prejudice in graphic print, L. Perry Curtis, *Anglo-Saxons and Celts: A Study of Anti-Irish Prejudice in Victorian England,* vol. 2 (Bridgeport, Conn.: Conference on British Studies at the University of Bridgeport, 1968), xviii. For more on classical physiognomy,

see Jennifer Montagu, *The Expression of the Passions: The Origin and Influence of Charles Le Brun's "Conférence sur l'expression générale et particulière"* (New Haven, Conn.: Yale University Press, 1994). I have discussed the historical relationship between physiognomy and drawing in greater depth in Chapter 3.

2. Starting with Johann Caspar Lavater's writings, most major modern physiognomic works devoted at least one section to national or group physiognomies. See, for example, George Corfe, *The Physiognomy of Diseases* (London: James Nisbet and Co., 1849); John Cross, *An Attempt to Establish Physiognomy upon Scientific Principles* (Glasgow: University Press, 1817); and Alexander Walker, *Physiognomy Founded on Physiology* (London: Smith, Elder and Co., 1834).

3. In this chapter, I use "Irish" to refer to Irish Catholics and Nationalists. Although there were many different kinds of Irish, the process that I examine is one that sought to eradicate distinctions rather than highlight them.

4. Sheridan Gilley, "English Attitudes to the Irish in England, 1789–1900," in *Immigrants and Minorities in British Society*, ed. Colin Holmes (London: Allen and Unwin, 1978), 81–110.

5. Entertainment was also a significant feature of Victorian anti-Catholic material.

6. Perry Curtis Jr., *Anglo-Saxons and Celts: A Study of Anti-Irish Prejudice in Victorian England* (New York, 1968), 22.

7. Tim Barringer, "Images of Otherness and the Visual Production of Difference: Race and Labour in Illustrated Texts, 1850–1865," in *The Victorians and Race*, ed. Shearer West (Aldershot: Scolar Press, 1996), 34–52; Donald M. MacRaild, "'Principle, Party and Protest': The Language of Victorian Orangeism in the North of England," in *The Victorians and Race*, ed. Shearer West (Aldershot: Scolar Press, 1996), 128–141.

8. As Dror Wahrman has demonstrated, notions of class and nationhood are highly contingent on prevailing political realities and the ways in which they are communicated. Although he acknowledged the importance of changes in social structures, he placed far more weight on the rhetoric and representation of political pressures in the formation of class identities. Dror Wahrman, *Imagining the Middle Class: The Political Representation of Class in Britain, c. 1780–1840* (New York: Cambridge University Press, 1995). Likewise, as Benedict Anderson argued in his classic work *Imagined Communities,* "nations" are built primarily through words and ideas rather than extant geographic or ethnic realities. Benedict R. O'G. Anderson, *Imagined Communities: Reflections on the Origin and Spread of Nationalism* (London: Verso, 1983). Both of these scholars rooted the origins of communal ties in formulations of language rather than in physical or economic structures.

9. Although colonialism played a role in the demarcation of racialized types and the attitudes toward them, this chapter focuses specifically on Britons rather than on the empire writ large. It is precisely because of the possibility of daily interaction with the Irish and the Jews that the imperative for visual identification was so strong.

10. Linda Colley, *Britons: Forging the Nation, 1707–1837* (New Haven, Conn.: Yale University Press, 1992).

11. For more on the development of print culture, see Celina Fox, *Graphic Journalism in England during the 1830s and 1840s* (New York: Garland Publishing, 1988); and James A. Secord, *Victorian Sensation: The Extraordinary Publication, Reception, and Secret Authorship of "Vestiges of the Natural History of Creation"* (Chicago: University of Chicago Press, 2000).

12. I have taken this formulation of the grotesque from Colin Trodd, Paul Barlow, and David Amigoni, eds., *Victorian Culture and the Idea of the Grotesque* (Brookfield, Vt.: Ashgate, 1999), 3.

13. As Sheridan Gilley has argued, there were both positive and negative representations of the Irish; the Victorian notion of Paddy as entertaining emerged from earlier positive representations that were increasingly belittling throughout the nineteenth century. Gilley, "English Attitudes to the Irish," 85.

14. By 1841, almost 20 percent of London's population was immigrants, 90 percent of whom were from other parts of Britain, including Scotland, Wales, and Ireland, and 10 percent of whom came from abroad. H. A. Shannon, "Migration and the Growth of London, 1841–91: A Statistical Note," *Economic History Review* 5 (1935): 82.

15. In 1841, Thomas Arnold characterized the modern period of history through four features common to the world's nationalities: language, religion, institutions, and race. The last was strongly identified with blood and biology; see Douglas A. Lorrimer, "Race, Science and Culture: Historical Continuities and Discontinuities," in *The Victorians and Race*, ed. Shearer West (Aldershot: Scolar Press, 1996), 12–33. Race in the nineteenth century is a voluminous and well-studied topic that I do not examine here. Rather, I explore the ways in which the racial imaginary was translated into visual manifestations. For more on Victorian ideas of race, see, for example, Shearer West, ed., *The Victorians and Race* (Aldershot: Scolar Press, 1996).

16. Dermot Quinn, *Patronage and Piety: The Politics of English Roman Catholicism, 1850–1990* (Stanford, Calif.: Stanford University Press, 1993).

17. Eliza Lynn Linton, "Passing Faces," *Household Words* 2 (7 April 1855): 261.

18. Quinn, *Patronage and Piety*, 183.

19. Like all identity categories, Irishness and Jewishness were unstable; the Irish in England were different from the Irish in Ireland, who were in turn different from the Irish in the United States. Likewise with Jews in different geographic locations. Michael de Nie, *The Eternal Paddy: Irish Identity and the British Press, 1798–1882* (Madison: University of Wisconsin Press, 2004), 9, 13.

20. The Irish political violence of the second half of the nineteenth century, including the Phoenix Park murders and the later home-rule debates, fueled further virulent political caricatures. Likewise, the spike in eastern European Jewish immigration following a rise in pogroms, as well as the anti-Semitism of the Jack the Ripper investigations, initiated further negative Jewish imagery. However, I am interested in the transition from individual to group depictions, which had already occurred by the second half of the nineteenth century.

21. Many scholars have discussed the relationship between anti-Jewish violence and Jewish emigration. For detailed numbers of Jewish immigrants to Britain, see Todd M. Endelman, *The Jews of Britain, 1656 to 2000* (Berkeley: University of California Press, 2002).

22. For more on depictions of Disraeli, see Daniel Pick, *Svengali's Web: The Alien Enchanter in Modern Culture* (Cambridge: Cambridge University Press, 2000).

23. As Paul Rich has pointed out, Victorian anthropological discourse often used the term *race* to refer to culture. Paul Rich, "Social Darwinism, Anthropology and English Perspectives of the Irish, 1867–1900," *History of European Ideas* 19 (1994): 777–785.

24. R. F. Foster, *Paddy and Mr. Punch: Connections in Irish and English History* (London: A. Lane, 1993). Foster referred only to the Irish. He noted that in fact, Matthew Arnold, J. R. Green, and Charles Kingsley suggested intermarriage between the Saxons and the Celts as a means to use Celtic speed to balance Saxon cloddishness. Edwin Samuel Montagu, the son of a Sephardi Jewish financier, was secretary of state for India from 1917 to 1922 and was an important advocate of Indian independence.

25. Sir John Fielding linked the Jews and the Irish in a letter to the secretary of state. He suggested that if these populations were kept under tighter control, there would be fewer robberies in London and more jobs available to London's English inhabitants. Quoted in Bernard Glassman, *Protean Prejudice: Anti-Semitism in England's Age of Reason* (Atlanta: Scholars Press, 1998), 81. Many economic historians have argued that the Irish labor force was critical for British industrial and technological development and infrastructure. For a discussion of this historiography, see Donald M. MacRaild, *Irish Migrants in Modern Britain, 1750–1922* (New York: St. Martin's Press, 1999). The role of the Irish in the English economy is a contested topic; for an opposing view, see Jeffrey G. Williamson, "The Impact of the Irish on British Labor Markets during the Industrial Revolution," *Journal of Economic History* 46 (1986): 693–720.

26. Similar tensions existed with respect to the Welsh and the Scots as well. The Welsh were vilified as foreigners primarily in the seventeenth century, while anti-Scot sentiment and propaganda reached its height in the eighteenth century as their self-government was dismantled. Historian Michael Duffy pointed out that the Scottish prejudice diminished a great deal in the late eighteenth century. Duffy argued for a sense of common identity from the shared experience of the Industrial Revolution and the growth of the British Empire. Likewise, the growing Irish Catholic threat served to unite the Welsh, the Scots, and the English against the Irish in the nineteenth century. Michael Duffy, *The Englishman and the Foreigner* (Cambridge: Chadwick Healy, 1986), 20. For more on print depictions of, and attitudes toward, the Welsh and the Scottish, see Duffy's book.

27. The two most prominent examples of conversion in England were Lord George Gordon, who converted to Judaism in 1787, and Benjamin Disraeli, who converted from Judaism in 1817. For depictions of Gordon, see Library

of the Jewish Theological Seminary of America, *The Jew as Other: A Century of English Caricature, 1730–1830; An Exhibition, April 6–July 31, 1995,* Frank Felsenstein and Sharon Liberman Mintz, curators (New York: Library of the Jewish Theological Seminary of America, 1995).

28. For a discussion of the Jew as contagion in late Victorian Britain, see Judith Halberstam, "Technologies of Monstrosity: Bram Stoker's *Dracula,*" *Victorian Studies* 36 (1993): 333–353.

29. *Hansard's Parliamentary Debates,* n.s., 28 (1830): 1325.

30. This text was first translated into English in 1892.

31. Thomas Carlyle, *Chartism,* as quoted in Friedrich Engels, *The Condition of the Working Class in England,* ed. David McLellan (New York: Oxford University Press, 1993), 102.

32. Ibid.

33. See, for example, Henry Mayhew, *London Labour and the London Poor,* 4 vols. (New York: Dover Publications, 1968), 1:34.

34. According to the *Catalogue of Political and Personal Satires* compiled for the British Museum by M. Dorothy George, the number of prints depicting Ireland and the Irish rose steadily from 1784 through 1832. Graphic print production increased generally at this time; what is significant is the specific focus on the Irish situation during the most heated political moments. Images of the Irish peaked, as one would expect, at the end of this period, in tandem with increasing political agitation. From 1784 to 1792, there were 59 prints listed, rising to 95 for the period 1793–1800. There was a significant rise in 1801–1810, to 115, coincident with the Act of Union with Ireland, discussed later. The period 1811–1819, relatively quiet in Anglo-Irish relations, saw a dip in the number of prints to 86. The number rose again to 100 for 1820–1827 and finally reached 140 in the scant four-year period 1828–1832, during which Irish political organizing was particularly active. This trajectory reflects caricaturists' attempts to deal with the increasing threat through humorous and mocking portrayals. M. Dorothy George, *Catalogue of Political and Personal Satires Preserved in the Department of Prints and Drawings in the British Museum,* vols. 5–11 (London: British Museum Publications, 1954). Although the British Museum's holdings do not include all the prints produced during this period, the collection is quite comprehensive and provides a good indication of the concentration of prints in various areas. The catalogue runs only through 1832.

35. Domestic and zoo animals played an extremely prominent part in the Victorian consciousness. For more on the role of animals in the nineteenth century, see Harriet Ritvo, *The Animal Estate: The English and Other Creatures in the Victorian Age* (Cambridge, Mass.: Harvard University Press, 1987). Ritvo argued that the animal fancies mirrored class distinctions. She charted the ways in which zoos acted as metaphors for imperial dominance, and she exposed in detail the relationship between Victorians and their pets, farm animals, and zoo animals.

36. 12 June 1798, British Museum (subsequently BM) 9228. Roy Douglas, Liam Harte, and Jim O'Hara, *Drawing Conclusions: A Cartoon History of Anglo-Irish Relations, 1798–1998* (Belfast: Blackstaff, 1998), 16.

37. Johann Caspar Lavater, *Essays on Physiognomy,* trans. Thomas Holcroft (London: Ward, Lock and Co., 1800), 340.
38. Ibid., 381.
39. Ibid., 471.
40. Ibid., 394.
41. Ibid., 477.
42. For examples of these prints, see Duffy, *Englishman and the Foreigner,* 21.
43. The Irish had many important internal distinctions that held little meaning for the English. For more on the heterogeneity of the Irish and the ways in which these came to be ignored during the nineteenth century, see MacRaild, *Irish Migrants in Modern Britain,* 6–8.
44. One of the major impetuses for the passing of the act was the 1828 election of O'Connell as the member of Parliament for County Clare, a seat he was unable to take; fearing a violent response from the Irish, the act was passed in 1829, allowing, among other things, O'Connell to sit in Parliament.
45. For the exact numbers of prints in various subject areas, see George, *Catalogue of Political and Personal Satires.*
46. De Nie, *Eternal Paddy,* 14.
47. My use of the masculine pronoun is not accidental. Paddy was always male, though not always a man per se. The major political and activist agitators, starting with O'Connell, were almost exclusively men. Thus the visual depictions of "Paddy" (as the Irish were termed) likewise focused almost exclusively on masculine monsters and apes. In fact, the few representations of female Irish tended to be flattering; *Punch* often depicted Hibernia as the epitome of classic Greek female beauty. See, for example, *Punch,* 29 October 1881. For more on different depictions of Hibernia, see L. Perry Curtis Jr., "The Four Erins: Feminine Images of Ireland," *Éire-Ireland* 33 (1998): 70–102.
48. A great deal of work has been done on satire and caricature in the eighteenth and nineteenth centuries. These studies deal with a wide range of topics on which I can touch only briefly. For more, see, for example, Diana Donald, *The Age of Caricature: Satirical Prints in the Reign of George III* (New Haven, Conn.: Yale University Press, 1996); M. Dorothy George, *English Political Caricature: A Study of Opinion and Propaganda* (Oxford: Clarendon Press, 1959); Richard Godfrey, *James Gillray: The Art of Caricature* (London: Tate Gallery Publishing, 2001); Mark Hallett, *The Spectacle of Difference: Graphic Satire in the Age of Hogarth* (New Haven, Conn.: Yale University Press, 1999); and John T. Hayes, *The Art of Thomas Rowlandson* (Alexandria, Va.: Art Services International, 1990).
49. Judith Wechsler, *A Human Comedy: Physiognomy and Caricature in 19th Century Paris* (Chicago: University of Chicago Press, 1982), 71–91.
50. *Past Present Future,* lithograph, January 1834. For more on the minimum clue, see E. H. Gombrich, *Art and Illusion: A Study in the Psychology of Pictorial Representation,* 4th ed. (London: Phaidon Press, 1972).
51. This is not to say that physiognomy was not well known and used in France, but rather that it did not hold the same immediate visual meaning that made it so useful for English physiognomists. However, British caricature was strongly influenced by French traditions and styles.

52. *Punch* 9 (July–December 1845): 255.
53. Douglas, Harte, and O'Hara, *Drawing Conclusions*, 38. Print by Robert Seymour, *Figaro in London*, 31 October 1835.
54. Caroline Fox, *The Journals of Caroline Fox, 1835–71: A Selection*, ed. Wendy Trewin (London: Elek, 1972), 42.
55. Ibid, 49.
56. Paddy was ubiquitous in a number of media, especially the theatre.
57. Foster, *Paddy and Mr. Punch*, 174. Foster pointed readers to *Punch* 1 (July–December 1841) as an example of pro-Irish sentiment. However, even in prints that demonstrated sympathy with the Irish, such as John Leech's "Justice to Ireland" (18 April 1846), the male Irish peasant in the drawing was still sullen and somewhat simian.
58. The stage Irishman was a ubiquitous figure of fun from the seventeenth century but, like visual representations of the Irish, became increasingly uniform in costuming and character during the nineteenth century.
59. John Leech, "The 'Repeal Face,' or, Mother Goose and the Golden Eggs," *Punch* 4 (1843): 37.
60. Walker, *Physiognomy Founded on Physiology*, 260.
61. Ibid., 262.
62. The sequence of Irish Frankensteins is reproduced in L. Perry Curtis Jr., *Apes and Angels: The Irishman in Victorian Caricature*, rev. ed. (Washington, D.C.: Smithsonian Institution Press, 1997).
63. In 1845, the population of Ireland was over 8 million people. By the end of 1851, the population had declined by nearly 3 million, over a million of whom died from starvation and related diseases; the rest emigrated to England and abroad, especially the United States and Canada. Cormac Ó Gráda and Kevin H. O'Rourke, "Migration as Disaster Relief: Lessons from the Great Irish Famine," *European Review of Economic History* 1 (1997): 22–23.
64. The British government officially declared the end of the famine (and famine relief laws) in 1849, although some contended that it ended with the agricultural improvements of 1847. Others argued that it continued well into 1851.
65. The Young Ireland movement grew out of the Irish nationalist newspaper the *Nation*, founded in 1842 by Charles Gavan Duffy. The organization became increasingly radical and initiated the Tipperary riots of 1848. Many of its members later joined the Irish Republican Brotherhood.
66. John Leech, "Young Ireland in Business for Himself," *Punch* 11 (1846): 70.
67. The term *degeneration* became a major focal point of debate in the last twenty years of the nineteenth century; here I mean it only to refer to the animal-like nature of the subject. For more on late Victorian degeneration, see Daniel Pick, *Faces of Degeneration: A European Disorder, 1848–1918* (Cambridge: Cambridge University Press, 1989).
68. The hat became a general costuming symbol for the stage Irish.
69. Douglas, Harte, and O'Hara, *Drawing Conclusions*, 45.
70. "How to Tame Ireland," *Punch* 14 (1848): 166.
71. John Leech, "Height of Impudence," *Punch* 11 (1846): 245.
72. "The English Labourer's Burden," *Punch* 16 (1849): 79.

73. George Jabet, *Notes on Noses* (London: R. Bentley, 1852), 3.

74. For more on Pritchard and the monogenist/polygenist debate about the singular or multiple origin of human races, see Nancy Stepan, *The Idea of Race in Science: Great Britain, 1800–1960* (London: Macmillan, 1982).

75. Engels, *Condition of the Working Class in England,* 103. Henry Mayhew, *London Labour and the London Poor,* 1:34.

76. "The Lion of the Season," *Punch* 40 (1861): 213; and "A Great Time for Ireland," *Punch* 41 (1861): 244.

77. See, for example, Wilhelm Hauff, "The Young Englishman," in *Tales by Wilhelm Hauff* (London: Bell, 1900), 151–169.

78. "The Missing Link," *Punch* 43 (1862): 165.

79. Ibid.

80. Of course, the total simianization of Paddy was not irreversible; many later images show Paddy as the animan of earlier days. See, for example, *Punch,* 28 December 1867, or the *Tomahawk,* 18 December 1869.

81. Adrian J. Desmond, *The Politics of Evolution: Morphology, Medicine, and Reform in Radical London* (Chicago: University of Chicago Press, 1989). For more on pre-Darwinian evolutionary discussions, see also Secord, *Victorian Sensation.*

82. The notion of Jews being identified by their noses has always been powerful; late eighteenth-century Jewish violoncellist Jacob Cervetto was nicknamed "Nosee," cries of which always greeted him when he performed. For a 1774 picture of Cervetto as Nosee, see Alfred Rubens, "Anglo-Jewry in Caricature, 1780–1850," *Jewish Historical Society of England Transactions* 23 (1971): 113.

83. This comment does not imply that geographic differences are irrelevant in the production of different characteristic facial structures. In fact, this variation is precisely what is ignored when different Jews are categorized as having a uniform face, that is, as "looking Jewish." For more on the various implications of this conflation, see Sander Gilman, *The Jew's Body* (New York: Routledge, 1991).

84. M. J. Landa, *The Jew in Drama* (New York: KTAV Pub. House, 1969), 120.

85. In comparison with the Irish, there were relatively few prints of Jews in the eighteenth century. This stands to reason because there were still very few Jews living in Britain. In 1753, the Jewish population was between 6,000 and 8,000; by 1830, there were over 30,000 Jews living in Britain. By 1850, there were about 35,000 Jews living in Britain, of whom 18,000 to 20,000 lived in London. Colin Holmes, *Anti-Semitism in British Society, 1876–1939* (London: E. Arnold, 1979).

86. Endelman, *Jews of Britain,* 48.

87. Ibid.

88. Rubens, "Anglo-Jewry in Caricature," 97, discusses the changes in Jewish caricature following the 1753 bill.

89. This does not indicate that the Sephardi banker/trader/stockjobber was totally accepted in English society. On the contrary, there was a great deal of resentment against these men, particularly when customers lost a great deal of money.

There was also a great deal of interreligious discrimination; for many assimilated Sephardi Jews, their peddling Ashkenazi or Tudesco (Portuguese for "German") coreligionists were an embarrassment from whom they made great efforts to distance themselves. Intermarriages between Ashkenazi and Sephardi Jews were relatively rare. By the early nineteenth century, there were between 12,000 and 15,000 Jews in Britain, of whom about 2,000 were of Sephardi backgrounds. Ashkenazim outnumbered Sephardim in Britain from around 1720, but because of the strong economic position of the Sephardim during the eighteenth century, it was they who affected the British awareness of Jewishness, such as it was. This shifted in the nineteenth century. Johann Wilhelm von Archenholz, *A Picture of England: Containing a Description of the Laws, Customs, and Manners of England; Interspersed with Curious and Interesting Anecdotes of Many Eminent Persons* (London: Pall Mall, 1797), 41. With the increased numbers of poor Jews during the nineteenth century, the British Jewish community had its own internal charity systems designed in part to ward off external criticisms of poverty and laziness. Endelman, *Jews of Britain,* 83.

90. Library of the Jewish Theological Society of America, *Jew as Other.*
91. Endelman, *Jews of Britain,* 60.
92. Archenholz, *Picture of England,* 177.
93. See, for example, Daniel Defoe, *The Villainy of Stock-Jobbers Detected: And the Causes of the Late Run upon the Bank and Bankers Discovered and Considered* (London: [s.n.], 1701).
94. The Cromwell negotiations are outlined in Manasseh ben Israel, *Menasseh Ben Israel's Mission to Oliver Cromwell: Being a Reprint of the Pamphlets Published by Menasseh Ben Israel to Promote the Re-admission of the Jews to England, 1649–1656,* ed. Lucien Wolf (London: Macmillan, 1901). There was already a small Jewish community in England when the Jews were officially allowed to reenter; they were a critical part of the negotiations.
95. Duffy, *Englishman and the Foreigner,* 17. Sir Solomon de Medina was the first English Jew to be knighted. It was 137 years before another Jew was similarly honored.
96. 12 August 1788, Rubens 877, BM 7368. "Rubens" refers to the catalogue of Alfred Rubens, now found in the London Jewish Museum. Blue and buff were Fox's election colors.
97. A number of caricatures outlined Jewish support for Fox, including BM 6795, 7344, 7363, and 7366. There was also a Gillray print from 1807, *Election Candidates,* BM 10732, in which a bearded but bareheaded Jew is shown taking the election oath.
98. Lavater, *Essays on Physiognomy,* 352–353.
99. London, 14 February 1792, printed for and sold by Carrington Bowles. Rubens 850.
100. Lavater, *Essays on Physiognomy,* 353.
101. Ibid., 396.
102. Ibid., 394.

103. Ibid., 392.
104. J. G. Spurzheim, *Phrenology, in Connexion with the Study of Physiognomy* (Boston: March, Capen and Lyon, 1836), 200.
105. Rubens 917, BM 10604.
106. Cross, *Attempt to Establish Physiognomy upon Scientific Principles*, 180. This comment is interesting because it is one of the few examples of a writer discussing the mechanism for change in physiognomic determinism.
107. Rubens 1514, BM 7424.
108. In fact, Jews were often depicted with or even as pigs as a particularly degrading marker of difference. For more examples of this trend, see Library of the Jewish Theological Society of America, *Jew as Other*, 58–64.
109. Ibid., 32. Jewish women also occasionally engaged in prizefighting; Endelman, *Jews of Britain*, 58.
110. For more on Daniel Mendoza, see the reprint of his memoirs, *The Memoirs of the Life of Daniel Mendoza* (New York: Arno Press, 1975). See also Library of the Jewish Theological Society of America, *Jew as Other*, 382; and Alfred Rubens, "Portraits of Anglo-Jewry," *Jewish Historical Society of England Transactions* 19, Sessions 1955–1959 (1960): 13–52.
111. March 1795, Rubens 889, BM 8626.
112. For more on English notions of Jewish criminals, see Gerald Reitlinger, "The Changed Face of English Jewry at the End of the Eighteenth Century," *Jewish Historical Society of England Transactions* 23 (1971): 34–43.
113. November 1809, Rubens 927, BM 11425.
114. Although there are examples of prominent Jewish politicians and financiers in the late nineteenth century, they did not represent the status of the community overall.
115. The franchise was not extended to all British men until 1917. Universal suffrage was achieved in 1928.
116. David Feldman, *Englishmen and Jews: Social Relations and Political Culture, 1840–1914* (New Haven, Conn.: Yale University Press, 1994), 1.
117. This tradition dated back to mean-spirited caricatures of Sampson Gideon, who was falsely believed to have used his influence to promote the failed Naturalisation Bill of 1753. Rubens, "Portraits of Anglo-Jewry," 16. Later attacks focused on rising Jewish politicians, including Lionel de Rothschild, David Salmons, and, of course, Benjamin Disraeli. For more on the depictions of these men, see also Alfred Rubens, "The Rothschilds in Caricature," *Jewish Historical Society of England Transactions* 22, Sessions 1968–1969 (1970): 76–87.
118. Rubens 997, BM 15804.
119. Rubens, "Rothschilds in Caricature," 98.
120. The notion of the Jewish nose has been analyzed in Gilman, *Jew's Body*.
121. George Jabet, *Nasology: or, Hints towards a Classification of Noses* (London: R. Bentley, 1848), 14.
122. "Aquiline," in *The Oxford English Dictionary*, 3rd ed. (Oxford: Oxford University Press, 1989), 597.

123. Jabet, *Notes on Noses*, 9.
124. For more on eighteenth-century physiognomic manipulation, see Roy Porter, "Making Faces: Physiognomy and Fashion in Eighteenth-Century England," *Études Anglaises* 38 (1985): 385–396.
125. Jabet, *Notes on Noses*, 89–90.
126. Ibid., 92.
127. Henry Mayhew, *London Labour and the London Poor*, 2:106. An 1832 discussion in the periodical *Guide to Knowledge* noted that "in spite of all our beadles and policemen, our way-sides and lanes are infested with Christian beggars—but who ever saw a Jew begging?" *Guide to Knowledge*, 15 September 1832, 104.
128. The change in Dickens's portrayal of Jews can be attributed to many factors, including literary range and increased liberalization in attitude. The latter is likely due in part to Dickens's correspondence with Mrs. Eliza Davis, the wife of a London Jewish banker who bought Dickens's home. Mrs. Davis protested Dickens's lack of sympathy for the Jews and argued that it was in marked contrast to his defense of other impoverished communities living in England. Deborah Heller, "The Outcast as Villain and Victim: Jews in Dickens' *Oliver Twist* and *Our Mutual Friend*," in *Jewish Presences in English Literature*, ed. Derek Cohen and Deborah Heller (Montreal: McGill–Queen's University Press, 1990), 41–42.
129. For a detailed analysis of Fagin with respect to Dickens's attitude toward Jews, see Heller, "Outcast as Villain and Victim."
130. As I noted in Chapter 1, the text and illustrations of *Oliver Twist* were an important source of evidence for Jabet's claims about noses.
131. Mayhew, *London Labour and the London Poor*, 1:106.
132. Henry Mayhew, *London Labour and the London Poor*, 4 vols. (London: Griffin, Bohn and Co., 1861–1862), 3:119.
133. "Is She a Jewess?" *Star*, 4 November 1837.
134. Mayhew, *London Labour and the London Poor*, 3:119.
135. Physiognomy and anthropology converged on racial distinctions. Lavater made detailed reference to the works of Petrus Camper and Johann Friedrich Blumenbach, as did later physiognomic writers. Interest in anthropological study became formalized in 1843 with the founding of the Ethnological Society of London. Because of a significant divide among members over ideas of race, a portion of the society broke away in 1863 to form the Anthropological Society. The two groups reunited in 1871 to establish the Anthropological Institute of Great Britain and Ireland. This group remained interested in differences between races, as is seen with the election of John Beddoe as its president in 1889. Among other works, Beddoe was the author of *The Races of Man* (1860) and *The Races of Britain* (1885), which argue for degrees of Nigrescence, as well as the hierarchy of development and intelligence among races.
136. Petrus Camper, Adrian Gilles Camper, and Georges Cuvier, *Observations anatomiques sur la structure intérieure et le squelette de plusieurs espèces de cétacés* (Paris: Dufour, 1820); Johann Friedrich Blumenbach, William

Lawrence, and William Coulson, *A Manual of Comparative Anatomy*, 2nd ed. (London: Printed for W. Simpkin and R. Marshall, 1827); Robert Knox, *The Races of Man: A Fragment* (Philadelphia: Lea and Blanchard, 1850).

137. I am not claiming that the experiences of colonized blacks and of the Irish were equivalent; as G. K. Peatling has pointed out, such comparisons "trivialize or misinterpret the plight of nonwhite victims of imperialism or subjugation." G. K. Peatling, "The Whiteness of Ireland under and after the Union," *Journal of British Studies* 44 (2005): 115. However, the imagery of blacks in the eighteenth century, both in Britain and in the empire, provided many of the iconographic models used by Victorian caricaturists. These images drew on hierarchical assumptions about race, as well as reinforcing the colonized status of the Irish in the larger British context. It was precisely because the Irish could not be immediately visually identified and treated accordingly that the physiognomic imperative was so strong.

138. Ideas about race did not emerge from imperial expeditions, but notions of empire drew the English directly into these discourses in their reading practices of travel literature, in advertisements and commercial expeditions, and especially in the way they related to Britons as a whole. See Anne McClintock, *Imperial Leather: Race, Gender, and Sexuality in the Colonial Context* (New York: Routledge, 1995), for a discussion of colonial consciousness and the civilizing mission of the imperial project. As David Dabydeen has argued, clothing (as opposed to nakedness) was an important rhetorical mark of the state of a black's civilization; unlike the Irish and Jewish hegemonic representations, depictions of colonized "savages" maintained a range of distinctions in status and type. David Dabydeen, *Hogarth's Blacks: Images of Blacks in Eighteenth Century English Art* (Athens: University of Georgia Press, 1987), 90.

139. Although much nineteenth-century caricature retained its political and radical roots, a large body of work was devoted to sheer commercial appeal, and it is the process by which these commercial drawings communicated meaning through physiognomic depictions that interests me here.

140. In particular, Giambattista della Porta and Charles Le Brun wrote about and provided models for the use of physiognomic principles in artistic work. See Giambattista della Porta, *De humana physiognomonia . . . libri IV* (Vici Aequensis: Apud Iosephum Cacchium, 1586); and Charles Le Brun in Montagu, *Expression of the Passions*.

141. As Celina Fox noted, "If all of these literary and allegorical references, taken from classical scholarship to popular sayings and slang, provided a framework for all types of graphic artist, so too did the prints of the 1830s present a spectrum of physiognomical depiction, ranging from the highest level of portraiture to stock types and gross caricature." Fox, *Graphic Journalism in England*, 96. There was indeed something for everyone from everywhere, and it was the physiognomic references that made images meaningful across boundaries.

5. Photographic Physiognomy

1. The first of the inexpensive "shilling monthlies," the *Cornhill Magazine* appealed to a well-educated middle-class audience who disdained the cheaper sensational publications but who nevertheless did not buy the expensive highbrow journals like *Blackwood's*. Launched in 1860, the *Cornhill* sold 120,000 copies of its first edition and sparked a stream of successful imitations, including *Temple Bar*. The imitations sold well, but the *Cornhill* retained the bulk of the market.

2. "On Physiognomy," *Cornhill Magazine* 4 (1861): 472.

3. Ibid., 473.

4. Ibid., 475. The *Cornhill* was echoing Lavater's own frustration with the value of physiognomic evidence presented by portraiture, whose "actual, incredible, imperfection" Lavater called "one of the greatest obstacles to physiognomy. Johann Caspar Lavater, *Essays on Physiognomy*, trans. Thomas Holcroft (London: Ward, Lock and Co., 1800), 175.

5. E. S. Dallas, "The First Principle of Physiognomy," *Cornhill Magazine* 5 (1861): 570.

6. Hugh Welch Diamond, "On the Application of Photography to the Physiognomic and Mental Phenomena of Insanity," in *The Face of Madness: Hugh W. Diamond and the Origin of Psychiatric Photography*, ed. Sander Gilman (New York: Brunner/Mazel, 1976), 19–24.

7. Ibid., 22–23.

8. Lavater, *Essays on Physiognomy*, 58. Lavater took a very active role in the execution of his own portraits in order to avoid communicating false physiognomic information.

9. For a comprehensive review of the status of physiognomy in the nineteenth century, see Sharrona Pearl, "As Plain as the Nose on Your Face: Physiognomy in Nineteenth-Century England" (Ph.D. diss., Harvard University, 2005).

10. Sander L. Gilman, ed., *The Face of Madness: Hugh W. Diamond and the Origin of Psychiatric Photography* (New York: Brunner/Mazel, 1976), 8.

11. Diamond, "On the Application of Photography," 23.

12. Jean-Martin Charcot suggested that hysterical states could be produced by manipulation, a concept pushed by his student Sigmund Freud, who used past experiences to explain and eradicate manifestations of mental illness. Both these approaches were contingent on a notion of interiority that explained mental phenomena.

13. Diamond's Royal Society paper suggested three uses for photographic physiognomy in the asylum: record keeping, diagnosis, and therapy. Diamond, "On the Application of Photography."

14. Kate Flint, *The Victorians and the Visual Imagination* (Cambridge: Cambridge University Press, 2000), 236.

15. See, for example, Susan Stanford Friedman, *Mappings: Feminism and the Cultural Geographies of Encounter* (Princeton, N.J.: Princeton University Press, 1998), and Lynda Nead, *The Female Nude: Art, Obscenity and Sexuality* (New York: Routledge, 1992).

16. Diamond was one of the few physiognomists who engaged with the question of change over time. Because physiognomy was a technology of immediate diagnosis and decision making, change was largely irrelevant for its most frequently used application, pocket physiognomy. Few of the polite and professional physiognomists addressed the question even as they sought to scientize the practice. Lavater touched briefly on the issue of change, noting that although the inherited body set out certain parameters, there was always the possibility of developing in different directions on the basis of a variety of environmental factors. The face itself, however, would be unlikely to change; as in the case of Socrates, a notoriously ugly man, people inclined to rise above their physiognomic fates would have to overcome the faces they were born with rather than change them. See Lavater, *Essays on Physiognomy*, 7, 84, 103, 105, and 235, for his comments on this question.

17. Diamond did, however, share with other medical physiognomists a belief in the value of physiognomy for diagnostic purposes.

18. The 1856 death of a Surrey Asylum patient, Daniel Dolley, sparked an investigation into the cruelty of his physician, Mr. Charles Snape, because of an anonymous letter alleging that the death was not from natural causes. The exhumation of Dolley's body found the heart to be absent, which Diamond had examined following the postmortem and subsequently burned. Diamond's investigation was based on his own dissatisfaction with the finding of natural causes in Dolley's death. Snape was acquitted of murder by the grand jury, but his livelihood and reputation were ruined. The lack of the heart made further inquiry impossible, and Diamond received severe criticism for his actions throughout the course of events, which led to his resignation. For details of the Dolley trial, see Adrienne Burrows and Iwan Schumacher, *Portraits of the Insane: The Case of Dr. Diamond* (New York: Quartet Books, 1990), 22–34.

19. Bloore, *Hugh Welch Diamond*, 4. Photography was an expensive and time-consuming hobby, and this led to a strong distinction between "amateur" and "professional" photographers. Amateurs, with time and leisure and without the profit-making motive or necessity, experimented with "art." However, professionals were providing a mechanical and reproducible "craft" service. For more on the distinction between amateur and professional photographers, see Jennifer Green-Lewis, *Framing the Victorians: Photography and the Culture of Realism* (Ithaca, N.Y.: Cornell University Press, 1996), 50–51. See also Grace Seiberling and Carolyn Bloore, *Amateurs, Photography, and the Mid-Victorian Imagination* (Chicago: University of Chicago Press, 1986).

20. Gilman, *Face of Madness*, 7.

21. "Testimonial to Dr. Diamond, of the Surrey County Asylum," *Asylum Journal of Mental Science* 1 (1855): 176. Details of this journal are discussed later.

22. "Dr. Diamond," *Athenaeum*, 3 July 1886, 17.

23. "Photography in Medical Science," *Lancet*, 22 January 1859, 89.

24. These photographs were exhibited a number of times in both London and Norwich under similar titles, including "Phases of the Insane" (1854), "Portraits of Insane Persons" (1856), "Studies of Insane Persons" (1857), and "Illustrations of Mental Disease" (1859). For a complete listing of Diamond's photographic exhibitions, see "Photographic Exhibitions in Britain, 1839–1865," www.peib.org.uk (accessed 21 May 2006).

25. Sir Charles Bell, *The Anatomy and Philosophy of Expression as Connected with the Fine Arts* (London: C. Bell, 1883); Alexander Morison, *The Physiognomy of Mental Diseases* (London: Longman and Co., 1843).

26. Étienne Esquirol, *Mental Maladies: A Treatise on Insanity,* trans. E. K. Hunt (Philadelphia: Lea and Blanchard, 1845).

27. "Exhibition of the Photographic Pictures at the Society of Arts," *Athenaeum,* 1 January 1853, 23. Diamond's widespread recognition was aided by the "wet-plate" or collodion process, invented by his former patient Frederick Scott Archer in 1851. This inexpensive process was the first to create a negative image, allowing unlimited reproductions of the original photograph.

28. Diamond, "On the Application of Photography," 24.

29. Ibid., 20; emphasis in original. Diamond used similar language in an 1852 letter to William Henry Fox Talbot, writing that his photographs were "most accurate & useful," unlike "Sir A's Morrison's [*sic*] delineations of the insane[, which] instead of being truthful are perfect caricatures." Hugh Welch Diamond, "Letter to William Henry Fox Talbot," *Talbot Correspondence Project* (London: Fox Talbot Museum/Lacock Abbey Collection, 1852), LA52–034.

30. J. M. Charcot, *Charcot, the Clinician: The Tuesday Lessons; Excerpts from Nine Case Presentations on General Neurology Delivered at the Salpêtrière Hospital in 1887–88 by Jean-Martin Charcot,* trans. Christopher G. Goetz (New York: Raven Press, 1987), 107.

31. Diamond, "On the Application of Photography," 20.

32. Ibid.

33. Roland Barthes, "The Photographic Message," in *Image, Music, Text,* ed. and trans. Stephen Heath (New York: Hill, 1977), 17.

34. Diamond published photographic articles extensively in the informational journal *Notes and Queries* between 1852 and 1854. His writings provided guidance for many aspiring photographers, medical and otherwise. Among those who followed in his diagnostic footsteps were doctors John Charles Bucknill, Daniel H. Tuke, Samuel Hitch, T. N. Brushfield, and especially Sir William Charles Hood. Another important asylum photographer was Sir James Crichton-Browne, whose pictures were examined by Charles Darwin as he researched *The Expression of the Emotions in Man and Animals* (1872).

35. For more on Diamond as a medical pioneer, see Sander Gilman, *Seeing the Insane* (Lincoln: University of Nebraska Press, 1996); and Gilman, *Face of Madness.* Diamond's work with amateur photographers is chronicled in Seiberling and Bloore, *Amateurs, Photography, and the Mid-Victorian Imagination.*

36. Robinson's 1858 photograph "Fading Away," in which he pictured a healthy fourteen-year-old girl who appeared to be on her deathbed, generated a storm of controversy. The issue was not the sensitive subject matter; death scenes were a common and widely appreciated pictorial subject. Rather, viewers felt betrayed by the manipulations of the photographer. Photography had a responsibility to record what was rather than what could be or especially, as the following 1865 comment about Robinson's photograph showed, what could not be: "Here photography is employed to portray the disembodied spirit winging its course to regions no mortal eye has seen. Apart from the liberty taken with a sacred subject which will jar on the feelings of many, the utter impossibility of such a thing ever being presented to the camera, the absolute certainty that the figure is that of a young woman in the flesh, travestying [sic] the ideal rendering which imaginative painters have given to spiritual beings, at once impresses the beholder with the untruth of the whole thing. It is not only not a fact or possible to be a fact, but it is alike untrue to nature and art, and carries its untruth and incongruity on the surface." Respice Finem [pseud.], "The Legitimacy of Combination-Printing," *Photographic Journal* (1865), as quoted in Green-Lewis, *Framing the Victorians*, 54–55.

37. Henry Peach Robinson, *Pictorial Effect in Photography: Being Hints on Composition and Chiaroscuro for Photographers* (Pawlet, Vt.: Helios, 1971).

38. Diamond, "On the Application of Photography," 21.

39. Ibid., 23.

40. Ibid.

41. Karl Marx, *Capital: A Critique of Political Economy,* trans. Ben Fowlkes, vol. 1 (New York: Vintage Books, 1977).

42. John Tagg, *The Burden of Representation: Essays on Photographies and Histories* (Minneapolis: University of Minnesota Press, 1993).

43. Moral management accompanied the removal of physical restraints from the mad in the eighteenth century and became an increasingly sophisticated technique until the size of large public asylums made its thorough application difficult. Some forms of moral management are still in use today, particularly in the treatment of eating disorders.

44. The term *art therapy* was coined by British artist Adrian Hill in 1942. Since the 1940s, art therapy has developed a number of different approaches, with a rich literature and a wide variety of options for those who wish to train in the field. The most comprehensive exploration of modern art therapy and its intellectual precursors can be found in Susan Hogan, *Healing Arts: The History of Art Therapy* (London: Jessica Kingsley, 2001).

45. Following the original optimism of the early asylums designed under the principles of "moral treatment," large public asylums found themselves overcrowded and unable to meet the needs of most of their patients. Rather than acting as short-term therapeutic options, Victorian asylums became long-term housing solutions for the mentally ill. For more on moral treatment and the construction of asylums, see Nancy Tomes, *A Generous Confidence: Thomas Story Kirkbride and the Art of Asylum-Keeping, 1840–1883* (Cambridge: Cambridge University Press, 1984).

46. This review, which appeared in the newly launched *Photographic News,* commented that the photographs "are neither interesting as works of art nor as photographs; it is well to know of the application, but we say it again, we do not want to see all the results. The photographs are perfectly hideous." "The Exhibition of the Photographic Society," *Photographic News* 1 (1859): 255.

47. Because Diamond was the superintendent of the female ward of the Surrey Country Lunatic Asylum, the bulk of his patients and subjects were women, although there are a few extant images of men. Conolly was particularly interested in female lunatics; his approach to cure was more amenable to saving so-called fallen women.

48. The Ophelia theme in Diamond's work has been examined in depth in Shari Addonizio, "Portraits of Madwomen: Another Look at Dr. Hugh Welch Diamond's Photographs of the Insane Female in Victorian England," *Athanor* 17 (1999): 53–39. For more on Ophelia images in the nineteenth century, see Elaine Showalter, *The Female Malady: Women, Madness, and English Culture, 1830–1980* (New York: Pantheon Books, 1985), 90.

49. John Hitchman, "Annual Meeting of the Association: President's Address," *Journal of Mental Science* 4 (1858): 7; emphasis in original. Hitchman began his career working at the Hanwell Asylum under the leadership of John Conolly.

50. See in particular the birds in the wallpaper of Holman Hunt's 1861–1863 painting *The Awakening Conscience.*

51. John Conolly, "Case Studies from the Physiognomy of Insanity with Plates 1–17," in *The Face of Madness: Hugh W. Diamond and the Origin of Psychiatric Photography,* ed. Sander Gilman (New York: Brunner/Mazel, 1976).

52. Ibid., 27.

53. John Conolly, *The Construction and Government of Lunatic Asylums and Hospitals for the Insane* (London: Dawsons, 1968), 61.

54. Conolly, "Case Studies from the Physiognomy of Insanity," 33.

55. Ibid., 37.

56. Ibid., 38.

57. The degeneration discourse became increasingly prominent during the second half of the nineteenth century with the writings of Max Nordau, Cesare Lombroso, and Bénédict August Morel. As a literary theme, degenerationist ideas can be found, for example, in the novels of Emile Zola, Robert Louis Stevenson, and George Du Maurier. Victorian novelists used family resemblances as a literary device to explain common familial behavior. See Daniel Pick, *Faces of Degeneration: A European Disorder, 1848–1918* (Cambridge: Cambridge University Press, 1989), for an analysis of nineteenth-century literary and scholarly writings on degeneration.

58. Puerperal insanity was the diagnosis given to new mothers whose states of mental imbalance followed immediately the birth of their children. Hilary Marland, *Dangerous Motherhood: Insanity and Childbirth in Victorian Britain* (New York: Palgrave Macmillan, 2004).

59. Diamond, "On the Application of Photography," 21.
60. J. C. Bucknill, "The Diagnosis of Insanity," *Asylum Journal of Mental Science* 2 (1856): 240.
61. Conolly, "Case Studies from the Physiognomy of Insanity," 60.
62. Unfortunately, there is no record of Diamond's case notes, so many aspects of his therapeutic approach are unknown.
63. Conolly, "Case Studies from the Physiognomy of Insanity," 60.
64. Diamond, "On the Application of Photography," 21.
65. Conolly, "Case Studies from the Physiognomy of Insanity," 62; Diamond, "On the Application of Photography," 21. As Charles N. Eberline has pointed out, Diamond's characterization echoes the words of Mark 5:15: "And they came to Jesus, and saw the demoniac sitting there, clothed and in his right mind."
66. Conolly, "Case Studies from the Physiognomy of Insanity," 48.
67. Ibid., 67.
68. Ibid., 67, 70.
69. Ibid., 71–72.
70. John Conolly, "The Physiognomy of Insanity," *Asylum Journal of Mental Science* 4 (1860): 49.
71. Ibid., 49.
72. Ibid.
73. Ibid., 50.
74. Ibid., 52.
75. Ibid., 53.
76. See also Henry Nelson O'Neil, *Destitute* (n.d.); Henry Nelson O'Neil, *Return of the Wanderer,* 1855; and J. R. Spencer Stanhope, *Thoughts of the Past,* 1859.
77. Thomas Carlyle, *Carlyle, "The Hero as Poet" and "The Everlasting Yea,"* ed. Tika Ram Sharma (Ghaziabad: Vimal Prakashan, 1987).
78. Lady Elizabeth Rigby Eastlake, "Art of Dress," *Quarterly Review* 79 (1847): 375.
79. Graeme Tytler, *Physiognomy in the European Novel: Faces and Fortunes* (Princeton, N.J.: Princeton University Press, 1982), 219–220.
80. Charles Dickens, *Bleak House* (New York: New American Library, 1964), 811.
81. Robert Gardiner Hill,, *Total Abolition of Personal Restraint in the Treatment of the Insane: A Lecture on the Management of Lunatic Asylums, and the Treatment of the Insane; Delivered at the Mechanics' Institution, Lincoln, on the 21st of June, 1838; with Statistical Tables* (London: Simpkin Marshall and S. Highley, 1839).
82. Michel Foucault, *Madness and Civilization: A History of Insanity in the Age of Reason* (New York: Pantheon Books, 1965). In 1792, Philippe Pinel, head of the Bicêtre asylum in France, put into practice his beliefs about the somatic nature of mental illness by removing the patients from their restraints. Under his stewardship, the Bicêtre and later the Salpêtrière were converted from madhouses to hospitals for the insane, complete with treatment and

possible cures. In 1796 in England, William Tuke opened the retreat at York for the humane treatment of the insane. These two pioneers, particularly Pinel, have been elevated to iconic status for their actions in "freeing the mad from their chains."

83. Hill, *Total Abolition of Personal Restraint*, 45.

84. Thomas Wakely, *Lancet 5* (1840): 377; emphasis in original.

85. Diamond's opposition to physical restraints is outlined in Andrée Lee Flageollé, "The Demystification of Dr. Hugh Welch Diamond" (M.A. thesis, University of New Mexico, 1994), 39.

86. John Charles Bucknill and Daniel Hack Tuke, *A Manual of Psychological Medicine: Containing the History, Nosology, Description, Statistics, Diagnosis, Pathology, and Treatment of Insanity; With an Appendix of Cases* (London: J. Churchill, 1858). This textbook went through four revised editions in twenty-nine years and was in use through the end of the century; see Gilman, *Seeing the Insane*, 176.

87. Daniel H. Tuke, *Rules and List of the Present Members of the Society for Improving the Condition of the Insane; and the Prize Essay Entitled "The Progressive Changes Which Have Taken Place since the Time of Pinel in the Management of the Insane and the Various Contrivances Which Have Been Adopted instead of Mechanical Restraint"* (London: John Churchill, 1854).

88. T. N. Brushfield, "Application of Photography to Lunacy," *Journal of the Photographic Society* 3 (1857): 289.

89. Diamond, "Letter to William Henry Fox Talbot."

90. For more on Victorian criminal lunacy, see Joel Peter Eigen, *Unconscious Crime: Mental Absence and Criminal Responsibility in Victorian London* (Baltimore: Johns Hopkins University Press, 2003).

91. "Twelfth Night at the Hanwell Lunatic Asylum," *Illustrated London News*, 15 January 1848, 27.

92. Conolly, "Physiognomy of Insanity," 22.

93. John Conolly, "The Physiognomy of Insanity No. 3, General Melancholia," *Medical Times and Gazette* 6 (February 1858): 53, as quoted in Burrows and Schumacher, *Portraits of the Insane*, 36.

94. Conolly, "Physiognomy of Insanity No. 3," 43.

95. Eliza Lynn Linton, "Passing Faces," *Household Words* 2 (1855): 263.

96. Morison, *Physiognomy of Mental Diseases*, 73.

97. Bucknill and Tuke, *Manual of Psychological Medicine*, 287–288.

98. Ibid., 288.

99. Ibid., 287.

100. David Dabydeen, *Hogarth's Blacks: Images of Blacks in Eighteenth Century English Art* (Athens: University of Georgia Press, 1987), 90.

101. Gérard de Lairesse, *A Treatise on the Art of Painting in All Its Branches*, trans. William Marshall Craig (London: Edward Orme, 1817), 5.

102. As quoted in Tytler, *Physiognomy in the European Novel*, 381.

6. Diagnostic Physiognomy

1. Johann Caspar Lavater was very explicit about his data-compilation agenda. He frequently noted that he lacked the anatomical skill to engage in a research program but offered his information for others to do so. See, for example, Johann Caspar Lavater, *Essays on Physiognomy,* trans. Thomas Holcroft (London: Ward, Lock and Co., 1800), 40.

2. Michael Lind, *The Next American Nation: The New Nationalism and the Fourth American Revolution* (New York: Free Press, 1995), 5.

3. Anthony S. Wohl, *Endangered Lives: Public Health in Victorian Britain* (London: J. M. Dent, 1983), 77–79.

4. The classic study is Daniel J. Kevles, *In the Name of Eugenics: Genetics and the Uses of Human Heredity* (Cambridge, Mass.: Harvard University Press, 1995). For more on the personal history of Francis Galton, see, for example, Nicholas Wright Gillham, *A Life of Sir Francis Galton: From African Exploration to the Birth of Eugenics* (New York: Oxford University Press, 2001).

5. E. P. Thompson, *The Making of the English Working Class* (New York: Vintage Books, 1966); Linda Colley, *Britons: Forging the Nation, 1707–1837* (New Haven, Conn.: Yale University Press, 1992). Joan Scott has demonstrated the ways in which Thompson's analysis of class was structured by his understandings of masculinity and femininity. Although Thompson cast class as apparently gender neutral, which Scott helpfully corrected, his work remains foundational in the field. Joan Wallach Scott, *Gender and the Politics of History* (New York: Columbia University Press, 1988), 42–45, 68–92. An interesting exception to this process of grouping is the emergence of the New Journalism, which, from the 1860s, replaced the traditional "we" with "I" in reporting and spoke out against anonymous writing and reviewing. Richard Salmon, "'A Simulacrum of Power': Intimacy and Abstraction in the Rhetoric of the New Journalism," in *Nineteenth-Century Media and the Construction of Identities,* ed. Laurel Brake, Bill Bell, and David Finkelstein (Hampshire: Palgrave, 2000).

6. Peter Mandler, *Liberty and Authority in Victorian Britain* (New York: Oxford University Press, 2006), 16.

7. James V. Werner, *American Flaneur: The Cosmic Physiognomy of Edgar Allan Poe* (New York: Routledge, 2004), 75–76.

8. The historical relationship between physiognomy and the fine arts has been well documented in a number of places. See in particular Jennifer Montagu, *The Expression of the Passions: The Origin and Influence of Charles Le Brun's "Conférence sur l'expression générale et particularière"* (New Haven, Conn.: Yale University Press, 1994).

9. Classification was not itself considered a science but rather a method to study science. Many nineteenth-century practitioners of science criticized those who mistook classification for science. For example, Dr. John Cross wrote in 1817 that "classification, which constitutes absolutely no part of science, but is indispensable to its acquirement in the present limited state of our faculties, has, like most good things, been carried to an extreme." John Cross, *An Attempt to*

Establish Physiognomy upon Scientific Principles (Glasgow: University Press, 1817), 7–8. Although physiognomy was a method of classification, it was also thought by many to be a science in its own right. For a review of the debates about the scientific efficacy of physiognomy, see Sharrona Pearl, "As Plain as the Nose on Your Face: Physiognomy in Nineteenth-Century England" (Ph.D. diss., Harvard University, 2005), 39–96. Even among those who were convinced of physiognomic efficacy, there were still numerous debates about the source of its legitimacy as a practice. For a discussion of the status of physiognomy as an art or a science, see Pearl, "As Plain as the Nose on Your Face," 64–66.

10. An example of an approach dealing explicitly with the scientific efficacy of physiognomy can be found in Lucy Hartley, *Physiognomy and the Meaning of Expression in Nineteenth-Century Culture* (Cambridge: Cambridge University Press, 2001).

11. Doctor and founder of phrenology Franz Josef Gall claimed that his initial insight into phrenology came out of a straightforward physiognomic observation: "The schoolmates most formidable to me were those who learned by heart with such facilities . . . All these [had] large prominent eyes." From this he concluded that "if memory were made evident by external signs, it might be so likewise with other talents or intellectual faculties." F. J. Gall, *On the Organ of the Moral Qualities and Intellectual Faculties: And the Plurality of the Cerebral Organs* (Boston: Marsh, Capen and Lyon, 1835), 58–59. For more on phrenology and especially its use as a self-improvement doctrine, see Roger Cooter, *The Cultural Meaning of Popular Science: Phrenology and the Organization of Consent in Nineteenth-Century Britain* (Cambridge: Cambridge University Press, 1984). See also Alison Winter, *Mesmerized: Powers of Mind in Victorian Britain* (Chicago: University of Chicago Press, 1998).

12. See, for example, J. G. Spurzheim, *Phrenology, in Connexion with the Study of Physiognomy* (Boston: Marsh, Capen and Lyon, 1836), 180–181.

13. At least three phrenology journals were published during the middle of the nineteenth century: the *Phrenological Journal and Miscellany* (1823–1847), the *Zoist* (1843–1856), and the *Phreno-Magnet or Mirror of Nature* (1843). The Edinburgh Phrenological Society was founded in 1820, followed by a host of others across Britain and the United States.

14. For this historiographical approach, see, for example, John Graham, *Lavater's Essays on Physiognomy: A Study in the History of Ideas* (Berne: Peter Lang, 1979), 35; Graeme Tytler, *Physiognomy in the European Novel: Faces and Fortunes* (Princeton, N.J.: Princeton University Press, 1982), xv; Lynda Nead, *Myths of Sexuality: Representations of Women in Victorian Britain* (Oxford: Basil Blackwell, 1988), 170; and Barbara Maria Stafford, *Body Criticism: Imaging the Unseen in Enlightenment Art and Medicine* (Cambridge, Mass.: MIT Press, 1991), 118.

15. Joachim Denis Laurent Zender, *Physiognomy and Craniology; or, A Manual of Phrenology* (Philadelphia: Published by the author, 1843). Other examples include John Abernathy, *Reflections on Gall and Spurzheim's System of*

Physiognomy and Phrenology (London: Longman, Hurst, Rees, Orme, and Brown, 1821); *Illustrated Annual of Phrenology and Physiognomy* (New York: Fowler and Wells, 1865); and Nelson B. Sizer and H. S. Drayton, *Heads and Faces, and How to Study Them: A Manual of Phrenology and Physiognomy for the People* (New York: Fowler and Wells, 1887).

16. Not all phrenologists adopted physiognomic connections; one of the major phrenological systematizers, Franz Josef Gall, strongly objected to Lavater and drew sharp distinctions between phrenology and physiognomy. For more on Gall's comments about Lavater, see Tytler, *Physiognomy in the European Novel*, 90.

17. Zender, *Physiognomy and Craniology*, 111; and R. B. D. Wells, *A New Illustrated Hand-Book of Phrenology, Physiology and Physiognomy* (London: H. Vickers, 1860; originally published 1843), 29.

18. Rather than dismissing phrenology and physiognomy as aberrations in the history of ideas, more recent scholarship has demonstrated the role that they played in introducing an element of materiality into studies of human behavior, thereby providing the intellectual framework for brain-localization studies. See Robert Young, *Mind, Brain and Adaptation in the Nineteenth Century: Cerebral Localization and Its Biological Context from Gall to Ferrier* (Oxford: Clarendon Press, 1970); and Anne Harrington, *Medicine, Mind, and the Double Brain: A Study in Nineteenth-Century Thought* (Princeton, N.J.: Princeton University Press, 1987).

19. Although phrenology was the subject of continued controversy, it had achieved many of the hallmarks of scientific respectability, including professional societies and journals devoted to its pursuit. For more on the development of phrenology in the nineteenth century, see Cooter, *Cultural Meaning of Popular Science*, and Winter, *Mesmerized*.

20. Alexander Walker, *Physiognomy Founded on Physiology* (London: Smith, Elder and Co., 1834); see 203-214.

21. Ibid., 210.

22. Ibid., 214.

23. William Hazlitt *The Collected Works of William Hazlitt*, ed. A. R. Waller and Arnold Glover, with an introduction by W. E. Henley (New York: McClure, Phillips and Co., 1902), 7:137.

24. George Jabet, *Nasology; or, Hints towards a Classification of Noses* (London: R. Bentley, 1848), 6.

25. Richard Daniel Altick, *The English Common Reader: A Social History of the Mass Reading Public, 1800-1900*, 2nd ed. (Columbus: Ohio State University Press, 1998), 320-321.

26. "Spirit of Public Journals: Dinners," *Mirror of Literature, Amusement and Instruction* 12 (1829): 124.

27. Physiologists, themselves struggling for recognition from the intellectual establishment, were particularly sensitive to the advantages offered by borrowing from physiognomic language and principles.

28. Mario Biagioli, "The Anthropology of Incommensurability," *Studies in History and Philosophy of Science* 21 (1990): 183-209.

29. Ibid., 184.
30. Although phrenology itself fell out of use, the ideas behind it are still very much in practice.
31. The historiography about phrenology as a self-improvement technique was pioneered by Cooter, *Cultural Meaning of Popular Science*.
32. An obvious exception to this, of course, was Lavater, who had numerous eager subjects vying for inclusion in his prestigious books.
33. Until and sometimes even after the nonrestraint approach to treating mental illness was ushered in by Philippe Pinel in France and William Tuke in England, the mad were often chained and sometimes violent, necessitating examination (when it happened) from a distance.
34. Lavater, *Essays on Physiognomy*, 83.
35. In 1884, German neurologist Hermann Oppenheim argued in a Darwinian lecture to the Organization of Berlin Psychiatrists that human expression was universal and appeared particularly unfettered in the faces of the insane. Hermann Oppenheim, "Beiträge zum Studium des Gesichtsausdrucks der Geisteskranken," *Allgemeine Zeitschrift für Psychiatrie* 40 (1884): 840–863.
36. Thomas Tryon, *A Treatise of Dreams and Visions: Wherein the Causes, Natures, and Uses, of Nocturnal Representations, and the Communications Both of Good and Evil Angels, as Also Departed Souls, to Mankind. Are Theosophically Unfolded; That Is According to the Word of God, and the Harmony of Created Beings; To Which Is Added, a Discourse of the Causes, Natures, and Cure of Phrensie, Madness or Distraction. By Tho. Tryon, Student in Physick* ([London]: T. Sowle, 1689), 261–262; emphasis in original.
37. Sir Charles Bell, *The Anatomy and Philosophy of Expression as Connected with the Fine Arts* (London: G. Bell, 1883). There were at least eighteen different editions of the book, spanning the years 1806 through 1912.
38. *Dictionnaire des sciences médicales* (Paris: Panckoucke, 1819); Étienne Esquirol, *Mental Maladies: A Treatise on Insanity,* trans. E. K. Hunt (Philadelphia: Lea and Blanchard, 1845). Esquirol was a student of asylum reformer Philippe Pinel.
39. Anne Secord has demonstrated the growing dominance of scientific language at the expense of local knowledge in her study of the gulf between gentlemen botanists and artisan naturalists in the nineteenth century. She showed that this gulf marginalized the amateur as a contributor to scientific knowledge, and she claimed that what Lorraine Daston has called "deep subjectivity," a highly personalized form of instinct and response, had become an illegitimate way of knowing. I am grateful to Anne Secord for pointing out the connection between this process and medical observation; see *Artisan Naturalists: Science as Popular Culture in Nineteenth-Century England* (Chicago: University of Chicago Press, forthcoming), 164–172. Observation and description have long been important components of the practice of medicine. Visual skill was particularly important for (male) physicians treating polite

female patients because propriety often forbade close physical examination. To this end, physicians often had recourse to midwives or other women to act as intermediaries when they were examining gynecological problems. Likewise, observation was a significant component of the medical doctrine of signs, whereby the examination of urine and pulse provided a measure of the nature and severity of the illness. For a discussion of the history of semiology in medical practice, see Ian Maclean, *Logic, Signs, and Nature in the Renaissance: The Case of Learned Medicine* (New York: Cambridge University Press, 2002).

40. Francis Galton, *Inquiries into Human Faculty and Its Development* (London: Macmillan, 1883), 6.
41. Lady Elizabeth Rigby Eastlake, "Physiognomy," *Quarterly Review* 90 (1851–1852): 63.
42. Ibid., 73.
43. Lady Elizabeth Rigby Eastlake, "Photography," *Quarterly Review* 101 (1857): 461–462. Eastlake was referring to the bushy and prominent mustaches stylistically associated with the Crimean.
44. Eastlake was particularly interested in clothing and environmental markings.
45. Eastlake, "Photography," 461.
46. Wohl, *Endangered Lives,* 77. The identification of criminals occupied a number of late Victorian minds, most notably Italian criminologist Cesare Lombroso, whose concepts of atavism determined the course of criminology studies for many years.
47. Most of Charlotte Brontë's characters possessed physiognomic and phrenological skills, a mark of her own commitment to these principles. See Sally Shuttleworth, *Charlotte Brontë and Victorian Psychology* (Cambridge: Cambridge University Press, 1996).
48. Charlotte Brontë, *Villette* (Oxford: Oxford University Press, 2000), 155.
49. Ibid., 139.
50. Alain Corbin, *The Foul and the Fragrant: Odor and the French Social Imagination* (Cambridge, Mass.: Harvard University Press, 1986), 5.
51. Chris Otter, *The Victorian Eye: A Political History of Light and Vision in Britain, 1800–1910* (Chicago: University of Chicago press, 2008), 93.
52. Henry Mayhew, *London Labour and the London Poor,* 4 vols. (London: Griffin, Bohn and Co., 1861–1862), 3:209.
53. Kate Flint, *The Victorians and the Visual Imagination* (Cambridge: Cambridge University Press, 2000), 3.
54. "Photography: Its History and Application," *Living Age* 92 (1867): 210. Diamond's therapeutic technique was built on the revelatory power of photographs, as I discussed in Chapter 5.
55. Joanna C. Scherer, "Historic Photographs as Anthropological Documents: A Retrospect," *Visual Anthropology* 3 (1990): 131–155.
56. The presentation of anthropological images in England is detailed in Brian Street, "British Popular Anthropology: Exhibiting and Photographing the Other," in *Anthropology and Photography, 1860–1920,* ed. Elizabeth Edwards (New Haven, Conn.: Yale University Press, 1992).

57. Jonathan Smith, *Charles Darwin and Victorian Visual Culture* (Cambridge: Cambridge University Press, 2006), 17.

58. Ibid., 181–182.

59. Although there is no doubt that *On The Origin of Species* had a profound impact on Victorian life and culture and was the topic of numerous drawing-room debates, scientific and learned-society meetings, periodical and newspaper articles, and caricatures and prints, the original sellout print run was only 1,250 copies. The next edition was still a modest 3,000 copies. Most of those discussing the book and its concepts had not actually read it.

60. Smith, *Charles Darwin and Victorian Visual Culture*, 199.

61. See Chapter 1 for a discussion of Darwin's nose.

62. Charles Darwin, letter to Charles Lyell, 21 August 1861. I am grateful to Matt Stanley for pointing me to these references. Darwin's letters are available from the Darwin Correspondence Project, http://www.darwinproject.ac.uk/ (accessed 1 June 2009).

63. See, for example, Charles Darwin, letter to Asa Gray, 11 October 1861.

64. Charles Darwin, *The Expression of the Emotions in Man and Animals* (London: HarperCollins, 1998), 10.

65. Ibid., 359.

66. Johann Caspar Lavater, *L'art de connaître les hommes par la physionomie, par Gaspard Lavater* (Paris: Depélafol, 1835).

67. Jane Browne, "Darwin and the Face of Madness," in *The Anatomy of Madness: Essays in the History of Psychiatry*, ed. W. F. Bynum, Roy Porter, and Michael Shepard (New York: Tavistock Publications, 1985), 153.

68. Charles Darwin, *The Expression of the Emotions in Man and Animals*, ed. Francis Darwin (New York: New York University Press, 1989), 295.

69. Browne, "Darwin and the Face of Madness," 161.

70. Darwin and Crichton-Browne had a lengthy correspondence from the late 1860s, throughout which Crichton-Browne sent Darwin packets of photographs taken in his asylum. Their correspondence is largely unpublished but is chronicled in Sander Gilman, *Disease and Representation: Images of Illness from Madness to AIDS* (Ithaca, N.Y.: Cornell University Press, 1988), 179–186.

71. Rosemary Jann, "Evolutionary Physiognomy and Darwin's *Expression of the Emotions*," *Victorian Review* 18, no. 2 (1992): 1–27.

72. Ibid., 13; and Smith, *Charles Darwin and Victorian Visual Culture*, 204.

73. "Review of *The Expression of the Emotions in Man and Animals*, by Charles Darwin," *Journal of the Anthropological Institute of Great Britain and Ireland* 2 (1873): 444–446; and "Review of *The Expression of the Emotions in Man and Animals*, by Charles Darwin," *Athenaeum* 2350 (1872): 591.

74. Darwin, *Expression of the Emotions in Man and Animals* (1989 ed.), 24.

75. Darwin turned to photography only after finding the evidence provided by painting and sculpture lacking because of artists' preference for beauty over truth. Smith, *Charles Darwin and Victorian Visual Culture*, 182.

76. Browne, "Darwin and the Face of Madness," 157.

77. For Darwin, I am referring, of course, to his near rejection as ship's naturalist and captain's companion for HMS *Beagle* on physiognomic grounds. Robert FitzRoy, the captain of the *Beagle,* was a dedicated physiognomist.

78. Raymond E. Fancher, "Francis Galton and Phrenology" (paper presented at the Proceedings TENNET IV, Montreal, Canada, 1993).

79. Gillham, *Life of Sir Francis Galton,* 57.

80. Fancher, "Francis Galton and Phrenology."

81. Karl Pearson, *The Life, Letters and Labours of Francis Galton,* vol. 1, *Birth 1822 to Marriage 1853* (Cambridge: Cambridge University Press, 1914), 144.

82. Composite photography was very different from the kinds of photographic techniques used by Diamond. For more on the technical details of Galton's composites, as well as the implications for the kinds of images they produced, see Josh Ellenbogen, "Camera and Mind," *Representations,* Winter 2008, 86–115.

83. Francis Galton, "Generic Images," *Proceedings of the Royal Institution* 9 (1879): 166.

84. Francis Galton, "Photographic Composites," *Photographic News* 29 (1885): 234–245.

85. As quoted in Gillham, *Life of Sir Francis Galton,* 219; emphasis in original.

86. Ibid., 216–217.

87. Alan Sekula, "The Body and the Archive," *October* 39 (1986): 3–64.

88. Francis Galton, *Finger Prints* (London: Macmillan and Co., 1892), 152.

89. Petrus Camper, Adrian Gilles Camper, and Georges Cuvier, *Observations anatomiques sur la structure intérieure et le squelette de plusieurs espèces de cétacés* (Paris: Dufour, 1820); Johann Friedrich Blumenbach, William Lawrence, and William Coulson, *A Manual of Comparative Anatomy,* 2nd ed. (London: Printed for W. Simpkin and R. Marshall, 1827).

90. Hunt founded the Anthropological Society of London in 1862 largely as a forum for his racialist views, which were unwelcome in the context of the humanitarian Ethnological Society. Hunt's model was Paul Broca's Société d'anthropologie de Paris, an organization devoted to large-scale examinations of the "the science of the whole nature of man." George W. Stocking, *Victorian Anthropology* (New York: Free Press, 1987), 247–248.

91. For a comprehensive overview of Victorian anthropology, including debates about the classification of different races, see Stocking, *Victorian Anthropology.*

92. Roland Barthes, *Image, Music, Text,* ed. Stephen Heath (New York: Hill, 1977), 44.

93. Elizabeth Edwards, *Raw Histories: Photographs, Anthropology and Museums* (New York: Berg, 2001), 38. In her exploration of the materiality of photographic meaning, Edwards focused primarily on the collections held by scientific institutions and individual scholars. Although I draw on Edwards's research, I am interested in how nonspecialists looked at anthropological and tourist photographs, and how their observations built on a shared

language of looking as knowing. See also Jennifer Tucker, *Nature Exposed: Photography as Eyewitness in Victorian Science* (Baltimore: Johns Hopkins University Press, 2005).

94. Steven Shapin and Simon Schaffer, *Leviathan and the Air-Pump: Hobbes, Boyle, and the Experimental Life; Including a Translation of Thomas Hobbes, Dialogus physicus de natura aeris by Simon Schaffer* (Princeton, N.J.: Princeton University Press, 1985), 22–79.

95. Benedict R. O'G. Anderson, *Imagined Communities: Reflections on the Origin and Spread of Nationalism* (London: Verso, 1983); Elleke Boehmer, *Colonial and Postcolonial Literature: Migrant Metaphors,* 2nd ed. (Oxford: Oxford University Press, 2005).

96. Kathleen Wilson, "Citizenship, Empire, and Modernity in the English Provinces, *c.* 1720–90," in *Cultures of Empire: Colonizers in Britain and the Empire in the Nineteenth and Twentieth Centuries,* ed. Catherine Hall (New York: Routledge, 2000), 157–186.

97. As analyzed in Simon J. Potter, "Webs, Networks, and Systems: Globalization and the Mass Media in the Nineteenth- and Twentieth-Century British Empire," *Journal of British Studies* 46 (2007): 623–624.

98. For a discussion of the relationship between photography and anthropology/ethnography, see Alison Griffiths, *Wondrous Difference: Cinema, Anthropology, and Turn-of-the-Century Visual Culture* (New York: Columbia University Press, 2002), 86–126.

99. Barbara Korte, *English Travel Writing from Pilgrimages to Postcolonial Explorations* (New York: St. Martin's Press, 2000), 85, 93.

100. Ibid., 86. Early anthropological photographs have been analyzed in Elizabeth Edwards and Lynne Williamson, *World on a Glass Plate: Early Anthropological Photographs from the Pitt Rivers Museum, Oxford* (Oxford: Pitt Rivers Museum, 1981). Until these photographs were displayed in a museum context, their viewership was largely limited to a tight network of anthropologists and scientists. Travel newspapers, cartes de visite, diaries, journals, and novels had images that reached a much wider audience.

101. Korte, *English Travel Writing.*

102. Talal Asad, "Ethnographic Representation, Statistics, and Modern Power," in *From the Margins: Historical Anthropology and Its Futures,* ed. Brian Keith Axel (Durham, N.C.: Duke University Press, 2002), 66–91; see 78.

103. George Levine, *Dying to Know: Scientific Epistemology and Narrative in Victorian England* (Chicago: University of Chicago Press, 2002).

104. Ibid., 18–19, 114.

105. The literature on Lombroso, Galton, and eugenics is extensive. For a study of physiognomy and its relationship to German eugenics in particular, see Richard T. Gray, *About Face: German Physiognomic Thought from Lavater to Auschwitz* (Detroit: Wayne State University Press, 2004).

106. Eastlake, "Physiognomy," 63; Galton, *Finger Prints,* 149.

107. Francis Galton, "Personal Identification and Description," *Nature* 38 (1888): 173–177.

108. For Faulds's approach to fingerprinting, see Henry Faulds, "On the Skin-Furrows of the Hand," *Nature* 22 (1880): 605; and Henry Faulds, "On the Identification of Habitual Criminals by Finger-Prints," *Nature* (1894): 548.

109. Alphone Bertillon, a French law-enforcement officer, created a system of measurements by which every criminal could be uniquely identified. Bertillon's method was discontinued following a series of incidents in which various officers received different results for the same criminals.

110. Sekula, "Body and the Archive."

111. Galton, *Finger Prints,* 17, 192–193; emphasis in original.

112. Carlo Ginzburg, *Clues, Myths, and the Historical Method* (Baltimore: Johns Hopkins University Press, 1989), 96–125.

113. The publication of physiognomy texts declined steadily throughout the nineteenth century, as chronicled in John Graham, "Lavater's *Physiognomy:* A Checklist," *Papers of the Bibliographical Society of America* (1961): 297–308.

114. The literature on Charcot is very rich; for a discussion and examples of his photography, see Georges Didi-Huberman, *Invention of Hysteria: Charcot and the Photographic Iconography of the Salpêtrière,* trans. Alisa Hartz (Cambridge, Mass.: MIT Press, 2003).

115. The conductor metaphor is taken from Winter, *Mesmerized;* see especially 318–320.

116. The key word here is "tried." As many of his contemporaries contended, and historians later analyzed, Charcot was a victim of his own beliefs; his subjects were likely responding to his cues and performing on command, skewing his results and causing a far higher concentration of hysterical model patients at the Salpêtrière than anywhere else before, at the time, or since.

117. J. M. Charcot, *Charcot, the Clinician: The Tuesday Lessons; Excerpts from Nine Case Presentations on General Neurology Delivered at the Salpêtrière Hospital in 1887–88 by Jean-Martin Charcot,* trans. Christopher G. Goetz (New York: Raven Press, 1987), 107.

118. Following a series of very public challenges, Charcot's theories were disregarded as full of evidentiary holes.

119. Anna O. was the pseudonym of Bertha Pappenheim, whom Breuer treated from 1880 to 1882. Pappenheim became a noted feminist and pioneered the practice of social work in Germany. Despite the success portrayed in Breuer's and Freud's writings, Pappenheim remained negative about her experiences with psychoanalysis until the day she died. I have called her a collaborator because it appears from Breuer's and Freud's account of her treatment that she was responsible for identifying the therapeutic value in recognizing the events that led to her symptoms.

120. For more on this incident and others like it, see Breuer and Freud's account of Anna O.'s treatment in Joseph Breuer and Sigmund Freud, *Studies on Hysteria,* trans. James Strachey (New York: Avon, 1966).

121. Frank J. Sulloway, *Freud, Biologist of the Mind: Beyond the Psychoanalytic Legend* (Cambridge, Mass.: Harvard University Press, 1992).

Conclusion

1. Modern physiognomic studies cover a range of approaches, from an examination of the neurological response to various visual stimuli to statistical analyses of the correlations between physical features and types of behavior. For an example of a neurological study and a review of current literature, see Martin S. Lindauer, "Perceiving, Imaging, and Preferring Physiognomic Stimuli," *American Journal of Psychology* 99 (1986): 233–255. More recently, the Wellcome Department of Imaging Neuroscience has conducted a series of experiments dealing with neurological responses to facial recognition and perception. Behavioral studies include correlations between webbed feet and child hyperactivity and between toe spacing and criminal tendencies. A review and analysis of this work can be found in Alan F. Collins, "Physical Appearance as a Sign of Temperament, Character, and Intelligence," *History of Psychology* 12 (1999): 251–276.

2. Such brain-imaging studies record the neurological expression of physiognomic perception.

3. Roger Cooter has chronicled the relationship between self-improvement and Victorian science in *The Cultural Meaning of Popular Science: Phrenology and the Organization of Consent in Nineteenth-Century Britain* (Cambridge: Cambridge University Press, 1984). See also Anne Secord, *Artisan Naturalists: Science as Popular Culture in Nineteenth-Century England* (Chicago: University of Chicago Press, forthcoming).

4. Karl Marx, *Capital: A Critique of Political Economy,* trans. Ben Fowlkes, vol. 1 (New York: Vintage Books, 1977).

5. Walter Benjamin, *Illuminations* (orig. pub. 1968; repr., New York: Schocken Books, [1986]), 217–252. Although Benjamin was not a member of the Frankfurt school, and remained on the periphery of this intellectual circle during his lifetime, he was an important teacher of Adorno, and his now extremely well-known work remains closely affiliated with this movement.

6. Emily Brontë, *Wuthering Heights* (London: Penguin Books, 1995), 57.

7. Graeme Tytler, *Physiognomy in the European Novel: Faces and Fortunes* (Princeton, N.J.: Princeton University Press, 1982), 228.

8. For more on physiognomy and World War II, see Richard T. Gray, *About Face: German Physiognomic Thought from Lavater to Auschwitz* (Detroit: Wayne State University Press, 2004). Before and even after the genocide propagated by National Socialism, countries across the world, including the United States, instituted forced sterilizations as part of active eugenics projects.

9. A few samples include Jo-Ellan Dimitrius and Mark Mazzarella, *Reading People: How to Understand People and Predict Their Behavior, Anytime, Anyplace* (New York: Random House, 1998); Gordon L. Patzer, *Looks: Why They Matter More Than You Ever Imagined* (New York: Amacom, 2008); and Leslie A. Zebrowitz, *Reading Faces: Window to the Soul?* (Boulder, CO: Westview Press, 1997). I invite the reader to do her or his own search to find further materials.

10. See http://www.uniphiz.com/physiognomy.htm (accessed 21 May 2008).

11. "Face Value," *Economist,* 26 January 2008, 78; Malcolm Gladwell, "The Naked Face," *New Yorker,* 5 August 2002, 38–50. The *Economist* article chronicled the research conducted by psychologists Nicholas Rule and Nalini Ambady at Tufts University, which has been widely published and cited. The *New Yorker* article was one of many profiles of the psychologist Paul Ekman and his work.

12. "Physiognomy: Facing the Truth," *Economist,* 21 August 2008, http://www .economist.com/science/displaystory.cfm?story_id=11959198.

13. Ranko Bon, "Physiognomy Resurgent: A Letter to the Economist (August 26, 2008)," *Residua Book XXXIII* (August 26, 2008), http://www.residua .org/book-xxxiii-2008/physiognomy-resurgent-a-letter-to-the-economist/.

14. Numerous biological anthropology labs are conducting this kind of research. One example is Peter Ellison's lab at Harvard University.

15. See, for example, J. S. Winston, B. A. Strange, J. O'Doherty, and R. J. Dolan, "Automatic and Intentional Brain Responses during Evaluation of Trustworthiness of Faces," *Nature Neuroscience* 5 (2002): 277–283.

Index